6/27

Mary Farrell's
BEYOND
the BASICS

How to Invest Your Money,
Now That You Know
a Thing or Two

MARY FARRELL

Simon & Schuster
New York   London   Toronto   Sydney   Singapore

SIMON & SCHUSTER
Rockefeller Center
1230 Avenue of the Americas
New York, NY 10020

Designed by Deirdre C. Amthor

Manufactured in the United States of America

1   3   5   7   9   10   8   6   4   2

Library of Congress Cataloging-in-Publication Data

ISBN 0-684-86811-3

to my children, Katherine and Stephen, the best investments ever made, and my husband Dan, the greatest asset ever acquired,

and to my father and in memory of my mother, for their lifelong commitment to family and belief in their children, and to Margaret, Frank, Bob, Kathy and Stephen, for their lifelong loyalty and laughter

Contents

Part III: Managing Your Investments for Tomorrow

16. Rethinking Retirement Planning:
    All the Rules Have Changed   236
17. Wealth Preservation: Strategies That Work   258
18. Where Do We Go from Here?   274

    Acknowledgments   281
    Index   282

Introduction:
Building on What
You Already Know

We have become a nation of avid investors.

Americans—for the first time—now have more money in securities than in bank accounts. Stocks and bonds, in both our personal and retirement accounts, comprise more of our net worth than our homes. There are at least 100 million of us—that's four out of ten people living in this country—who hold securities, either directly or through mutual funds. That's the highest percentage of ownership in U.S. history. By now the reasons for this dramatic growth in investing are well known. More and more Americans have been attracted to investing by the 1990s bull market, which year after year has provided many of us with double-digit returns. And we have been drawn to the stock and bond markets—some of us reluctantly—by the 401(k) revolution as well, which has required us to take charge of our own retirement planning by choosing the ways in which our retirement assets are invested.

The aging of the massive baby boom generation—a group that is 78 million strong—is giving investing for retirement a particularly high priority in the nation's consciousness. It is easy to understand why. The age at which people retire keeps falling—it is now somewhere around 61—and the oldest members of the baby boom generation reach 54 in the year 2000.

Another intriguing fact underscores our need for investment expertise: the largest wealth transfer in U.S. history will take place over the next few decades. Today's generation of retirees is the first that by and large hasn't liq-uidated its assets in retirement. Thanks to Social Security and Medicare—and those monthly pension checks and health care benefits that a good number of retirees receive—many have not had to dip extensively into their savings. The result? They will leave a tidy sum to their children and grand-children. In fact, according to Federal Reserve estimates, they may be leav-ing behind estates valued in total at $8 trillion. Their children, grandchildren, and in many cases great-grandchildren want to know how to invest this in-heritance wisely, in order to reap the full benefits.

Searching for More Information

Because of the expanding role of securities in our household financial assets, there has been a growing demand for investment information, and every-where we turn there is another book, magazine, newspaper, newsletter, Web site, television program, call-in radio show, or seminar telling us what we should do with our money. There is no shortage of information. But all the clutter obscures a lot of what could help—and even if you eventually get to the truly useful information out there, much of it is too simplistic if you al-ready have experience in investing.

I've learned this from traveling throughout the country, listening to the questions I'm asked while giving financial seminars for PaineWebber, and from reading the letters I've received after appearing on *Wall $treet Week With Louis Rukeyser* (where I also occasionally fill in for the host). People who already have some experience with investing tell me that they want to learn more, and invariably they point to the same two areas:

- They want to know how they can *build on the knowledge they have,* in order to make smarter decisions that will allow them to accomplish their financial goals sooner, and with less risk.
- They are interested in *understanding the competing vectors that drive the markets.* They figure—correctly—that if they can comprehend those forces, they can harness them to serve their own investment needs. (For example, an informed decision about the right time to buy stocks or bonds requires some knowledge about interest rates.)

In *Beyond the Basics* we will address both sets of questions, questions that not surprisingly overlap. Of course, nothing in this book should be construed as giving specific legal or tax advice; as always, readers should consult with their own advisers regarding their specific situation.

Here's What I Am Going to Assume

I begin with the premise that you know something about investing and are interested in financial theory only if it can help you accomplish real-world goals: preparing for a better retirement; paying for college for your children or grandchildren; gaining more financial freedom. This book is not for the novice, but it's not for the expert either. We will be discussing everything from how you can benefit from the long-term changes that are reshaping the economy (see chapter 8, "Tools for Success: Why Thematic Investing Can Give You an Edge") to where Social Security fits into your overall investment plan (chapter 16, "Rethinking Retirement Planning: All the Rules Have Changed") to why time in the market is more important than market timing (chapter 2, "Time in the Market: Gaining the Edge").

This is a book with a point of view: that common stocks are the best means to build wealth over the long term.

The goal throughout will be to build on the knowledge you already have. We will do that in two ways: first, by showing you how to better use the tools you already have when it comes to making financial decisions, and second, by introducing you to some new concepts that will make your investment decisions easier and more productive.

Part I
Reviewing the Basics

1

Successful Investing Defined

I'd like to introduce you to three investors, three people who appear, on the surface, to have nothing in common. I promise you they do. They also happen to be related to me, but that is not the common link.

My Father

My father is the classic long-term investor, still holding some of the stocks he purchased back in the 1950s (although the companies he bought may have merged or changed names along the way). His modest purchase of 100 shares of Irving Trust several decades ago has today become 2,680 shares of Bank of New York. Similarly, small purchases of Travelers Insurance, where he worked for forty-five years, grew to thousands of shares of Citigroup, thanks to the mergers and splits that have taken place over the years.

As the son of Irish immigrants, my father believes strongly in the American dream, and his investing reflects that belief. He has always purchased growth stocks. Beginning modestly in the 1950s, he had built a reasonable portfolio by the sixties, but used most of it to educate his six children. By the time the last child had graduated from college, in 1976, my father was already retired. He began slowly to rebuild his portfolio, just in time for the bull market. It is fair to say that the stock market gave my parents a far more financially secure retirement than they ever dreamed possible.

Dad bought carefully, and had a long-term investment horizon. Although conservative by nature, and certainly in no position to lose money, he bought stocks, not bonds—something he was never going to let me forget, no matter what my job was on Wall Street.

A quick story will make the point. A few years ago our bond strategist came into my office and strongly recommended that I increase the percentage of fixed-income investments in my personal portfolio. It was sound advice, and I bought some bonds for my father's account as well. (My father was ninety years old at the time.) When he received the statement confirming the trades, he called to inform me he wanted to invest in growth stocks, not bonds—period. I got the message.

My parents had simple goals: to educate their children and, if they were lucky, to have something left over for retirement. Although there was never a time when my parents had a lot of spare cash—I guess that goes without saying when you come from a family as large as mine—they always found some money to invest, and over a sixty-year horizon it paid off handsomely.

My Brother Frank

My brother Frank is a philosophy professor with little interest in the market, except as a tool to give him the financial security he needs to pursue his real passion in life, writing. He is also extremely conservative. To his credit, Frank maximizes his contribution to his retirement plan on a pretax (through his 403[b]) and posttax (through his nondeductible IRA) basis, and invests these retirement monies in stocks. Because he reviews his retirement account statements only quarterly, he is comfortable with the ups and downs that come from being in equities. He knows he will not need his retirement money for well over a decade, so he has no intention of worrying about every little bump in the market.

But his other investments, the ones outside his retirement accounts, reflect a substantial conservative bias. Believing he is already sufficiently exposed to stocks through his 403(b) and IRA, Frank has invested more heavily in bonds through his brokerage account, which handles investments designed to help make the cost of daily living a little easier. Given the equitylike re-turns of the fixed-income markets of the last fifteen years, this has been a successful strategy. Going forward, however, my brother may need to get more comfortable with stocks, given that we expect to see much more mod-est returns in the bond market in the future.

Still, he has done well. Frank's goal has been twofold:

- to build enough financial security to continue taking summers off to pursue his writing, which he has been able to do thanks to the returns his bond portfolio is producing
- to fund an early retirement, which appears to be a distinct possibility, given how well his retirement investments have done so far

My Sister Kathy

My sister Kathy, a busy lawyer with four children and little interest in the market, began investing painlessly through mutual funds, preferring not to be bothered with ongoing decisions about specific stocks. But as time went on and she became more comfortable with investing, she graduated to buying individual equities, adding gradually to her retirement and other accounts. Her income has decreased significantly in recent years as she has scaled back her job responsibilities in favor of spending more time with her children. Still, she and her husband never fail to fund their Keogh and retirement plans, regardless of tuition and other financial pressures. While they have a high tol-erance for risk (which is appropriate, given that they are still in their forties), their goals are conservative, just as our parents' were: they want to educate their children and provide a secure retirement for themselves.

What Do They Have in Common?

I am sure you spotted the common threads. None of these people started in-vesting because they had an excess amount of cash and didn't know how to spend it. And none began with the resources to fund a large, well-balanced portfolio. But they did start with a belief in the stock market, and they began investing early, to make sure they would have a pleasant retirement and (in the case of my dad and my sister) be able to educate their children. Saving regularly has always been a part of their budgets (although there have been times in their lives, as in everyone's, when saving was not possible). Only over time have they been able to accumulate a balanced portfolio. Although they have very different risk tolerances and have quite different sums of money to invest, they all recognize investing as a means of reaching financial goals.

They have one other thing in common: *they all are successful investors.* They have accomplished—or will, before they retire—what they set out to do with their money. I don't know any better definition of success.

The Moral

These stories make an important point. When it comes to investing, there is no one right answer. One size does not fit all. *You* have to determine what you want to accomplish, and then *you*—perhaps with some help—need to make sure that it happens.

The only person who can define what financial success looks like for you is you.

Providing some of that help is what this book is all about. The goal is to show you new ways to apply the knowledge you already have, so you can accomplish your financial goals faster, and to give you new concepts that can make your financial life easier.

After nearly thirty years of working with investors, I have noticed that people who achieve their financial goals have five things in common. Successful investors take the following actions.

They clearly identify their goals

Everyone has different goals and different needs. You may be investing to buy your dream house; your friend's primary concern might be putting his children through college; and a colleague may be focusing on an estate plan for her elderly parents. But while our goals are unique, we all need to be clear about what we want to accomplish.

Establishing a time horizon for achieving your objectives is critical. Long-term investors will be less concerned about short-term market fluctuations and so are more likely to be heavily invested in stocks. Shorter-term goals require different—and by definition more conservative—investment strategies.

They develop and implement an investment plan

Some successful clients have constructed elegant plans—complete with spreadsheets, bar graphs, and pie charts. Others have sketched out their goals in broad terms, keeping everything else in their head. It doesn't matter *how* you do it. What is important is that you *do* it.

For some people this can be difficult. Sometimes the most conscientious savers are haphazard investors. Tucking money into a variety of vehicles such as IRAs, 401(k)s, and accounts designed to put the children through college can be smart; but in itself, that is not an investment strategy. You need to start by determining the value of your current assets and liabilities, as well as your current income and expenditures. Then you need to develop a coherent plan, one that is unique to you and designed to meet your goals. This plan should include an asset-allocation strategy and should realistically estimate the returns you expect to receive from your investments.

They make saving an integral part of their budget

Without regular saving, it is difficult to find the money you need to invest and build wealth—unless you are fortunate enough to inherit a fortune or win the lottery. And given the demands on your financial resources throughout virtually every period of life, unless saving is a priority and as much a part of your budget as the mortgage, it isn't likely to happen. The success my father has had is the best example of what can happen if you make saving (and investing those savings) a serious priority.

They regularly review and update their plan

A single, static plan can't accommodate changes in your personal and professional circumstances, much less those in the markets over the next five, ten, or twenty years. The successful investment plan is one that changes and evolves. The best investors review and update their financial plan regularly—at least once a year, and more often as circumstances warrant—in order to take all these changes into account.

They continue learning

The people who are successful investors read business and investing magazines; they join investment clubs; they scour the Internet. Or they decide to take a more passive role, and choose to work with a financial adviser or another investment professional who will do the legwork for them. But even then, you have to have a base of knowledge to make effective decisions.

That brings us to an important point.

Tools for Success

The more tools you have at your disposal, the more successful you can be. But having the right tools is only half the battle. You need to know the best way to use them.

That's why we will revisit concepts you already understand—things like asset allocation and long-term investing—to show how they can be applied more efficiently.

For example, you already know that for your long-term goals, stocks—and mutual funds that invest in stocks—are your best choice. We will build on that knowledge, discussing where you can find the best stocks and funds. And we will go further, showing you how you can take advantage of shifts in the economy—from technological changes to the host of opportunities sparked by the aging baby boom generation—to potentially increase your investment returns.

Realistic Expectations

The bull market that began in 1982 has delivered extraordinary gains in both the stock and bond markets. During this remarkable period, stocks have often returned more than twice the 11 percent they have averaged since 1926. And the sharp decline in long-term interest rates rewarded bond investors as well. Not only did they benefit from high interest rates in their bond yields, but many obtained strong capital gains as well. The result was total returns that looked like those traditionally generated by equities. Completing the cycle, as rates came down, along with inflation, stock prices rose sharply as future earnings were more highly valued and investors became willing to pay more to own companies that could provide them.

All this has raised expectations of some investors about how well their investments will do going forward. It is important to put what has happened in perspective and, in the process, to underscore that we expect the performance of both stocks and bonds to return to the much more moderate historical levels in the foreseeable future.

Let's deal with stocks first. For nearly twenty years, bullishness has prevailed. Since 1982, not only did earnings rise, but the price investors paid for those earnings rose as well, and the market soared. Since the 1982 bottom, the earnings of S&P companies are up 229 percent, but the price of the S&P 500 Index is up 1,118 percent. The market P/E (price of the market divided by its earnings) rose from under 7 to over 30. Essentially, the repricing that occurred in the market—as investors recognized that we were shifting from a high-inflation environment to a low one—is behind us. The bull market has matured. It is likely to continue, but at a more measured pace as future gains are triggered by earnings gains in the companies themselves, rather than expanding P/Es. Since that is the case, we can expect stocks to once again return the 11 percent or so they have delivered over time, rather than the generous 20 and 30 percent–plus gains that we experienced in each year from 1995 to 1999, with NASDAQ delivering an extraordinary 85.6% in 1999. Five back-to-back years with these gains are unprecedented in stock market history.

We expect a similar picture in the bond market. If we view the high inflation of the last three decades as the aberration it was, it is realistic to assume that inflation, currently near historically low levels, will remain there. But with low inflation probable, interest rates are likely to remain in the $4^1/_2$–$6^1/_2$ percent range; and fixed-income instruments, both long and short term, are unlikely to compete with the returns from common stock. It is just not realistic to expect bonds to contribute much in the way of capital gains, given that interest rates have fallen as much as they have and future declines are likely to be incremental. For long-term investors, equities are the best place to be.

It is essential to keep these things in mind and not get swept away with the emotions of the day, which can prompt unwise investment decisions. Because so many investors today have experienced only a bull market, and these extraordinary gains, it is important to have realistic expectations for the future, when gains are likely to be more moderate.

Conversely, when there are serious declines, some investors get so demoralized that they forget how well stocks have performed over the long term. With technology making trading so much easier and faster, expect to see volatility, along with regular (and sometimes severe) corrections.

It is important to hold on to the investment wisdom you have gained over the years, no matter what people around you are saying or how frequently they are trading.

But even with the proper tools and the wisdom to use them, you have to implement your investment plan. And that is what successful investing is all about: building on your knowledge to create an investment plan that meets your goals and objectives over time—and then making that plan happen.

2

Time in the Market:
Gaining the Edge

The key to successful investing is a simple one: time.

To people who might otherwise worry about the daily fluctuations of the stock market—because movements of hundreds of points, either up or down, in the Dow Jones Industrial Average are now commonplace—there are few more comforting charts to look at than the one below, which shows the two-hundred-plus years of stock market history. It neatly captures why, when it comes to investing in stocks, you want to be a long-term investor.

Dow Jones Industrial Average

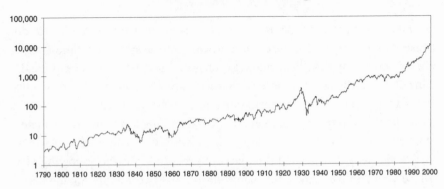

Source: PaineWebber

There are two impressive things about this chart. First, as you can see, the long-term trend line is positive.

Second, the chart puts the crash of 1929 (and the ensuing bear market) and the crash of 1987 (and the brief slump that followed) in perspective. If you spend a minute looking at the trend line, you realize that what happened in 1929 and in its wake was a painful aberration. And as devastating as October 1987 was—and as hard as this may be to believe for those who were working on Wall Street at that traumatic time—it appears as only a modest dip when placed in historical context.

Investors fear the risk of being in the market during the corrections that are characteristic of any bull market. And that fear is quite understandable. In this age of instant global telecommunications, those corrections can be swift, painful, and worldwide. So, there is no doubt that being in the market during an abrupt downturn is a risk that comes with investing.

But there is a greater risk: not being in the market at all. The market has appreciated, on average, 11 percent a year since 1926, so the odds favor those in the market.

As we will discuss toward the end of the chapter, you need the kind of growth the stock market has traditionally produced to offset the twin evils that haunt every investor: taxes and inflation. But for now, let's see why you must be in—and stay in—the market if you hope to accomplish your financial goals. As you will see, market timing just does not work.

Things Are Moving Faster

Over the last several decades there has been a tendency for the market to condense its movements—both up and down—into ever shorter time frames. For example, a typical bear market (generally defined as a stock-price decline of at least 20 percent) used to have a duration of about eighteen months. But thanks to the fact that information gets to everyone everywhere so much more quickly today, bear markets don't last as long anymore. Immediately after the crash of 1987, for example, there were two months of weakness—then a recovery that pushed the market to record highs the following year. Those who panicked and sold shares during that two-month volatile period missed the ensuing recovery. Those who held on, painful though those two months were, found their patience rewarded.

Since we now live in a time when market moves happen more quickly than ever, an investor trying to avoid the corrections is just as likely to miss the upswings. Just like corrections, moves to the upside are happening far more quickly.

A quick look at the numbers tells why it is so important to be in—and to stay in—the market. In the ten-year period ending December 31, 1998, there were 2,528 trading days. An investor who held stocks throughout that entire period—the quintessential buy-and-hold strategy—enjoyed a compound *annual* return of 16 percent, without even factoring in whatever dividends he may have received during that time.

But an investor who missed the top ten performing days—just one day a year, on average, during this period—saw her return drop to 11.8 percent annually. Missing the top forty performing days—merely being out of the market once a quarter during the decade—reduced her returns to a paltry 4.5 percent a year, a heavy penalty for faulty market timing.

You could take the reverse side of this argument and say that someone who was not invested during the ten worst-performing days would certainly have had enhanced results. However, this misses the point. Your primary objective as an investor is not to avoid losing money by not investing any. It is to make money. You have to be in the market to benefit from it. And once you are in it, as the chart on the next page clearly shows, you want to stay in it.

Given this compelling evidence that buy-and-hold is clearly the way to go, why don't more people do it? It certainly isn't due to a lack of knowledge. A colleague of mine, a twenty-year Wall Street veteran who understands the ins and outs of market movements as well as anyone, watched with more and more worry as the market's slide reached nearly 20 percent in

January 1, 1989, to December 31, 1998

Investment Period	S&P Annualized Return*
Fully invested for all 2,528 days	16.0%
Less the 10 best days	11.8%
Less the 20 best days	9.0%
Less the 30 best days	6.6%
Less the 40 best days	4.5%

Sources: PaineWebber and Standard & Poor's
* The return figures are actually slightly higher. Whatever dividends an investor received during this period were not included in calculating the annualized return.

the late summer of 1998. (The Dow ended up falling 19.5 percent, just missing, by 0.5 percent, a 20 percent decline—the classic definition of a bear market.) Now, this is a woman who knows long-term-performance numbers cold and also knows that, historically, markets have always come back after a dramatic decline like the one we were experiencing that summer. And yet, after watching the value of her shares fall on what seemed to be a daily basis for weeks and weeks on end, she sold everything—about ten days before the market dramatically turned around and headed for record highs.

Buying on the Dips

It is hard to hold on during a down market. It is even more difficult to think of declines as buying opportunities—but they usually are. If you just look at the chart at the beginning of the chapter, you'll realize history shows that if you are a long-term investor, this is exactly what you need to do. For an investor with a long-term plan, periods of market declines provide an excellent opportunity to continue building toward long-term goals.

Given the unprecedented bull market of the 1990s, stocks have reached the point where they certainly are not cheap. That makes the strategy of buying during corrections particularly important.

Corrections tend to present some of the few times that investors can buy high-quality stocks at less than top dollar. Recognizing that no one ever buys at the exact bottom every time, the long-term investor can comfortably buy during a correction, confident that even if stocks continue to slide, the ensuing recovery should reward patience.

Some investors I have talked to agree completely with what I have just said, but they tell me they find it hard to "pull the trigger" and buy during periods of market declines. For them, the frequently forgotten strategy of dollar-cost averaging makes sense. Dollar-cost averaging is nothing more than a form of disciplined investing. You put a fixed amount of money into the market at regular intervals. When the market is high, you get less stock for your money; when it is low, you can buy more. But over time you will accumulate a sizable portfolio.

When most people talk about dollar-cost averaging, they focus on the fact that the strategy lets you buy less when the market is rising. However, it works well even in periods of declining markets, as the example below shows—proving that it is a potentially worthwhile strategy to have in place during the next market correction.

The take-away message should be clear: buying on the dips, no matter

Dollar-Cost Averaging During a Declining Market

Month	Amount Invested	Share Price	Shares Acquired
January	$1,500	$30	50
February	$1,500	$25	60
March	$1,500	$20	75
April	$1,500	$15	100
May	$1,500	$10	150
Total	$7,500	*	435

Source: PaineWebber
* *The average share price during this steady decline was $20—the sum of what the stock was trading for during the five months you were employing this strategy, divided by five. However, by using the dollar-cost-averaging method, you would have paid just $17.24 a share (the $7,500 you invested, divided by the 435 shares you ended up buying).*

how you do it, assures your participation in a market that has been positive over the long term. (It also allows you to benefit from the power of compounding—a concept that we will explore in detail later in the chapter.)

I know that words about disciplined investing may seem to ignore the high level of emotion that accompanies the decision to put your money into the stock market and leave it there. Watching the value of one's assets—and the future security those assets represent—decline sharply can be a wrenching emotional experience, no matter how long you have been investing. Indeed, as we have seen, it can be difficult for even the professionals, who should know better, to maintain cool heads amidst chaos.

There is an old saying on Wall Street that "the market climbs a wall of worry": that is, there are periods when stocks keep rising despite concerns about corporate earnings, inflation, a "long-overdue correction," and the like. Similarly, it is often just when things look darkest that the market, which tends to anticipate events of all kinds, begins a recovery.

With those two facts in mind, you might want to try to climb your own wall of worry during the next market decline and step up your stock purchases, or at least make sure that you stick with your dollar-cost-averaging program. History says you will be rewarded if you do. History also shows that people who panic and sell into declining markets tend not to do well, because they rarely get back in a timely manner.

There have been times in the course of market history when common stocks were not the best-performing asset. During the high-inflation years of the 1970s and 1980s, interest rates soared along with inflation. When short-term interest rates were in the high teens, and the thirty-year Treasury bond yielded over 14 percent, a simple investment strategy was rolling over CDs or buying long-term Treasuries. This was an easy and extremely safe way to come up with returns that topped the 11 percent that stocks have produced annually since 1926. (But of course, holding long-term fixed-income investments during a period of rising rates is a disastrous strategy—something we will explore in detail when we discuss bonds later on.)

That era of high inflation, however, was an aberration in U.S. economic history, sustained by a series of poor policy choices on the part of the government and the Federal Reserve. But since 1980—thanks to much sounder policies from a conservative and more knowledgeable Federal Reserve, aided more recently by the government's running surpluses rather than deficits—

inflation is now back down to its historical rate. Barring some major change in Washington and a return to those high-spending, high-inflation days (and it never pays to underestimate the ability of our elected leaders to do foolish things), we believe stocks are the best way to build wealth.

Why People Don't Get into the Market

Some people I have worked with don't worry about selling before they should. They have a different problem. Instead of getting out of the market too soon, they don't buy at all. They are convinced that the market is at an all-time high, and there is nowhere to go but down.

Given the strength of the current bull market, their position is understandable. It is also wrong. Every investor fears buying at the top of the market. But again, the key to investing success is time in the market, not market timing.

Let's use some real numbers to prove the point that worrying about buying at a market top is not a good reason for staying away from stocks. Even an investor who had the unlikely bad timing of buying at the top of the market each and every year during the period we talked about before—January 1, 1989, to December 31, 1998—would still have had excellent results.

What exactly would have happened to returns if an investor had consistently bought at the exact top over the past decade? Not very much.

The annual return over the last ten years for someone who put $1,000 in the market at the beginning of each year would have been 17.9 percent (again excluding dividends received). But if another investor had incredibly bad timing and invested the same $1,000 in each of those years on the day the market reached its peak for the year—and even I am not that unlucky—his annual returns would have been 15.1 percent during those ten years, a moderate discount.

What's important to note about the table on page 32 is that the "mere" 15.1 percent return you would have received, if you had picked the absolutely worst possible times to invest, significantly outperformed long-term U.S. government bonds with their 11.3 percent return, and dwarfed the 4.9 percent yield on T-bills.

Of course, it is unlikely that any investor would be unlucky enough to

Even Being Unlucky Wouldn't Have Been a Bad Thing

If you invested $1,000 each year between January 1, 1989, and December 31, 1998, here is what would have happened to your investment.

	Ending Value	Rate of Return*
S&P 500	$27,629	17.9%
S&P 500 if you bought at the highest point each year	**$23,482**	**15.1%**
Long-term government bonds	$18,864	11.3%
Treasury bills	$13,133	4.9%

Sources: Ibbotson Associates and PaineWebber
* *Again, the return figures are actually slightly higher. Whatever dividends an investor received during this period are not included in the returns shown above.*

consistently buy at the top each year, but conversely, neither is it likely that anyone would be lucky enough to buy at the bottom.

The lesson here? Don't worry about investing at the top, and don't worry about finding the exact market bottom before you invest. The key, again, is to be invested.

Bear Markets

Declines of 20 percent or more in the stock market over extended periods of time do occur, and the astute investor will be prepared to respond with appropriate strategies. We saw that during the high-inflation period of the 1970s and into the 1980s: sophisticated individuals reduced—*reduced,* not eliminated—their stock holdings and shifted their money into bonds, to take advantage of yields that exceeded the historical returns of stocks. So, clearly we are not advocating being 100 percent in stocks at all times. You need to adjust your asset mix as market conditions change.

We don't know what will bring this bull market to an end, but good companies can perform well even in less than perfect markets—that's why you always want to keep a portion of your long-term money in stocks. As we enter the new millennium, common stocks continue to offer the best potential for long-term investors, just as they have historically.

There is another advantage to staying significantly invested. History shows that the longer an investor's holding period, the greater the chances are of making a positive return on investment.

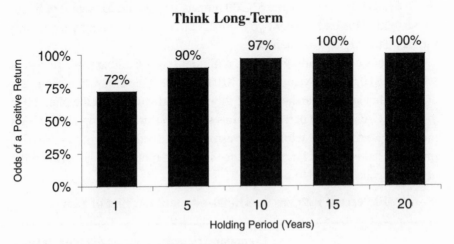

Think Long-Term

Sources: Ibbotson Associates and PaineWebber

The chart clearly shows the story. With a one-year holding period, the odds of a positive return have been 72 percent. For a five-year holding period, the odds improved to 90 percent. For ten years, 97 percent. If your holding period was fifteen years, market return has been positive 100 percent of the time.

The Power of Compounding

If time is a powerful ally of the investor, so too is compounding. In fact, it may have an even more beneficial effect.

Let's assume that a mutual fund investment of $1,000 is set up for a child at birth. Let's also assume that this is an equity mutual fund, and that the long-term compound annual growth rate (CAGR) of this fund is 10 percent. If this fund is never touched over the course of the child's life (no deposits or withdrawals) and all dividends are reinvested, by the time the child is 18, this fund will be worth over $5,500.

However, if the fund is held until the child is 65—again with no additions or withdrawals and with dividends reinvested—the original $1,000 will be worth over $490,000! This results from the effects of compounding.

Compounding is the process of interest earning interest. Interest earned in one period itself earns interest during subsequent time periods. For example, if $1,000 earns 10 percent over the course of a year, at the end of the year it is worth $1,100. In year two, the $1,100 returns 10 percent, for a gain of $110, so the total at the end of year two is $1,210. In each subsequent year, the return is on the higher base number.

How does compounding work in a mutual fund? Compare two investors who save $10,000 per year in their 401(k) plans. One starts when she is 21, and the other starts when he is 30. If they both retire at 65 and the plans have yielded a CAGR of 10 percent, the investor who started saving at 21 would have over $6.5 million, while the investor who started at 30 would have $2.7 million. That is quite a large difference for just a nine-year gap between the ages when each started to save.

10 Percent Returns on $1,000—Amount at End of Year

	Compound return	Simple return
Year 1	$1,100	$1,100
Year 2	$1,210	$1,200
Year 3	$1,331	$1,300
Year 4	$1,464	$1,400
Year 5	$1,611	$1,500

With both time and compounding working for you in long-term investments, you have two very powerful allies. The moral: invest early, reinvest your dividends, and keep your investments working for you. (Also, get your children started early. See chapter 15, "Investing for Your Children: Possibilities and Pitfalls.")

Don't Try to Time the Market

One final thought about *time in the market, not market timing*. I have been amused over the last few years by the fluctuating recommendations of technical analysts, the classic market timers. They read charts and various other measures of historical performance, and then make judgments about the future direction of the market. They can change their opinions remarkably quickly, going from bullish one day to bearish the next, and possibly bullish the week after that.

While the calls—and the comments justifying their rapidly changing opinions—can be interesting, and sometimes downright entertaining, I don't think they provide much value to the serious long-term investor. After all, you want to buy shares in specific companies to benefit from future earnings and dividends, not trade the market or stocks. Unless you want to pay round-trip commissions getting in and out of stocks, and don't care that any short-term gains will be taxed as ordinary income (instead of at the lower capital gains rate that applies to investments held more than a year), you should ignore the technical analysts' short-term calls. I would prefer to read tea leaves.

Inflation: Deadly

Let's focus on something implicit in everything we've talked about so far: you need to be in the market long-term to offset the invidious power of inflation.

While most investors intuitively understand that stocks are riskier than bonds, and that bonds are riskier than short-term fixed-income instruments like Treasury notes or CDs, far fewer are truly aware of the devastating impact inflation can have on savings and especially fixed-income investments.

Inflation erodes the value of all fixed-income assets; that is the key reason the bond market is so sensitive to signs of inflation. The *nominal* value of the investment will not change due to inflation: a $1,000 bond will still return $1,000 at maturity. However, the *real* value—approximately the nominal value minus inflation, or what $1,000 will be able to buy when the bond comes due—will change depending on the rate of inflation.

Let's see how this works. Buying a bond seems like a fairly safe proposition. You loan the government, agency, or corporation a fixed amount of money for a set amount of time—let's suppose $1,000 for thirty years. The borrower promises to pay you a fixed amount of interest (in the form of negotiable coupons) during those thirty years, for the use of your money, and pledges to return your original $1,000 at the end, as well.

It seems like a relatively risk-free proposition. However, if the rate of inflation is greater than 0 percent while you hold the bond, the $1,000 that is returned to you will not be worth as much as the $1,000 you loaned. And the coupon, or return interest, will be worth less as well. So, before you commit to an investment, inflation expectations need to be factored into the projected returns.

In the high-inflation years of the seventies and eighties, money in savings accounts lost substantial amounts of purchasing power over time. A $10,000 nest egg at the beginning of 1970 had purchasing power of only $3,000 by 1990.

But even low inflation can be devastating over extended periods of time. The chart opposite shows what would have happened if in 1926 you had invested $1,000 in three-month Treasury bills, in long-term government bonds, and in stocks. While the least-risky Treasury bills had the worst performance, as you would expect, at least the return was positive.

But look at the *inflation-adjusted* returns. The three-month Treasuries yielded a compound annual growth rate during the seventy-two years from 1926 to 1998 of less than 1 percent, and bonds just over 2 percent. The equity investment provided the best protection against inflation—by a dramatically wide margin—yielding a real annual rate of return of 7.9 percent.

Taxes: Another Threat

Now consider the onerous effects of taxation. The returns from the three-month Treasury bills are fully taxed at ordinary income tax rates (39 percent

Accumulated Wealth 1926–1998 (1926 = $1,000)

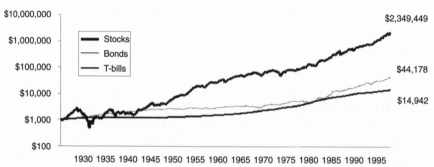

Source: Ibbotson Associates

Accumulated Wealth After Inflation (1926 = $1,000)

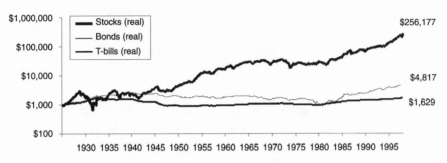

Source: Ibbotson Associates

for the higher-income earners today, and often far more when state and local income taxes are added on). On an after-inflation and after-tax basis, the *real* returns from short-term instruments, including savings accounts and CDs, can easily slip into negative territory. What this means is, *you can actually lose money in such "risk-free" investments.*

That isn't hyperbole. It's fact. Let's use historical numbers to show why that is so. Let's say you have $1,000 to invest and you put it in a CD. Historically, cash equivalents have returned 3.7 percent a year. So, at the end of the year, you would have $37 in interest. Not great, but at least it is a positive return, right?

Well, not quite. We haven't accounted for taxes or inflation.

Let's say you are in the 28 percent tax bracket. After you pay the $10.36 you owe (28 percent of $37), you are left with $26.64. That means your real return (what you received, minus taxes you have to pay) is 2.66 percent. But we still have not accounted for inflation. Inflation typically averages 3.1 percent, according to figures compiled by Ibbotson Associates, so that reduces your real return to minus 0.44 percent.

You've lost money.

In contrast, remember that appreciation in stock prices is taxed at the very favorable long-term capital gains tax rate, currently 20 percent. So, not only are returns far greater from stocks, but thanks to capital gains treatment, you get to keep more of them.

Of course, investors should always keep some money in short-term liquid instruments to provide money for emergencies, and there may be investment environments when returns from short-term fixed-income investments are advantageous, but generally speaking, common stocks are far better investments for the long term.

The conservative investor who avoids stocks as a way to minimize risk should be aware that the "risk-free" short-term instruments such as CDs and savings accounts can be very risky, even in a low-inflation environment, once inflation and taxes are factored in.

It is important to remind yourself that the perceived risk-free investments such as CDs, money market funds, or savings accounts may in reality turn out to be very poor investments that don't protect your assets from taxes and inflation. Inflation plays havoc with fixed-income investments. As we saw, inflation erodes both the purchasing power of the value of a bond and the value of the coupon (interest) payments you receive. As a result, in periods of rising inflation, bond buyers will demand a higher coupon, or interest rate, to compensate them for the lost value.

How It Works with Equities

For equity investors, things are a little different. Equity prices reflect the future value of the earnings and dividends that the company will deliver, so investors will simply pay less for the shares in a high-inflation environment, but more in a low-inflation environment, where those future returns will be worth more.

Some charts may be illustrative. While these charts are theoretical, historical pricing of the market, as we will see in a moment, shows that our theory is borne out. They essentially show how the market and how growth stocks are priced in different inflation environments.

In a 10 percent inflation environment, the market would be expected to sell at about 5 times earnings. (The price/earnings ratio is a shorthand way of measuring the price the market pays for earnings. If a stock sells at $10 and has $1 earnings, we say its P/E ratio is 10: the $10 share price divided by the $1 earnings. For the market, we use the price of the market index—the S&P 500—and divide it by the total earnings of the five hundred companies that make up the index.)

As the inflation rate moves to 2 percent, the market would be priced at 25 times its earnings. (In these examples we are assuming that earnings are growing 7.0 percent annually.)

But look what happens in the same environments to a stock that is grow-

S&P 500 P/E Versus Inflation Assuming 7% Earnings Growth

Source: PaineWebber

ing 15 percent a year, or at a rate that is more than twice the market as a whole. At a 10 percent inflation rate, this growth stock barely gets a premium, selling a little over 5 times its earnings. But as inflation slows to 2 percent, the growth stock will sell at 55–65 times its earnings. Clearly, this argues for purchasing growth stocks in a low-inflation environment.

The chart opposite may partly explain a phenomenon that must seem mystifying to many investors. Here's the scenario: A growth stock favored by investors is selling at a premium multiple but now reports earnings a few pennies short of expectations. This seemingly very modest shortfall results in an extremely sharp correction in the stock price. What happened?

It is the price of disappointment.

As investors adjust their projected growth rates downward even by just a few percentage points, the price paid, or multiple, deleverages, contracting more than the growth ratio.

The market has proven these theories to be correct. Back in the late fifties and early sixties, when inflation was below 2 percent, the market sold at over

Growth Stocks' P/E Versus Inflation Assuming 15% Earnings Growth

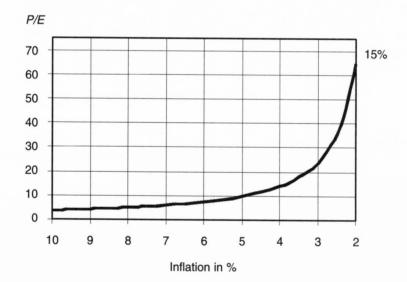

Source: PaineWebber

The Price of Disappointment:
P/E Drop When a 25% Growth Rate
Becomes a 20% Growth Rate

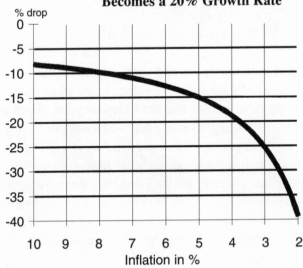

Source: PaineWebber

20 times its earnings, and many of the growth stocks of the day were trading at over 50 times their earnings. For example, Polaroid sold at over 100 times earnings, IBM traded at 77 times, and Avon Products had a P/E ratio of 51.

Conversely, in 1982, prior to August, when inflation was 14 percent, the market sold at less than 8 times earnings overall, while the growth stocks, with a few exceptions, barely traded at a premium.

The unprecedented gains for the S&P 500 from 1995 through 1999 (up 37.4, 23.1, 33.1, 28.6, and 19.5 percent, respectively) essentially repriced the market to reflect the low-inflation environment we enjoy today. With productivity generating growth without inflation, the government producing surpluses, and the Internet increasing competition and thereby reducing prices, we expect the market's price to continue to reflect this low-inflation environment. However, because it is unlikely we will see inflation fall below the 2 percent or so it averaged in 1999, it seems reasonable to assume that future market gains will have to come from earnings gains and not a further repricing of the market.

When Inflation Is High

As inflation increased in the seventies and early eighties, Americans took their money out of stocks and put it into fixed-income investments and real estate to take advantage of higher interest rates and rising prices. Hard assets, like real estate, are the assets of choice in a high-inflation environment because they tend to appreciate along with inflation. Americans instinctively understood there were two benefits to borrowing to finance a larger home or a second home: first, home prices would keep on rising along with inflation, and second, they would be able to pay their mortgages with ever cheaper dollars down the road.

But in the new millennium, we expect inflation to remain modest. That favors investing in financial assets.

When Inflation Is Low

Although inflation dominated economic life in the 1970s and 1980s, in the current lower-inflation environment we are starting to hear concerns about deflation, or falling prices. Indeed, in a number of areas (particularly many commodities), prices have been declining. Should investors be concerned and adjust portfolios to reflect a deflationary environment?

Before we answer the question, let's first put it in context. Falling prices are not necessarily negative for an economy. When caused by collapsing currencies and huge debt positions—such as occurred in a few Asian countries during the economic crisis of 1998–99—they can devastate an economy. But if improving productivity causes deflation, these price declines can be benign.

For example, in the post–Civil War period (between 1865 and 1905, to be exact), commodity prices declined by nearly 60 percent. But the U.S. economy experienced strong growth, and not coincidentally, the stock market rose sharply. The total return during that 40-year period was nearly 1,500 percent. The growth and the accompanying price declines were fueled by sharp productivity gains owing to two major technological leaps:

- the completion of the transcontinental railroad, which opened vast western markets to eastern manufacturers
- the creation of national communications, thanks to the widespread introduction of the telegraph

These developments spawned a huge increase in entrepreneurial activity and produced enormous productivity gains, which led to lower prices.

The analogy with today is obvious. For the last thirty years we have experienced declining prices in computers and related products. Virtually every year consumers can buy more powerful computers more cheaply. This has been a healthy development for our economy and has resulted in strong productivity increases, which in turn are reducing the price of everything from software to telephone calls. The Internet will contribute greatly to productivity and efficiency in the years ahead, and has already been responsible for sharp price declines. (Think of what has happened to book prices as a result of aggressive discounting by on-line booksellers.) These factors should allow us to continue to enjoy healthy growth with stable or declining prices. Since that is the case, deflation—should it arrive full force—is unlikely to cause you to radically restructure your portfolio.

The lesson for investors is simply this: it is the real, after-tax returns that count. Over time, common stocks—with the historically superior returns and the advantage that comes from being taxed at the long-term capital gains rate—have best protected investors from inflation (and have benefited in some periods of deflation as well). Short-term instruments, such as savings accounts and CDs, while perceived as nearly risk free, have achieved poor real (that is, after inflation is accounted for) after-tax returns. These short-term instruments are still a part of a balanced portfolio, and certainly during certain periods of high short-term interest rates should be overweighted. But they have been a risky proposition for long-term investors, and going forward, common stocks are likely to deliver better returns.

Summing Up

What have we learned from these two centuries of stock market history, and how can you benefit from it?

First, the obvious: the deck is stacked in the long-term investor's favor. Just think back to the chart that opened the chapter, showing that the long-term trend line in stock market history is steadily upward. And thanks to Ibbotson Associates, we have good records of the stock market's performance from 1926 on; the data shows that the market has appreciated on average about 11 percent a year during that time, which includes the crashes of 1929 and 1987. That's pretty impressive. After all, your money doubles in slightly less than seven years if it compounds at an 11 percent annual rate.

Second, no matter how positive the long-term trend line, there are going to be down days, weeks, months, and (even though it has been a while), years. As unnerving as such downturns can be, if you are a long-term investor you have to accept them. If you try to time the market, you can lose big, as we have seen.

The temptation is always to sell in a market correction. As tempting as it is, you know from experience that is not the way to go. Leave market timing to the traders, and calls about upcoming market swings (real or imagined) to the technical analysts. Individual investors profit by owning good-quality companies that are successful over the long term. When you buy a stock, you are buying a future stream of earnings and dividends. These are generally not dramatically affected by short-term market fluctuations. Your commitment to a solid company with superior prospects shouldn't be either.

Third, while worrying about buying at a market top is a legitimate concern, the historical data shows there is not much danger long-term. The bigger worry is missing out by not being in the market in the first place.

Fourth, start investing early. As we have seen, compounding can be an incredibly effective force.

After twenty-eight years on Wall Street, I can confidently say I know no one who has consistently timed the market correctly, avoiding the days when stocks fell the most and being 100 percent invested during rapid climbs. A far better strategy is to set strategic long-term goals, own companies you can have confidence in, and prepare to ride out the inevitable storms. Use those periods of volatility not to panic but to review your goals and holdings, and maybe even add to your existing portfolio.

You know that's what you should do. But in a market that is fluctuating as widely as this one, it never hurts to be reminded of the basics—and time in the market, not market timing, has been the basis for success during the last two hundred years.

That trend is likely to continue.

3

Diversification, Asset Allocation, and Risk

We are about to delve into the world of portfolio theory, which can, I know, get arcane at times. I make you three promises before we begin:

- The jargon that the theorists are fond of using will be explained.
- We will be brief.
- If you work through the material, you will have a better understanding of how you can increase the overall return of your investment portfolio.

With that understanding, let's get under way.

When considering any investment—be it stocks, bonds, or even cash equivalents—it is important to think about the risk involved. How certain are you that the investment you are contemplating will produce the returns you expect?

The word "certain" is important. A common measure of risk used by finance professionals is the variability of returns, which is normally measured in terms of standard deviations from either the mean or the average return.

That's less complicated than it sounds. A plot of an asset's returns over time shows that they center around the mean. Risk arises when the probability is high that in any one year, there could be a wide range of returns, running from a large loss to a large gain. So, the further the return ranges from the mean, the riskier the investment.

Obviously, if an investor is going to take on the risk that his returns might sometimes be negative, he'll need to be duly compensated. That's why, historically, risk and return have had a positive correlation: investors require additional compensation for bearing additional risk.

Conversely, the more certain an investor is of the expected return, the less risky the asset is considered to be and the less of a risk premium he will demand. That's why a Treasury bill typically returns less than a stock; with a Treasury bill the downside is fairly limited, and so is the upside.

The chart on page 48 shows four asset classes—Treasury bills, Treasury bonds, large-cap stocks, and small-cap stocks—and how each compares to the others on a risk/reward basis. The chart shows that between 1926 and 1998 the average annualized rate of return for T-bills was 3.2 percent, while its annualized standard deviation over the same period was 3.8 percent (a very narrow range). At the other end of the spectrum, the average annualized rate of return for small-cap stocks was 17.4 percent, but the annualized standard deviation was 33.8 percent (a comparatively wide range). So, small-cap stocks have been far riskier investments than Treasury bills, Treasury bonds, and large-cap stocks.

If we examine a more recent time frame, from 1980 to 1998, the results are somewhat different. The standard deviations of stocks and Treasury bills

Risk and Return of Various Asset Classes (1926–98)

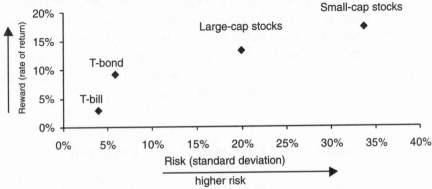

Source: Ibbotson Associates

Risk and Return of Various Asset Classes (1980–98)

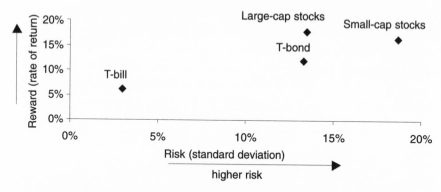

Source: *Ibbotson Associates*

have declined from the earlier period, while they have increased for Treasury bonds. The average rates of return, however, have *increased* for all asset classes except small-cap stocks.

This outcome seems counterintuitive, but these last nineteen years have truly been an exceptional period in our financial history.

There are other risks that also should be evaluated when making different types of investments. We have already talked at length (in chapter 2) about inflation risk. But there are more factors to be concerned about, including exchange rate risk, country/political risk, business risk, and liquidity risk.

Liquidity risk refers to how easy it is to buy or sell an asset, and generally refers to the risk on the sell side. The New York Stock Exchange and the National Association of Security Dealers provide liquidity, or ease of buying and selling, for most securities. But the liquidity for smaller companies often leaves much to be desired. When an investor wishes to sell shares in a firm with a tiny market capitalization, there may be few interested buyers, which forces the seller to take a low price to unload the stock.

Containing Risk with Diversification

"Don't put all your eggs in one basket" may sound old-fashioned, but it still remains sound advice in investing. Diversification is perhaps one of the most important tools available to investors who are looking to reduce the overall risk within their portfolios.

The term "diversification" describes two possible investing scenarios:

1. holding different classes of assets in a portfolio
2. investing in different securities within the same asset class

Both approaches are designed to reduce risk. Let's take each individually.

Diversifying among asset classes helps to even out the risks associated with each type of asset. That is why you might have a portfolio composed of stocks, bonds, and cash equivalents. The particular risk of any asset can be offset to some degree by the specific variability of the other assets in the portfolio.

Diversifying within an asset class—for example, within stocks you might choose to own a dozen large-cap growth stocks, a handful of small-value stocks, and an S&P 500 Index fund—can help smooth out the returns within a particular sector of your portfolio.

Studies have shown that a well-diversified stock portfolio should contain roughly thirty stocks: in an all-equity portfolio, the maximum benefits of diversification are reached when the portfolio contains thirty different companies' stocks. Do you have to own that many? Apparently not. Other studies indicate that *most* of the benefits of diversification can be achieved from portfolios containing twelve to eighteen stocks. I would certainly feel secure with eighteen; others may want a broader spread.

Diversification is a way to spread your risk among different kinds of investments. Asset allocation refers to the different weightings you give to each asset category—stocks, bonds, and cash equivalents—that you use to diversify. Thus, you can see that asset allocation should be the middle step in the investing process.

- First, you should determine the expected return from each asset category.
- Second, you need to decide which combination of the three asset classes—stocks, bonds, and cash equivalents—will offer you the best potential return, given the risk you are willing to accept.

- Only then do you take the third step: you select the asset you want to buy within the class.

The weakness of any discussion about diversification and asset allocation is that there is no one right answer as to what makes up the perfect portfolio. Each of us has to decide the appropriate level of diversification given the cost and timing of our goals and our risk tolerance. I have always been over-weighted in stocks because I believe in them and my horizon is still long-term, but within the stock category I have diversified with different types of stocks and mutual funds.

But that's just me. Your circumstance could be remarkably different.

The issue is further clouded by the fact that returns for an investor who holds stocks, bonds, and cash, in whatever proportion, will never be as high as from the best-performing asset. Particularly in a bull market as strong as this one has been, that makes the merits of asset allocation less apparent. Being 100 percent in common stocks over the past few years would have produced a better return than any combination of stocks and bonds you could have devised.

A typical asset allocation if markets are selling in balance—that is, if each asset class is performing as it has historically—might be 60 percent stocks, 32 percent bonds, and 8 percent cash. But since markets rarely sell in balance, these weightings must be adjusted for current conditions. Back in 1981, when three-month Treasury bills yielded 17 percent, investment accounts should have been heavily overweighted in these cash equivalents. With stocks' historical return of 11 percent, 17 percent guaranteed by the U.S. government was clearly a superior investment, and one that was available with less risk. Similarly, as short-term rates came down, the double digits still available in the long-term fixed-income markets were more than competitive with stocks. Today, with rates far lower, common stocks should have the highest weightings.

Recognizing there is no typical investor and that only you know what your objectives and risk tolerance are, you have to tailor asset allocation weightings to your own situation. For a baby boomer investing through a retirement account, such as an IRA or 401(k), it would be reasonable to have a much higher weighting in stocks, given the long-term nature of the objective. If current income is needed from investments, that must be taken into account.

If the money is required for upcoming tuition or other payments, risk must be reduced.

But not only should the cost and timing of your goals drive your asset allocation; market conditions should as well. There are rare occasions—such as the declining inflation environment of the 1980s—when it might make sense to use bonds to accomplish your long-term goals.

The point here is simple. As you adjust your portfolio to reflect your changing circumstances (there is a new child or grandchild, for example), take a moment to see if the overall market has changed since you last adjusted your portfolio, and respond to that change as well.

You don't allocate assets to maximize performance. You do it to minimize risk. For example, if the stock market goes into a correction or a bear market, you may benefit from the returns in the fixed-income markets.

One final point about risk. The unique risk of an asset is known as "unsystematic risk." This is the risk that characterizes only one individual asset, and it is a risk that can be eliminated through diversification. For example, the risk that the management of the ABC Corporation will make strategic blunders is unsystematic risk. Only ABC's managers have the ability to make internal decisions that can ruin the company's future. The managers of XYZ Co. have the ability to give their shareholders heart palpitations, but are likely to have very little influence on what happens at ABC, unless they are a direct competitor.

Risk that cannot be diversified away is known as "systematic risk." This risk is inherent in all assets. It is caused by macroeconomic factors and will remain even in a diversified portfolio of assets. For example, a nationwide recession will affect most companies and is therefore considered systematic risk.

A final thought on asset allocation. Everything we have just talked about should help put long-term stock market performance into perspective. As we have seen, the longer your holding period, the greater the likelihood of positive returns. And you also should have a greater appreciation of the true risk in the market. For the long-term investor, stocks become less risky over time, and the "safe" fixed-income instruments, when viewed in the light of inflation, become far more risky, as we saw in chapter 2.

Diversification reduces risk, but it also precludes the spectacular success that comes from owning one investment that becomes a major home run. The risk associated with going for broke with one investment, or a limited number of investments, is unacceptably high, and the chances of success are unacceptably low. That's what makes diversification a necessary part of an overall investment strategy.

Is It Time to Rebalance?

Asset allocation can never be considered in a vacuum. It must reflect your changing personal situation as well as changing market conditions.

Since asset classes perform at different rates, you need to reassess your asset allocation periodically. But there should never be a blind adherence to numbers. You may become more comfortable with stocks over time and allow your allocation to move up. On the other hand, you may need to rebalance your investments. Let me explain.

Up until now we have stressed the need to consider stocks as a key portion of your portfolio if you are investing for a long-term goal, such as retirement. However, it is possible that stocks are already a greater portion of your portfolio than you imagine—and indeed a greater portion than you want—through no fault of your own. For being unintentionally overweighted in stocks, you can blame the bull market. With stocks having outperformed most other investments by such a wide margin over the past few years, the percentage of your retirement portfolio allocated to equity investments may have increased—perhaps substantially.

Let's use a simple example to show what could have happened. Say in 1989 you had a portfolio of $200,000 and you had set your asset allocation at 65 percent stocks, 25 percent bonds, and 10 percent cash equivalents. You

$200,000 Portfolio in 1989

		Percentage of the Total Portfolio
Stocks	$130,000	65%
Bonds	$50,000	25%
Cash	$20,000	10%
Total	$200,000	100%

Source: PaineWebber

would have had $130,000 in stocks, $50,000 in bonds, and $20,000 in cash, as the table above shows.

Over the ten-year period from 1989 to 1998, both stocks and bonds have substantially outperformed their historical averages. Stocks have climbed 19.2 percent; bonds have increased by about 11.7 percent a year; and cash by 5.3 percent annually.

Assuming that you didn't put any more money into your accounts during those ten years, the stock portion of your portfolio would have climbed to $752,846 in value; your bonds would be worth $151,183; and the cash component would have risen to $33,521. Those are pretty impressive gains. But look at what has happened to your asset allocation.

Because your stocks have grown so much faster than your bonds and cash, they now represent more than four-fifths of the portfolio; and bonds and

That $200,000 Has Become a $937,550 Portfolio Today

		Percentage of Portfolio
Stocks	$752,846	80.3%
Bonds	$151,183	16.1%
Cash	$33,521	3.6%
Total	$937,550	100.0%

Source: PaineWebber

cash——which used to make up about a third——have fallen to less than 20 percent combined.

As a result of the bull market, you may be taking on more investment risk than you originally planned. As you know, while stocks have historically produced the highest returns, they also carry the highest level of volatility. It is important that your total portfolio reflect your current objectives and desired level of risk. If it doesn't—as a result of a run up in stocks or some other factor—it may be time to rebalance.

That holds true whether you're an aggressive investor or a conservative one, or fall somewhere in between. As our example shows, you can't simply choose an asset-allocation strategy and let it take care of itself. Keeping an investment strategy working is an ongoing activity. You probably want to review it at least once a year, since different investments may grow at different rates.

Before we talk about the factors to consider in rebalancing your portfolio, let me make one probably superfluous note. Rebalancing your portfolios is not the same as market timing—switching asset allocations because you think the market is going to rise or fall in the short term. When you rebalance, you are making adjustments in what you own to make sure your holdings reflect your long-term objectives.

Factors to Consider When Rebalancing

When you rebalance your portfolio and/or change your asset allocation strategy, you need to consider three things:

Time Horizon

How long will it be until you will need the money from this investment? Obviously, the more time you have until you require the money, the more you can afford the higher risk (but potentially greater returns) that come from being in stocks.

Investment Goals and Overall Financial Situation

Performance of your investments is just one reason that may cause you to re-balance. You should also consider it whenever you experience a major event in your life, such as retirement, the death of a spouse, the birth of a child or grandchild, or a disability suffered by you or a family member.

Risk Tolerance

Have changes in market conditions—a long run up in stocks, for example—left you with a portfolio that contains more (or less) risk than you would like? Or conversely, are stocks now so much more attractive than bonds that you are willing to put a higher portion of your funds into equities?

Summing Up

Risk tolerance is different for each individual. Despite all the charts and graphs, it remains a personal decision. If an investment makes you uncomfortable, no matter what its long-term investment history, then it is not the right investment for you.

Generally, riskier investments are more suitable for individuals with longer investment horizons. If you have ten or more years until you reach a major goal, then you should feel comfortable having the majority of your money in stocks. Your goal is far enough away that you can ride out the invariable bumps that come from investing in stocks. If you need the money within the next year or so, or you are investing primarily for current income, you cannot afford the volatility that comes with placing that block of money in stocks. You need more conservative investments.

But again, asset allocation is an individual decision, and only you can determine the appropriate balance for your situation.

4

Investment Information:
Easy to Find, Hard to Evaluate

I have been appearing on *Wall $treet Week With Louis Rukeyser* for many years. Occasionally I am reminded of just how many.

When I travel, it is not unusual for someone to come up to me and in the course of our conversation ask about "little Stevie," my son. They tell me they remember seeing me on *Wall $treet Week With Louis Rukeyser* when I was nine months pregnant—and by that point there was no missing the fact that I was pregnant—and they'll recall how Lou announced my son's birth with full fanfare the next time I was on the show.

I am always touched by their interest. At some point during our talk, they may ask, "So, how old is little Stevie now?"

I tell them little Stevie, who now just wants to be called Steve, is a high school junior, who at six feet tall towers over his mother.

They are always surprised about "how quickly the time has gone," and to be honest, I am too. While I have been appearing on *Wall $treet Week With Louis Rukeyser* for eighteen years, I have hardly been there from the beginning. Lou has been doing the show for thirty years—an extraordinary record, but even more so given that *Wall $treet Week With Louis Rukeyser* really launched business programming on television. Back when Lou started, few thought an investment program would be interesting enough to draw a large audience, much less during prime time on Friday nights. And I don't think anyone would have predicted a record-breaking run.

Not only were business shows virtually nonexistent when Lou started, but *Wall $treet Week With Louis Rukeyser* was on public television, hardly the major force it is today. To make matters worse, the show is done live on Friday nights, and broadcast from Owings Mills, Maryland, a forty-minute cab ride from downtown Baltimore, and not exactly the center of financial activity. With those three strikes against it, it is a tribute to the show's content and quality that it is still, thirty years later, the most widely watched business program on television.

Business news has proliferated to the point where there are now television channels devoted solely to the financial markets and business in general.

Moreover, the Internet has added enormously to the information available. Want to know a stock's history, chart its performance against its peers, and see what twenty industry analysts think about its long-term viability? That is available with a click of your mouse, which will also give you an up-to-the-second quote on the stock's current price, a history of the last ten trades, its fifty-two-week high and low, P/E ratio, dividend yield, beta, and just about every other statistical measure you can think of. Technology and telecommunications have made information instantly available globally.

There are certainly advantages to all of this. Clearly, the more quickly information gets out to everyone, the more level the investment playing field becomes. Today some companies invite investors to listen in on the conference calls that they hold periodically with Wall Street analysts. These calls allow investors to hear firsthand from the company instead of being forced to rely on someone else's account and interpretation of what was said. But I would be quick to stress that after the call is complete, you probably will want to consult experts in the field—the very people the call was intended for—to get their take on what was said. Odds are they will have a greater understanding of nuances and context than you do.

But having all this information available does raise an interesting question: is it too much of a good thing?

For the investor with a long-term plan and the discipline to follow it, a daily deluge of information isn't necessarily helpful—even assuming the information is accurate and unbiased, which is not always the case.

Reader/Listener/Viewer, Beware

When there are problems with the accuracy of what is reported, the problem may not necessarily be with the people doing the reporting. For the most part, the financial media—especially the brand names such as *The Wall Street Journal, Investors Business Daily,* the *Financial Times, Forbes, Fortune, Business Week, Money, Smart Money, Worth,* the *Economist,* CNBC, CNN and CNN-fn, Fox and Bloomberg—do a masterful job of reporting the financial news, particularly given the relentless time constraints they are under.

The problem may lie in one of three areas:

- the news they are reporting (what they are told may turn out not to be true)
- who they use as sources and as guests
- the natural tendency to try to make each bit of information seem as important as possible

Let's take each of these points separately.

To show how information may turn out to be inaccurate, let's take a closer look at data you would expect to be unambiguous and certainly unbiased: government reports about how well the economy is doing. The federal government collects, analyzes, and disseminates reams of information about the economy: new housing starts, first-time unemployment claims, export sales, changes in the producer-price and consumer-price indexes. You name it, they track it.

One of the government's best-known reports is on the gross domestic product, the aggregate measure of the sale of goods and services in this country. Invariably, the government releases its quarterly report on GDP at 8:30 A.M. Eastern Time. Reporters at many of the television networks, not just the ones devoted to business news, break in to tell viewers what the report says, and analysts on Wall Street scramble to take a close look at the numbers and to interpret what they all mean.

The bond market reacts immediately, and when the stock market opens an hour later, there are often huge moves—either up or down—based on what was in the government report. This is just what you would expect, of course.

If the economy is growing much faster than everyone predicted, investors may worry that the Federal Reserve will raise interest rates. Since an increase in rates would slow the economy and increase corporate operating costs, stocks usually fall—sometimes very dramatically—based on a fear that rising interest rates will lead to lower corporate profits.

Conversely, news that the economy is modestly perking along (suggesting that the Federal Reserve will hold rates steady) or that it is slowing down a bit (so that the Fed might cut interest rates to get it going again) can cause the market to jump up.

As we said, this is just what you would expect.

Investing based upon any short-term judgment on the economy is risky because the state of the economy is not only difficult to estimate; it is difficult to measure—even years after the fact.

But here's something you wouldn't expect. The initial numbers often turn out to be dramatically wrong. Let's take a look at some GDP reports to show just how wrong.

Growth of Gross Domestic Product (GDP)

Quarter, Year	Preliminary Number	"Final Number"	First-Year Revision	Fourth-Year Revision
Q1, 1985	0.7%	0.3%	3.7%	4.9%
Q1, 1989	5.5%	4.3%	3.7%	3.2%
Q1, 1993	1.8%	0.7%	0.8%	−0.1%
Q1, 1997	5.6%	5.9%	4.9%	???

Source: Department of Commerce; Bureau of Economic Analysis

Consider the year 1985, which illustrates why investors should not react immediately—or at all—to much market-moving data.

The initial number released showed that the economy in the first quarter of 1985 had grown 0.7 percent. That was modest growth at best. The final number, issued after the government had more time to assess the data, showed that things were actually worse: the economy had grown at a rate of 0.3 percent, or very slowly. That is just slightly more than 1 percent on an annualized basis, which means the economy was barely expanding. That kind of negligible growth worries the stock market. If companies can't increase earnings, stock prices could fall.

But the government, to its credit, keeps going over the numbers and comparing them to historical norms, in an attempt to be as precise as possible. The first set of revisions, issued more than a year after the fact, showed that instead of being dead in the water, the economy had actually been humming along in the first quarter of 1985, growing at a very respectable, and indeed aggressive, 3.7 percent.

And by the time we had a firm reading of what had actually happened—four years later—it turned out that we hadn't been anywhere near a recession at all. We had been in the midst of a booming economy. The economy was growing at the rate of 4.9 percent a year—we just didn't know it.

So, it just doesn't make any sense to deviate from a long-term financial plan in response to some bit of economic news, no matter how breathlessly it is delivered. By the time a truer picture is known, the market has moved on.

It is far better to keep yourself focused on your long-term goals than to respond to every bit of economic data: first, because data is subject to change; and second—perhaps more important—because the economy, or GDP, is not the market. And that's fortunate, because the market has obviously been appreciating far faster than the economy has been growing.

Today, with 42 percent of the earnings for the Standard & Poor's 500 Index coming from outside the United States, a substantial portion of the market's earnings are driven by economies elsewhere on the globe. This is good, for it allows U.S. companies access to emerging markets that are growing much more rapidly than our own. It also benefits U.S. companies by diversifying their exposure to more than one economy.

Many of the goods that U.S. corporations sell abroad are actually produced abroad by their foreign subsidiaries. These sales are not included in our gross domestic product, yet they are significant, equal to about 25 percent of our GDP, and more than double the size of exports. While they are not counted in government statistics, they do accrue to corporate earnings.

A final note on the U.S. economy: nearly 25 percent is accounted for by the government and real estate sectors, neither of which is represented in the earnings of the market.

What all this means is that GDP is actually a poor indicator of corporate earnings—which are a much better predictor of market performance. Relying on government statistics, statistics that will often be radically revised, is a mistake. And while reacting to data that may not be relevant and might ultimately be wrong is not prudent, relying on what you hear in the media from an expert commenting on the market can be seriously detrimental to your financial health.

Whose Agenda Is It, Anyway?

The problem with the information presented in the financial media rarely stems from the reporters themselves. While occasionally you might hear of a reporter, editor, or producer using his position improperly, that's the rare exception. Most work very hard to deliver timely and accurate information.

The same cannot always be said of their sources, or the people who appear on their radio and television programs. Some of these experts may lack substantial knowledge in areas of investing or, worse, have a hidden agenda.

Let's deal with lack of knowledge first. I spend much of my time studying what is going on in the equity markets. In addition to my education and twenty-eight years of experience in the market, I have access to some of the best researchers and analysts in the business: the people who work for my firm, who use all the resources available to them—including some fairly complicated, proprietary quantitative models—to make investment recommendations for our clients.

I am glad that all of our hard work pays off. But still, it takes all the time, effort, and resources we have to select a list of stocks we believe are best for our clients. When it comes to estate planning or retirement concerns or the potential performance of bonds or derivatives, I need to consult with experts before I can even think of offering an opinion.

I know how much work I need to do to keep up in my single area, and so I wonder how some people can be held up as experts in every segment of business and finance, from investment strategy to stock picking to bond analysis to a discussion of foreign markets.

You may sense that someone is inflating his or her level of expertise, but it can be far more difficult to tell what the expert's personal agenda is, and that agenda may be far different from yours.

If you see an analyst, strategist, or fund manager on television, listen to her on radio, or read a quote from her in a newspaper recommending a particular stock, you may not know her true reason for doing so. It certainly could be she thinks the stock is undervalued. But there could be other motivations as well.

- Does she—or her firm—own the stock? Are they buyers, or sellers? Is her personal stake in what happens to the stock price affecting what she is telling you to do?
- Did her firm take public the company she is recommending? By telling the world that owning the stock is a good deal, is she trying to support her client's stock price, not only to justify their underwriting fee but also to show potential clients what her firm can do for them?
- Is the stock she is recommending underperforming, and is her company trying to boost the price—talking up the stock—to reduce its losing position and make its overall performance look better when her firm reveals how well its selections did at the end of the quarter?
- All of the above?

Now, the expert may indeed think the stock is a good buy and be talking about it in the hope that it will impress investors who will hire her and her firm in the future. Or she may have a hidden agenda, and her true motivation may not be immediately obvious. The more scrupulous media sources—be they money managers, major investors, heads of pension funds, or equity strategists—will be up-front about any potential conflict of interests they may have. A stock analyst or money manager will say, "These are our top holdings," or, "This is what we are recommending to our clients." A large investor might state, "This is what I own," or, "This is what we are buying now."

If the expert is not totally open, the person interviewing them might ask some probing questions, or in reporting the piece might note what the source does or does not own. But if they don't inquire, and you don't see or hear any disclaimers, you should be listening or reading with at least one eyebrow raised when someone is recommending what they would do with your money.

Why would a media outlet give space to someone with a hidden or self-serving motivation?

- They may not know about it.
- Conversely, they may assume everyone knows about the conflict. (You would expect the CEO of a company to say his stock is undervalued, or the head of a mutual fund company to emphasize his firm's superior performance and stock-picking prowess.)
- It's possible that the source is such good copy that reporters and producers are willing to downplay the conflict (the source in question has been a bear—but a very entertaining bear—during every leg of the bull market).
- They may simply be pressed to fill time.

The last point should not be overlooked, especially when it comes to what you see and hear on the all-business radio and television stations. The people who program those stations have much time to fill. The stock and bond markets are open only so many hours, and they may have to fill up many hours a day, often seven days a week, with some kind of business-related information. And while each outlet probably has a dream list of guests of the highest pedigree that they would like to have on every day, those guests are not always available.

When your first choice is not available, you go to your second, and when you can't get her, you move on to your third, and so it goes straight down the line. At some point, conflicts of interest and hidden agendas may come to the fore. That's especially true of the lesser-known and less-popular shows. The best guests want to be seen by the most people. Given the choice between appearing on a prestigious or nationally syndicated show and one that has a more limited audience, you can figure out where they are going to appear. That leaves the other shows—and other reporters and producers—scrambling for guests.

And scrambling for ratings and readers. It will come as no surprise to you that magazines compete for circulation—the more readers, the more they can charge the advertisers trying to reach them—and television programs, even those devoted to business news, battle for viewers for exactly the same reason. Even business shows need to obtain ratings. Given this competition, it is not surprising that media outlets tend to hype whatever content they have.

Thus, you might do better to think of all the business magazines and radio and TV programs as primarily a source of background material and entertainment rather than as your primary source of investment advice.

Information is not knowledge, and knowledge is not wisdom. This is worth remembering when it comes to the investment information you find in the media.

The Internet Gets Its Own Special Section

Everything we discussed about financial information is perhaps doubly true when it comes to finding and evaluating information on the Internet. (We will be talking about how to use the Internet as a tool in chapter 5.)

The good news—of course—is that thanks to the Internet, investors now have access to news and information that were available only to professionals a few years ago. If you want to find out about an over-the-counter stock that sounds intriguing, the latest quote on gold in London, or what Japan's balance of payments was last month, it is all available at the click of a button. You have access to much of the same data that professionals use in making their investment decisions and recommendations. There is no filter.

But there is something to be said for the filter that journalists provide. Like all other professionals, journalism is roughly a meritocracy. The higher you go up the ladder at a media outlet or publication—or the more prestigious the place you work for—the more likely it is that you deserve to be there. My experience with financial journalists has been very good. The vast majority work very hard, with readers' and viewers' interests at heart, to provide high-quality programming and information.

It is certainly possible for someone with questionable credentials or a hidden agenda to get on the air or be quoted in a story. But the fact is, someone—a reporter or producer—decided that the person being interviewed had some credibility before they brought this person to the public's attention. Unless they are doing man-in-the-street interviews, reporters and producers don't select people at random. They look for sources who are at least marginally qualified to offer an opinion.

On the Internet there is no such filter. Anyone can post anything about anything. Are you certain that Amazon.com is heading for a big fall because of a hush-hush decision by the Council of Little Green Men on Mars to interfere with the company's database? You can post your exclusive report in a chat room or on your Web site, or e-mail it to millions. It will look—at first blush, anyway—just as official as anything else out there.

The point is that some of the information you find on the Internet will be valuable; some will be as valuable as Martian green cheese; and some will be an outright fraud. You have to decide what the information is worth, based on your experience, on what you hear and read elsewhere, and on consultation with the people who help you make your investment decisions.

There should be a special place in purgatory for chat rooms that provide financial advice. They are the worst of all possible worlds. You don't know who is talking, you don't know the motivation behind their comments, and there is no immediate way to judge the value or truth of what these anonymous people are saying. They are accountable to no one.

While I am usually for less, not more, government regulation, it is worth noting—and a good thing for investors—that the New York Stock Exchange and the National Association of Securities Dealers highly regulate what member firms' employees can and can't do or say, regulations that provide much protection from conflicts of interest, unethical behavior, and fraud.

The Moral of the Story

What does all this mean to you? When it comes to evaluating the financial news and information you see, read, or hear, "Buyer (listener/viewer/ reader), beware." Even government data can be seriously flawed.

Given virtually unlimited news sources, limit yourself to a few brand names that you find most relevant to your personal goals and that you can develop confidence in. Make use of your public library to familiarize yourself with what is out there before selecting the magazines, newspapers, and newsletters that will be part of your regular reading. Make judgments about which television programs provide information that will help you make decisions. Be discriminating.

And finally, as far as your long-term goals are concerned, the financial information you hear and read is best thought of as a potential source of news, or perhaps entertainment, but rarely as an investment directive.

If an influential analyst thinks a pharmaceutical company's new drug is a bust, odds are it will depress the stock short-term. But one miss probably won't have a lasting effect on long-term earnings, if the pharmaceutical company has lots of drugs in the development pipeline. The long-term investor who has faith in the company can ignore that one failure.

I began the chapter talking about *Wall $treet Week With Louis Rukeyser,* so let me end it the same way. I am always grateful for my experiences on the program and the chance not only to work with Lou and the distinguished panelists but also to meet so many of the best minds in finance. One of my fondest memories is of meeting Nobel laureate Milton Friedman.

I doubt if anyone who knows me well would say I'm assertive, much less aggressive, but I overcame my natural shyness to hitch a ride with Milton Friedman, whom I had admired greatly since my days as an economics major in college. Professor Friedman was the honored guest on *Wall $treet Week With Louis Rukeyser* one night when I was a panelist. Since he doesn't live in New York, I was surprised to recognize him as he stepped off the same Metroliner I had taken to Baltimore. My regular cab was waiting, but I realized I had the chance of a lifetime if I could summon the courage to ask Professor Friedman for a ride in the car the show had sent to pick him up. Quickly paying my cabdriver, I approached Professor Friedman, implying I was stranded, and he generously consented to give me a lift. I already knew, of course, that he was a brilliant and creative thinker, but in that ride to Owings Mills I learned that he is also charming and personable. I count this personal time with one of the leading economic thinkers of the twentieth century as a true honor (and the autographed copy of the book, written with his wife, that he graciously gave me remains one of my prized possessions). The forty-minute ride to the studio was far too short.

5

The Internet:
A Tool, Not a Strategy

The Internet is revolutionizing how we live and accelerating the expansion of the Information Age. Few areas will be untouched by it. Already we have seen its impact on how we shop, get information, and communicate. While there are certainly reasons to be cautious when using the Internet, there can be major benefits for investors. Used as a tool, the Internet can be of great benefit in terms of both information and trading, if one is very careful.

Information

Before the Internet, information was extremely difficult to obtain. You'd go to the library, and you'd also network. Sometimes at the end of all your efforts you'd think you had covered all the bases, but often it seemed you had to make decisions before you were convinced that you knew everything you possibly could.

The Internet changes all that. Information is now much easier to come by. You can cover a lot more ground more quickly, especially when it comes to finding financial information and investing. But judging the quality of what you find is still up to you, and you must be careful. Misinformation runs rampant on the Internet. Because virtually anyone can post just about anything, there is no guarantee that the people providing advice on-line are knowledgeable about the investments they are discussing—and perhaps touting. There is no guarantee that what they post is true.

Periodically, I receive a "blind cc" e-mail between two people I have never met, or even heard of. The first person tells the second he has discovered—thanks to a newsletter that I have never been able to locate—a wonderful stock that he is urging his friend to buy. The implication, of course, is that I should too.

The Internet allows this kind of solicitation to become commonplace, and it makes information easy to replicate and broadcast. All of this can lead to misrepresentations—at best. Many of the message boards and chat rooms where investors exchange ideas are risky places to gain information to help you invest. In fact, the SEC has pinpointed chat rooms and message boards as breeding grounds for fraud, warning (with a certain amount of understatement) that a tip from an anonymous Internet subscriber may not be the best source of investment strategy.

Between 1998 and 1999, complaints to the SEC about Internet chat rooms and bulletin boards more than tripled. But the SEC can monitor only a small fraction of the advice given on-line. It is up to you to evaluate what you read, see, and hear. Investment fraud is probably as old as investing itself. The Internet just allows dishonest people a new and much more efficient medium for reaching their marks.

For example, people who offer tips may be involved in what is known as a pump-and-dump scheme: they rally interest in a stock to drive the price up, they short it, and then they make a fortune when the truth becomes known and the stock falls. (Shorting a stock means borrowing shares, selling them, and replacing them later at what—you hope—will be a lower price. This strategy is employed when an investor believes a stock is going down.)

The converse of this scam is also prevalent. Someone buys a significant position in an unknown, thinly traded stock and then posts raves about the company on every Web site and message board they can find, or via e-mail. As other people buy the stock, the value of the promoter's holdings soars, and then he sells out, before all the hype about the stock cools down and people realize that the company is grossly overvalued.

As always, you need to cross-check all the information you receive. It is here that a broker or financial adviser you trust can be especially valuable.

Perils and Pitfalls of Internet Trading

There is no doubt that the Internet has caused an explosion in on-line investing, revolutionizing—and further democratizing—investing in the process.
Just look at the numbers. Internet transactions now account for about a third
of all trades made by individuals. Indeed, it is estimated that by the end of
1999 more than 6 million households will have traded stocks over the Internet. That number is more than triple what it was in 1997. And according to
The New York Times, an estimated 20 million people regularly log onto the
Web for stock quotes and news.

Not surprisingly, the free-market system has responded to this demand.
There are now more than a hundred companies that handle on-line trading—
some full-service brokerage firms (including my own) and others that just
deal with stock trading. At the end of 1996, there were less than a dozen offering the service. So, if you want to trade on-line, you have a lot of options,
from buying and selling strictly on your own to having an account that includes trading on your own but getting advice as well. In fact, responding to
clients who want to make the transactions on-line but still want the services
associated with a financial adviser, many firms now offer an array of account types, often fee based, that can meet varying needs—a very healthy
development.

That's the good news. But there are several pitfalls you should be aware of
when considering Internet trading, even if you have already made the move
to trading on-line.

The first problem is relatively minor, but worth understanding. Outages
can occur on the Web. To avoid problems, it obviously helps to have a backup
plan. Check to make sure the brokerage firm you are using (or plan to use)
offers other methods of trading (by phone, for example) so you are not left
without access in the event of an outage. It is important to have a brokerage
firm that is easy to contact. The lowest-commission firms, the ones known as
deep discounters, often sacrifice customer assistance in exchange for low
fees. (As always, if you want to discount this advice because I work for a
full-service firm, you can. But it just makes sense to know the firm's abilities
and limitations before you become a customer. And the inability to manage
your investments, should there be a problem getting on-line, is a concern.)

The second problem is a bit more troubling. What you see is not always what you get when you trade over the Internet. Even if you receive a notice that your "order has been executed" after you have entered your trade on-line, it does not mean that your trade has gone through. It simply means the brokerage firm has received it. The actual buying and selling could occur later. Obviously, if the stock you are trying to buy goes up in the interim, you'll end up paying more than you thought. Similarly, if you are trying to sell into a declining market, you could get less than you expected, given the "order executed" message.

But perhaps the greatest concern is that the ability to buy and sell at the touch of the button may tempt you to become more of a trader than is prudent, if you have a long-term investment strategy.

In studies done by NFO Worldwide, a Greenwich, Connecticut–based research firm, a common theme quickly became apparent: Internet trading is boosting the confidence of investors to artificially high levels, and as a result they are taking ever greater risks. On-line investors told researchers that being able to monitor their stocks, as well as the latest financial news, on-line made them feel more in touch and connected with their investments, allowing them to be more aggressive with trading. Many log on at work and home throughout the day to monitor their investments' progress. The net result? They trade more frequently.

That's a problem. As we have emphasized, you don't want to be a (day) trader; you want to be a (long-term) investor. NFO found that of investors who have been trading on-line for less than a year, 16 percent are "heavy" traders—they have traded more than ten times in the last six months. The number of heavy traders jumps to 30 percent among investors who have been trading on-line for more than a year.

To some degree, certain on-line brokerage firms may have helped to foster all this activity, by fostering unrealistic expectations, something that SEC chairman Arthur Levitt has commented about publicly. Specifically he has complained about the marketing hype by on-line brokerage firms, which frequently portray investors who have achieved overnight success and riches beyond what most of us can imagine, thanks to trading on-line. (Remember the man who was able to afford his own island, thanks to on-line trading?) Chairman Levitt was concerned that these firms were not painting a realistic picture.

His message is being reinforced by others. In a recent series of ads, major on-line brokerage houses are trying to counter unrealistic expectations and frenzied trading. But although some companies are sending a message about trading responsibly to investors, many ads still play on the consumer's desire for fast money. That appeal, coupled with the long bull market and the facility of trading on-line, has desensitized too many on-line investors to risk.

And many on-line investors have forgotten about a very crucial factor: taxes. Short-term gains are taxed at ordinary income tax rates, not the more favorable long-term rates for stocks held over twelve months.

Day Trading

Perhaps the biggest risk comes in the most extreme form of Internet trading—day trading.

Day trading has been around for a decade, but due to improvements in technology and the stock market's rise, it has proliferated over the last year and a half. In order for day traders to be profitable, they must be nimble enough to get in and out of stocks at just the right moments. While we call it day trading, the people who engage in this exercise rarely hold on that long to the stocks they buy. They dart in and out of stocks in a matter of minutes, trying to make a killing on $1/16$ or $1/8$ moves at a time. With day trading, there is no concern for what a company's earnings are, how much market share it has, or how fast it's expected to grow. The only point of interest for the day trader is the stock's price and the direction it's moving. While extreme volatility in stock prices can work in the day trader's favor, it can also be the enemy. In a fast-moving market, getting out of a stock when its price is sliding can be a challenge, and losses can accumulate rapidly. When stock prices are generally rising, day trading can seem pretty simple and lucrative. However, in mid-1999, when the price of Internet stocks (favorites of day traders) fell, many of those day traders who could once do no wrong were suddenly seen for what they truly were: lucky.

"Personally I don't think day traders are speculating, because traditional speculation requires some market knowledge," SEC chairman Levitt said when asked about the phenomenon. "They are, instead, gambling, which doesn't."

It is estimated that about five to ten thousand people have quit their regular jobs to trade full-time at day-trading firms. By all estimates, it is only a select few who can actually make a living at day trading. The North American Securities Administrators Association studied one day-trading firm and reported that 70 percent of the day traders there had lost money, once all their trades were netted out.

It's not enough to be quick and intuitive at the day-trading game. There are additional costs that must be considered. Day-trading firms charge customers monthly fees to use their equipment, and/or require customers to make a certain minimum number of trades per month. Excessive trading is almost encouraged at these firms by arranging loans for customers or between customers. Customers then use leverage to make ever larger bets, and risk losing ever larger sums.

All that said, let me underscore something that I am sure you already know. Trading on the Internet and investing on the Internet are of course different things. *Day trading*—moving in and out on the market quickly by using the Internet as a trading vehicle—throws research and analysis out the window. *Investing* through the Internet involves research and commitment. When investing, information found on-line is used to make informed decisions about stocks and companies that one can buy.

Day trading involves guessing whether the next move of a stock's price will be up or down. Investment is about staying committed to a stock over a long period because of a belief that the company will do well. That doesn't change, whether you buy the stock yourself on-line or execute the trade through a broker. How you actually buy is the least important part of the investment process.

The idea of using research to find a stock that you can hold on to for the long term brings us back to where we started when we began talking about the Internet as a research tool.

Using the Net

Where do you begin if you want the Internet to make the process of finding good investments simpler? Anywhere you like, really.

Let's say that you don't have a clue about what you want to invest in—and you don't want to meet with a financial adviser of any kind until you do. If you are starting at ground zero, you probably want to look for trends you can capitalize on in the future. Most trends have a demographic component, so you'll probably want to begin at the source: if you are interested primarily in American companies, your first stop could be the U.S. Census Department. (The federal government has done a remarkably good job over the last couple of years putting information on-line. The Census Department is a case in point.)

How do you find its Web site? It's simple, even for us slow-to-adapt technology users. You call up a search engine—say Yahoo.com or Lycos.com—and type in "U.S. Census Department." What pops up is the on-line address of the U.S. Census Bureau Site Search, a place that contains thousands of separate research papers completely indexed.

Rummaging around the site, you find confirmation that the median age in this country is climbing. But you also learn that people are retiring earlier. Armed with those facts, you go searching for lifestyle articles in some of the country's major newspapers (NYTimes.com and the LATimes.com, for example) to give you some idea of what all these relatively young people are doing in retirement. What you find is intriguing. You might have guessed that many of these people are working part-time—often turning a hobby into a small business—and it is possible that you could have anticipated that they are devoting more of their time to studying the market. But the articles make clear a fact that might be surprising. These younger retirees are doing that studying in real time, investing heavily in technology to do so. They are buying personal computers and signing up for Internet services so they can keep track of their investments second by second. Logically, then, it follows that the makers of computer equipment, the peripherals (the infrastructure that allows the personal computer to connect to the Internet), and on-line service providers could be possible investment opportunities.

But which companies? The Net can help here as well. Not only does virtually every publicly held company of significant size have a Web site, but most use them to facilitate interaction with investors—and potential investors—to a surprising degree.

For example, go to Microsoft.com, and not only can you get copies of all the company's latest financial filings with the SEC, but you can be hooked into the conference calls the company holds with Wall Street analysts when it announces its quarterly earnings. At Dell.com it is possible to see—and hear—the company's annual meeting through the firm's Web site. (And some firms will let you ask a question, via the Internet, while the meeting is taking place.)

With all this information, you are inching closer to making a decision. But you must do much more than just find a company in a growing industry. You have to analyze the company's financials, understand the competition, and be sure the industry/company will continue to be attractive. The Internet makes it possible to find a company that meets all these criteria.

The logical decision at this point would be to check in with your financial adviser for a second opinion. You certainly can pick up the phone, but initially that may not be necessary. Many of the largest brokerage firms make their recommended lists available on-line, in addition to posting the research reports on dozens, and often hundreds, of companies. And here I admit my bias. I think it is very difficult for the average person to do the research job on his own. Why not take advantage of the vast resources of the major firms' research departments? But you can't stop there. Research and lists of recommendations given freely over the Internet are only a tool, not the final word on what to invest in. Again, these recommendations might be old or about to be updated, might be for investment banking clients with whom the firm wants to maintain a good relationship, or otherwise not appropriate. Any stock purchase must be considered in the context of your overall financial plan.

After taking these steps, the discussion with your financial adviser can be more productive. You have done the research, so you have a pretty good sense of the company you are thinking of buying, and by checking on-line, you know what your brokerage firm thinks of the stock. The conversation with your adviser can then focus on where this investment fits—or doesn't fit—within your portfolio. You can also talk about the timing of buying it. It is a much more efficient way to invest.

You can, of course, also use the Internet to trade on-line. You can open an account with one of the many firms that have on-line trading and do your buy and sell transactions simply. Or you can choose a firm that offers the ability to do on-line trading within the context of an account that also provides advice and other services. With all the changes in the financial services industry, many generated by both technology and competition, the client today can choose from an array of accounts that meet his particular needs.

The Internet is changing our lives across the board, from retailing to education to investing and just about everything in between. Used wisely, the Internet can be a valuable tool to help achieve your investment goals.

6

Creating the Best
Financial Team

I work for an investment firm that offers advice through its financial advisers (we call them advisers, not brokers, because it better describes what they do—help our clients with all aspects of their financial lives), research department, retirement planning services, and a network of attorneys our clients can call on to help them with issues like estate planning. So, if you want to discount anything I have to say about the benefits of working with a full-service brokerage firm, I will understand.

Yet even though I work for an investment firm, and therefore am in the "finance business," I have a professional who does my taxes, and there are attorneys I consult when I have legal questions about how to handle my money. They were particularly helpful when I got married recently. It was the second marriage for both my husband and me, and with four children between us, it got complicated. And even though I have spent nearly thirty years on Wall Street and know something about stocks, I know a lot less about bonds and fixed-income investments, so my financial adviser is a big help there. And I was glad I had him when my mother passed away. I didn't know very much about how things like probate worked or how estates got settled, so it was a relief to have this professional supervising a team who took care of many details during a difficult time.

I am telling you a bit about myself because it underscores an important point about *you*. You have to decide what kind of help you need, and you have to decide how you want the interactions with the professionals you hire to go.

Everyone is different, so there is no one right answer when it comes to the question of advisers. Some people don't use them at all, while others give them total discretion to make all their investment decisions, content to get a report once a quarter, or once a year, about how well their investments are doing.

But even the people who decide to delegate everything are driving the investment process. They have made a decision—to let someone else decide everything for them. That's fine—for them.

However, if it's not fine for you, or if you are not happy with the way your money has been handled up until now, you have to decide how you are going to change the situation. You have to decide where you need some assistance.

Experienced investors actually have an advantage when it comes to finding advisers. They know what they don't know, and so they can set out to fill specific needs. This flies in the face of conventional wisdom, which says the less you know, the more help you need. That's why you might hear someone say, "For people who don't know very much, buying through a full-service brokerage firm makes the most sense. It is worth paying the commission to get the hand-holding and advice you need."

That doesn't make much sense, if you think it through. If someone truly doesn't know anything about investing, they don't know enough to make any kind of informed decision about where to put their money. They don't even know what they don't know, let alone the areas in which they need help. What good is it to have a professional standing by if you don't know how to use his services, or even what you should ask him?

If I meet a true novice who asks me for a recommendation about advisers, I may tell them: "Establish a cash reserve for emergencies that is immediately accessible in a money market fund, put your long-term funds in an index fund that mirrors the performance of either the S&P 500 or Wilshire 5000, and start reading everything about investing that you can get your hands on. You want to get yourself to the point where you at least know what questions to ask, and identify where you need help."

Experienced investors are already at that point.

Deciding to work with a professional should be an emotional and financial decision. Emotionally, finding the right professional—someone with whom you feel rapport— should make you feel better. Financially, the professional you hire should generate more in savings and/or higher returns than you are paying her. (If not, you have to wonder if she is the right person for you, no matter how good she may make you feel.)

Can't You (Continue to) Do This Yourself?

Before we talk about finding the right professionals to help you, it is probably best to review a threshold question you probably asked yourself once you accumulated a little money: do you need any help managing your investments at all? If you have been handling all your financial decisions yourself—and you are happy with the results you have had so far—my answer would be, "No, you don't need an adviser."

Dealing with all aspects of your money—including estate planning—is a serious business requiring not only a certain aptitude and interest but a serious time commitment as well. There aren't many people who have the time, talent and willingness to do all this successfully on their own. (As we have already seen, I am not one of them.) But there are some. If you are one of them, I have only one suggestion. You might want to consult with a professional periodically to double-check how you are doing, particularly in complicated areas like estate planning with all its legal intricacies.

This is a strategy many investors use when it comes to handling their personal tax returns. They buy one of the tax-preparation software packages, and perhaps one of the oversized paperbacks the big accounting firms publish each year about how to prepare your taxes. They gather all their information and records, and then fill out the forms themselves. When they have completed their return, they take it to their accountant to see what they've missed or what advice and/or suggestions she might offer.

What about the rest of us?

Deciding to work with professionals is really a three-part process. You must

1. determine what you are trying to accomplish
2. ascertain where you are going to need help in accomplishing those goals
3. then find the best professionals to assist you in reaching those goals

Let's take the steps one at a time.

What Are You Trying to Accomplish?

Knowing where you want to go is the first step to figuring out what road to take and whom you want to help with the driving. If you are young, the answer to "What are you trying to accomplish?" can be as simple as, "I want my money to grow as quickly as possible, with the least amount of risk." In that case, the solution might be finding the stocks or mutual funds that take advantage of the thematic-investing ideas we'll talk about in chapter 8. The answer really could be that uncomplicated.

For most of us, however, things are no longer as simple as they once were. As we get older and gain more resources, the answer to "Tell me what you want to accomplish" becomes more difficult. And as your goals become more complicated, so do your options.

Clearly, some of your choices are easier than others. Need to create an estate plan? Go to a lawyer who is an expert in the field. Do you have a tricky capital gains/investment question? See a CPA or lawyer who specializes in those areas. We will talk about how to find these experts—and what you should expect from them—in chapter 11. But when you need to draw on these people is usually quite clear.

It gets trickier, however, when you have overlapping goals that all require immediate funding. For example, you want to

- buy a new house *and*
- put the kids or grandkids through college *and*
- secure your retirement

—simultaneously! In situations such as these, you have to work harder to find the right adviser.

What kind of advisers should you be working with? Again, you are going to drive the process, relying heavily on people who can help you in areas where you are not strong. And you are the best person to determine which those are. But first, let's begin with the most popular financial adviser there is: the broker/account executive.

Brokers/Account Executives

If you decide to work with a broker—or are already working with one—and he does not work for one of the big, brand-name firms, you are probably making a mistake. There is no hidden agenda or special pleading in my statement; it is just one of those cases where bigger really is better.

There are numerous advantages of going with a major firm, be it regional or national. Brokers hired by the brand-name brokerage houses get more extensive training than they do at smaller firms. Most have good research departments to draw on. (The thematic ideas we'll talk about in chapter 8 grew out of the work of my firm's proprietary research.) And at the large firms there are strict limits on what brokers can and cannot recommend. The idea is to serve the client with appropriate recommendations that are in line with the firm's best research resources.

But if you go with a large firm—or your existing broker works for one—how can you make sure you are getting the most out of the relationship?

For starters, remember it is a relationship. And if any relationship is going to work long-term, the person you are dealing with must *listen* to you. Your circumstances are unique, and it is important that your broker hears what makes you different from his "typical" client. If there is a special-needs child at home you are concerned about providing for, if you have health concerns, if your major concern is making sure that your children or grandchildren are provided for—your broker needs to know it. If your existing broker—or the one you are thinking about hiring—spends most of the time talking, especially if what he primarily talks about is the firm's recommendation of the day, you definitely want to rethink the relationship.

However, listening is only part of the process. Your advisers should actively be trying to *understand* your objectives and your circumstances. In this regard, I am always amazed at the number of brokers who fail to meet the client's spouse.

With many couples one person handles the finances, and invariably that is the person who deals with the account executive about the couple's investments. But what happens if that person dies? The surviving spouse, who may not have as good an understanding of the couple's finances as her partner did (to use a far too typical example), is now forced to learn quickly while relying on someone she may not know and may not have built trust with. It is not a good situation, and one that could have been avoided with some up-front planning.

And that brings up an important point. The need for understanding affects both parties—the customer and the broker. Just as the account executive needs to listen to you in order to understand your investment objectives, you need to understand the approach that your broker brings to investing. No, your objective here is not necessarily to make him happy. It is to understand whether you and the broker will make a good team as you work to achieve your goals.

While brokers are trained to understand many kinds of investments, they are only human. They come to their job with certain inclinations and they will personally prefer one type of investment to another. If the broker is partial to small Internet stocks, and you are investing to generate current income, it is something you both need to be aware of up front. And if the account executive's biases and yours don't match, it is incumbent upon you to tell him. When it comes to investing, it is unnecessary to try to conform to someone else's biases. After all, we are talking about your money, not the broker's. At the end of the day, you are the one that must be happy.

Professional Money Management

Some people want more of a hands-on approach than their broker or account executive can provide. Not only do they want investment advice, but they want professional money management as well.

When I talk to investors who think they want professional management, I always start with the table below, which outlines in broad terms the choices you have and what it will cost you to exercise them. (These are simply rough parameters. Specific amounts differ from firm to firm, and from money manager to money manager.)

What's perhaps most interesting about this table is that it reminds us of something most experienced investors have long forgotten: mutual funds give you professional management. We have become so used to thinking of mutual funds as a source of diversification that we often don't remember that they are also a way of gaining professional management inexpensively. After all, it is a professional manager who is deciding what the fund buys and sells.

To gain this kind of experience, you need to find a manager whose philosophy matches your own—his investment approach, of course, will be spelled out in the beginning of the fund's prospectus—and you let him do the rest.

Managed accounts, which are also called wrap accounts, are a hybrid, somewhere between owning a mutual fund and having your own personal money manager. These wrap accounts are gaining popularity. You generally pay a flat fee, based on account size, which covers the cost of advice, trading,

Differences Between Types of Money Management

	Mutual Fund	Managed Account	Individual Account
Minimum investment	$1,000	$100,000	$1 million or more
Fees (as a percentage of money being managed)	1.25%–1.75%	1%–2%	1.2% plus commission
Taxes	No control	Some control	Customized control

Source: PaineWebber

and investment and management fees. (This is usually paid quarterly.) Wrap accounts have the advantage of eliminating an inherent conflict that occurs when you pay for transactions: there is no incentive for the account executive to buy or sell.

These accounts work a little bit differently at each investment firm, and there are numerous variations, but the basics are the same. Generally your financial adviser assists you in developing a long-term investment strategy— within your risk parameters, to meet your objectives—and then identifies suitable investment managers from a list of managers who participate in the program. If you are investing for current income, you will get matched up with a specialist in that field. Is your objective long-term growth? Your broker will come up with several managers that would be appropriate.

The main advantages here are twofold:

> *First,* you have access to managers whose normal minimums are $1 million or more. And you have the chance to diversify with several different styles of investing, by allocating your assets to managers with different approaches to the market.
>
> *Second,* you receive an ongoing performance and allocation review to make sure you—and the money manager you selected—are staying on track.

Your adviser will monitor the performance of the money manager you selected to ensure he is performing in line with what you would like to accomplish. Your adviser will also monitor your allocation (for example, stocks versus bonds) to ensure it remains in line with your objectives and risk profile.

Finally, should you have sufficient resources, you can hire a money manager who will report directly to you.

Which way you go is up to you, of course. The table opposite synthesizes and summarizes the advantages of each.

No matter which professional you retain, you'll want to know whether the person you've hired to invest your money is performing well. And it is here that even the most experienced investors can make a mistake. An experienced investor will read that the S&P 500 was up 18 percent for the year, see that his investments climbed only 15 percent during the last twelve months,

Types of Accounts: An Overview

	Mutual Fund	Managed Account	Individual Account
Ease of diversification	Maximum	Maximum	Varies
Liquidity	Maximum	High	Varies
Personal service	Varies	Varies	Moderate-high
Total assets* under management	$5 trillion +	$202 billion	$6.5 trillion

Source: PaineWebber

and conclude that the people running his mutual funds or managed accounts, or his personal money manager, have not measured up.

What he'll forget is the way he set up his portfolio. To smooth out the volatility that comes by being completely in stocks, our hypothetical investor, like many others, decided to go with a mix of stocks, bonds, and cash. But that increased tranquillity comes at a price. Bonds and cash rarely outperform stocks, particularly in a bull market, so a portfolio made up of stocks, bonds, and cash is more than likely to underperform an all-equity portfolio. It just isn't fair to compare a blended portfolio to a pure-stock benchmark.

You have to be careful in deciding which target—and you can err by setting the benchmark too high or too low—you want your adviser to help you aim for.

A second problem occurs when investors inadvertently hold the manager's investment style against her. I own a mutual fund run by a money manager who is known for making aggressive bets in the market. Over time, I have been very satisfied with her performance. But there were certain periods when she significantly underperformed the market. It was helpful to remind myself that her aggressive style, which was the reason I selected her fund, often results in variations in return.

That said, if your adviser consistently underperforms the agreed upon benchmark, you obviously have to review her performance and consider a change. Just remember: as in all investing, performance should be measured over a long term.

How Do You Work with These People?

A major change is occurring in the relationship between client and financial adviser. Traditionally, brokers gave advice to clients and were paid by commissions on the transactions. Today, investors can choose from a broad array of account types that meet virtually every investor's needs. The definition of full service now includes trading on the Internet, for example, and I think these developments are a great advantage and will result in better service to clients. The old paradigm that investors paid for the transaction and got the advice for free is giving way to payment for advice, with the transaction becoming free.

This puts more of the onus on the investor to determine what relationship best meets his or her needs. There are numerous options, from on-line trading with no advice to full-service money management to an array of hybrids that offer various levels of advice and service with varying costs for trading. Investors today have to make the choice of what best suits their needs. This should be well thought out beforehand and be an important discussion in the initial meeting with a financial adviser.

As in every relationship, there has to be give-and-take. But unlike most of your other relationships, the one you have with your financial adviser can—and indeed should—be one-sided in your favor. Your adviser is the one who should be doing most of the giving. For example, she should work with you in a manner in which you are comfortable. If you don't want a phone call every few days with her firm's latest investment recommendations, she should respect that. If you want frequent contact, she should respect that as well.

No matter how long some people have been investing, they find it hard to talk with their financial advisers about working styles, fees, and objectives. That's understandable. If that describes you, here are some questions that both investors and advisers say have helped frame the discussion about what it will take for them to have a successful relationship:

- How do you envision us working together?
- What types of accounts and methods of payments do you offer?
- How often should we meet to review my portfolio and objectives?
- What do you expect from me as a client?
- Are there specific things you would recommend to help me become better educated about investing?
- What process do you recommend to determine if I need to rebalance my portfolio?
- How often should I review performance?
- What should I expect in the way of returns?
- What is a reasonable time frame in evaluating performance?
- Am I taking enough (too much) risk to achieve my goals?
- How much do I need to retire on my terms?

Where Do You Find These People?

In a perfect world, advisers would be easy to find. You would talk to a friend whose financial situation is similar to yours and ask for the names of the advisers she used, professionals who had her well on her way to accomplishing her goals. You'd talk to her advisers, develop confidence in their investment philosophies, and have an investment counselor for life.

Unfortunately, the world is rarely perfect. If you can't find anyone you like by talking to your friends and associates, your next step is to mine existing contacts. Does your CPA have a money manager he would recommend? Does your estate lawyer have any recommendations about financial advisers? Failing that, another option is to call some of the brand-name firms and ask to speak to the branch manager who runs the office near you. Explain specifically what you are looking for (for example, you want to invest for current income) and ask the manager for a recommendation. Meet with that person. If you don't mesh, move on to the next name. If you find someone you like, give him or her a small amount of your money to handle, and see how it goes.

A personal recommendation of someone you trust is obviously a better way to establish a relationship, but attending educational seminars or meetings put on by firms is a good way to get an idea if the firm's investment style is compatible with your own. It can give you a much greater knowledge base that can ultimately enhance your relationship with your financial adviser, and you might even find yourself hiring the adviser who put on the seminar.

Needless to say, never make an investment generated by a cold call over the phone. Cold calling is a time-honored way of establishing new relationships, and some highly productive ones have started this way. But it should prompt a meeting with the financial adviser, not a hasty investment decision that may or may not fit in with your overall investment goals. You don't want to work with someone who wants to make a quick sale rather than getting to know you, your personal situation, and your financial goals. Be particularly wary of a broker who seeks to rush you, implying that you'll miss out if you don't commit immediately. Hang up on this predator.

You're in Charge

When it comes to finding advisers, there is no off-the-shelf solution. The perfect financial adviser for me could be someone absolutely wrong for you. You have to work to find the people who are going to be right for you, and you have to devote time and effort to the relationship you have with them, keeping your ultimate financial goals in mind at all times. But that only seems fair. It is your money.

Part II

Managing Your Investments for Today

7

Aligning Your Investments:
Finding the Right Fit

It seems as though everyone's approach to investing is different. Some people will analyze an opportunity from every conceivable angle—twice. Others may be more intuitive when it comes to deciding what to buy.

But no matter how different their approaches may appear, the best investors follow a checklist—although some of them may only keep it in their heads—before they make any purchase. They know the answer to each and every one of the ten questions you'll find listed below. If they are not certain they know—and are comfortable with—the answer, they don't buy.

You probably already ask yourself most of the following questions, as a matter of course. But it doesn't hurt to compare your mental checklist to that of other savvy investors to make sure that you're not missing anything.

Don't expect perfection when you answer these questions. As you've learned by now, knowing and anticipating every possible contingency in investing is impossible. If you are looking for absolute certainty, you'll never buy anything. The goal here is to increase your comfort level by a significant degree before you make any changes to your portfolio.

Perhaps the most interesting aspect of this list is the first two questions sophisticated investors ask. The answers frequently make them move in a different direction from the one they anticipated—and sometimes they don't end up buying anything at all.

The Best Investors Can Answer These Ten Questions

Are all your bases covered?

Before you invest, you need to make sure that the basics have been taken care of. They are so fundamental that it is easy to forget them. Depending on your circumstances, "fundamental" can range from making sure you have a sufficient cash reserve—to cover not only a financial emergency but also any opportunities that require quick action—to double-checking that there won't be any margin calls in your future (we discuss those later). It can be as simple as making sure that you have paid off all credit card and nondeductible debt (including outstanding margin loans) or ensuring there will be enough cash on hand to cover an upcoming balloon payment.

Often the best way to make money is by not wasting it. If you don't remember to do the routine things, you might find yourself being forced to sell assets at a loss to raise cash quickly, or carrying nondeductible debt, two great examples of wasting money.

Have you done all your rebalancing?

We talked in detail about the concept of rebalancing, which is a particular form of asset allocation, in chapter 3 ("Diversification, Asset Allocation, and Risk"). The key concept is that assets grow at different rates, depending on what is happening in the marketplace. During the recent bull market, for example, the value of stocks has increased far faster than bonds and cash. If ten years ago you had two-thirds of your money in stocks, and the rest in bonds and cash, you might well have 80 percent of your money in stocks today, even if you haven't added another dime to any part of your portfolio. That's how quickly stocks have grown. The best investors rebalance their accounts as appropriate—making sure they have the levels of stocks, bonds, and cash they are comfortable with—before they make any new investments. After all, if you think you have too much money in stocks, you don't want to add to your equity holdings until you have redressed that imbalance. Rebalancing periodically has another advantage. It lets you take advantage of market conditions that may have changed dramatically. A stock weighting that you created for one set of circumstances—a low-inflation environment—may be out of whack in another, such as soaring interest rates. Remember, however, that rebalancing is not done in a vacuum, but always in the context of market conditions. In this bull market, it has paid to be overweighted in stocks, and given the fundamentals of the market, adherence to a fixed asset allocation would not have been prudent.

Do you know this investment inside and out?

While this question certainly is important if you are entering into a currency-hedging transaction or another complicated strategy, it needs to be applied to the more run-of-the-mill purchases as well. How, exactly, does that company whose stock you are thinking of buying make its money? Who are its competitors? Why will the company do, or continue to do, well? If you can't answer these questions with certainty and conviction, you should ask yourself the next question:

Why are you buying it?

In theory, the answer to this question should naturally follow from the last. You know exactly what you are buying—a company that you expect will be a major player in an emerging field you like—and so you are buying the stock in order to get in early on an important emerging trend. If you can't clearly answer the earlier question—do I know this investment?—you won't be able to answer this one either. But even if you know what you are about to purchase, you still may not have a good answer to this question. If you don't, you shouldn't buy.

Is this the best example?

Having done all your research, you have concluded that buying a large-cap growth fund is the way to go. But are you certain that the fund you are thinking of investing in is the best large-cap growth fund there is? You have done all this work to find the right asset class; take the extra step and make sure you also find "best in class."

Are you going to need the money soon?

Remember the basic rule of thumb: if you are going to need the money in the foreseeable future (to pay college tuition, for example), you want to be investing that money in such things as short-term Treasuries, intermediate-term bonds, and cash equivalents like CDs and money market accounts.

Do you have time on your side?

This is the converse of the previous point. If you are investing for the long term, stocks are the best place to be. There is, for example, no real reason to have cash equivalents in your retirement account if you aren't going to be drawing down the money within the next ten years.

Do you already own it?

People fall in love with the same type of investment over and over again. The question to ask is whether what you are thinking about buying is similar to something that you already own. If you have ten individual stocks that fall in the large-cap growth category, do you really want to own a large-cap growth mutual fund as well? Would you be better off diversifying a bit?

Does it fit?

We talked earlier about the importance of having a sense of what you want to accomplish with your money. That's a good thing to keep in mind here. To oversimplify, that piece of undeveloped land that has just come on the market might look extremely cheap, but if you are investing for current income, you may want to pause a minute—or two or three—before you sign the purchase and sale agreement. And even if an opportunity seems to fit, it may not. For example, you have designed an asset-allocation plan that calls for having 20 percent of your portfolio in fixed-income investments. The bond fund you are considering—yes, the one with the terrific yield—will push you substantially over that. Do you still want to make the move? You have spent a great deal of time creating an asset-allocation plan. Don't discard it just because an intriguing opportunity has come along. On the other hand, you should be flexible enough to take advantage of great opportunities if they can be incorporated strategically in your overall plan. A financial plan should not become a straitjacket.

Is it a SWAN?

Always ask: Can I live with this investment? A friend who is a senior mutual fund executive recommends only SWAN, or sleep-well-at-night, funds. I think that is good advice for all investments. If you can't live through market corrections, or if the ups and downs of technology stocks give you sleepless nights, you should review not only what you are thinking of buying, but also what you already hold.

Taking a moment to apply your internal checklist can save you time, money, and headaches in the long run, and equally important, it can keep you from deviating from your financial plan.

8

Tools for Success:
Why Thematic Investing Can
Give You an Edge

After twenty-eight years of observing investing strategies, I am reminded again and again that the most successful investors have achieved wealth not through market timing, short-term trading, or pursuing hot tips or investment fads, but by owning high-quality companies over a long-term time horizon. When you own a common stock, you own the rights to the future stream of earnings and dividends, and you can hold this stock indefinitely, without incurring capital gains tax on its rise in value until you sell. When you have confidence in the companies you own, you can live through the ups and downs of market cycles, convinced that ultimately your investment will be worth a lot more than you paid.

Much of Wall Street research is focused on the short, or at best intermediate, term, reflecting perhaps the orientation of many of today's professional investors, who might more accurately be called traders. Yet the case for long-term investing is clear. But even if you are committed to long-term investing, the question remains: what stocks should you buy?

One simple answer is: purchase index funds. This is a perfectly justifiable position to take. The logic, which you have heard a dozen times, goes like this: Once you buy an index fund you can sit back and relax. The fund will mirror the performance of the specific benchmark you selected—the S&P

500, for example, or the Wilshire 5000, which is designed to mimic the performance of all publicly traded stocks—and you don't have to do a thing. After all, these funds generally comprise proportionally weighted shares of the stocks that make up the index, so the value of your fund will rise and fall by roughly the same amount the index does. (The actual return you'll receive will probably trail the index by a fraction, because of the expenses associated with running the fund.) Indexing has been a good strategy in these years of unprecedented gains for the market.

The net result of owning an index fund? You will do as well, or as poorly, as the benchmark itself. That phrase "or as poorly," however, underscores one of two major problems with investing through index funds.

First, you don't have any protection when the market falls. If the S&P 500 drops by 10 percent, for example, the value of your S&P index fund is going to fall by that amount as well.

The second problem? In a rising market you are going to do only as well as the index as a whole. By definition, you can't do better than the benchmark if you invest in an index fund. If the S&P 500 climbs 8 percent in a given year, you will be up 8 percent—not 10, 12, or 20 percent.

Given these limitations, many people wonder if there is a different strategy they can use, one that will give them a chance of not only equaling the market's performance but actually exceeding it. We think there is—long-term thematic investing. Identifying trends before they emerge allows investors to select companies that have the potential for superior growth over a long period of time in the years ahead. Equally important, this discipline avoids companies that are likely to go the way of the buggy whip, icebox, and eight-track tape player in the future.

Here's how it works.

The creation of an investment theme begins when strategists with experience in the equity and fixed-income markets review empirical data, examine economic statistics, gather insights from colleagues, and add their own analysis. Through discussion and debate, ideas are formed and tested and a proposed investment theme emerges.

Next, the theme's assumptions are put to the test. The strategists get together with the fundamental analysts, who each have the responsibility for covering a specific industry, and ask them the questions that determine the theme's validity. Specifically, we try to learn from them:

- Do these assumptions make sense?
- Do you see any of these trends emerging in the industries and companies you follow?
- If so, how can investors be positioned to benefit?

The insights of these analysts give a different dimension to the debate, serving to validate, alter, or refute the theme as originally proposed. Strategists and analysts then work together to identify the specific investment opportunities that evolve from the theme in its final form.

Why do we spend so much time on this approach? Technological advances, demographics, political change, or structural changes in the economy can all significantly affect the business environment and the direction of the stock and bond markets. Companies cannot control their environment, so understanding the changes—and more important, anticipating those changes—is crucial to making a judgment about the future potential of any company, and any investment.

And those changes can have an impact on almost everything. Some of the major changes of the last few decades have been the globalization of the marketplace, the aging of baby boomers, the decrease in manufacturing and increase in the service sector of the American economy, and the explosion of technology, most recently the Internet. You'd be hard pressed to find any sizable company anywhere that was not affected by these trends.

While the themes are created so that investors can benefit from the trends in the years ahead, there is always risk that external factors can devastate even the most reasonable forecasts.

One that comes to mind is the sharp decline in the prices of drug stocks in 1993 when the idea of a national health care plan was pursued. Despite favorable demographics of an aging population, global domination by U.S. drug companies, and R&D budgets that filled the pipelines with potential new products, the possibility of the end of a free market for drug pricing overwhelmed these fundamentals and made the drug stocks, at least temporarily, bad investments. The point? Even long-term themes may prove short-lived, and like all investments must be reevaluated regularly and objectively. We will return to this idea later on in the chapter.

Where Will the World Be Tomorrow?
A Quick Introduction to Two Major
Investment Themes

Trends are always obvious in retrospect, but anticipating them requires more than a crystal ball. No one can foresee the future, but there are still many things that can reasonably be foreseen. Consider demographics. Studying changes in population growth has proven to be a reliable way to forecast changes in society and gain a good window on changes in the economy. Because it takes a change in birthrates, or in immigration policy, or a catastrophe to change the nature of the population, there is a certain predictability about the future, something we can see if we take a quick look at all those Americans born between 1946 and 1964.

The baby boomers, who make up about one-third of the U.S. population, have always exerted undue influence on the society and the economy by virtue of their numbers. After World War II, they crowded the maternity wards. They overfilled the schools in the 1950s and 1960s, flooded the job market in the seventies and eighties, and in the process pushed housing prices up as they got their first apartments and started buying their first homes.

Along the way, they created numerous investment opportunities. For example, all you had to do in the 1970s was to look at the ever-increasing percentage of women in the workforce to know that fast food companies, along with a myriad of other services that save the limited time of dual-income couples, would thrive.

Looking ahead, what additional themes will be fueled by the baby boomers? As they are now moving through their peak earning, spending, and saving years (ages 45–54), they will continue to have a disproportionate influence on the economy. Since they represent the largest segment of the population, and since their spending power is leveraged by the number of dual-income couples in the group, clearly companies that can provide the products and services they want should be winners.

Investing in companies that will benefit from changing demographics and lifestyles has been a sound strategy.

Let's take a quick look at another important trend.

Few things have shaped our lives more than technology in the last decade, and the story has just begun. The Internet will likely have a far greater influence in the future both on our personal lives and on business, providing more opportunities for investors. Technology has led U.S. economic growth over the last few decades and should continue to do so. Major technological revolutions ultimately surpass even the greatest expectations (railroads grew 10,000 percent between 1860 and 1910; car/truck production rose 2,400 percent between 1908 and 1916). The Internet is likely to fall into that category. As in any rapidly changing technology, the risks are high, but the rewards for the ultimate winners will be great.

Predicting the exact winners and losers from technology is more difficult than demographic predictions, but just a casual glance at the landscape starting in the late 1970s—the shift from mainframes to personal computers, the concurrent rise of software, and ultimately the Internet—would have convinced you that there was something vital going on in this sector of the economy as well. Technology is another major investing theme.

Baby boomer spending and investing habits and technology are not the only two possible forces that will affect the economy in coming years. Labor shortages could be a problem. Cultural changes could radically change the economy as we know it. The government may alter the tax structure, with unintended consequences. Those are just three of the countless scenarios that could have a major impact on your investment decisions.

As always, you have to sift through all the data and identify the forces you believe will have the *most* impact on the markets. And it is clear to us, by doing extensive research, that the aging of the baby boom population—which is now entering its peak earning, spending, and investment years—and technology will be among the biggest factors shaping the economic landscape in the decade ahead.

We came to this conclusion partly by the process of elimination and partly from what we have experienced so far.

Politicians today—be they Democrats, Independents, or Republicans—are all arguing against the rebirth of big government. So, public spending is not likely to be a driving economic force anytime soon. At the same time, corporations are determined to remain "lean and mean." That leaves us with two choices if the economy is going to grow.

First, we are going to have to do more with what we have. That's where technology comes in. As we continue to automate the way we do business—ordering computer to computer, for example—productivity increases. Technology-related companies—component makers, suppliers, distributors, retailers, service companies, and the like—have piggybacked on the growth of the information industry, expanding exponentially the growth opportunities associated with this theme. While this exciting, if at times risky, investment trend is already under way, we think it has a long way to go.

So, doing more with less—which could be the title of our technology section—is one way we expect the economy to keep growing.

Second, we will need consumers to continue to buy. Just because consumers are the logical choice to keep the economy humming doesn't mean they will do it. If we enter a recession—or we are faced with roaring inflation—they are likely to turn off the spending spigot and wait for the bad times to end.

But neither substantial inflation nor a major recession appears on the horizon. Real wages are likely to continue to climb, thanks to both an increasing demand for labor in this expanding economy and slow labor-force growth due to our aging population. Tight labor markets lead to bigger paychecks, and more disposable income for workers. And productivity improvements mean those rising wages are not inflationary.

So, betting on consumers seems to be the way to go. And the largest, fastest-growing, and most influential segment of the population is baby boomers—those 78 million Americans born between 1946 and 1964.

With the broad ideas sketched out, let's look at those two themes—baby boomers and technology—in more detail.

Theme 1:
The Baby Boomers Shape the Future

Relying on baby boomers to shape the economy is nothing new, of course. The postwar baby boom inaugurated a new era in American society, simultaneously spawning numerous investment themes that would play out over the ensuing decades. Whatever the boomers do has an impact, simply because there are so many of them.

Baby Boomers Are the Fastest-Growing Segment of the Population
% change by age group, 1995–2005

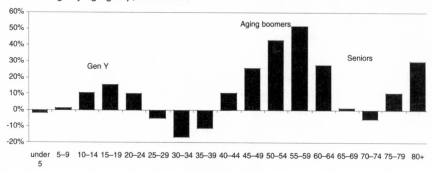

Source: Census Bureau

Clearly, how they spend and invest will influence which companies will do well going forward.

Unfortunately, figuring out how baby boomers will spend their money is not quite as easy as looking at what happened in the past. Here's a quick example of why you can't predict the future by looking in a rearview mirror. Starting in the early 1960s there was a major run up in the stocks of companies that were associated with coffee—growers, processors, and wholesalers. This was a can't-lose situation, some analysts said. The baby boomers were getting older and were about to reach the age where they would shift from milk and soft drinks to coffee.

A significant portion of them never did. Americans now consume more soft drinks than any other beverage, including water, by a wide margin. Coffee sales never fully recovered, although the rise of brand-name premium coffees and coffee shops suggests a comeback at least in the upscale end of the market.

The point is, we know that the boomers spend very differently than their parents. Most of their parents experienced the Depression, when nearly one-third of the labor force was out of work, banks were failing with no protection for depositors, and breadlines were not uncommon. Not surprisingly, the boomers' parents tended to be more conservative, taking on less debt and saving more for the future. The boomers grew up in unprecedented prosperity, with ready access to credit, and tended to be spenders right from the day they got their first allowance. We expect that trend to continue.

Peak Earnings Years

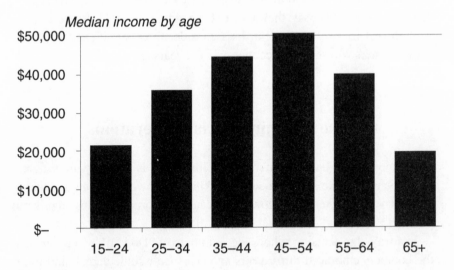

Median income by age

Source: Census Bureau

To help understand boomer spending patterns, PaineWebber hired the two leading experts on consumer behavior, the Gallup Organization and Yankelovich Partners. Working with Gallup, PaineWebber conducted a proprietary survey of baby boomers, asking about their actions, thoughts, and feelings about work, leisure, and consumption. Then to help analyze what we found, we turned to Yankelovich, which has for nearly thirty years been compiling comprehensive data about consumers' preferences, habits, and lifestyles.

At the broadest level, this research confirmed some of the things that you might have expected. Baby boomers are now older—the oldest are now in their mid-fifties—and indeed wiser. They are not the ebullient youths of the 1960s, nor the conspicuous consumers of the 1980s. They have evolved yet again, but still you can hear echoes of their past.

This generation has always been intrigued by the new—whether it be the latest forms of music, lifestyles, or ideas—and that trend continues, but this time in a slightly different form. Today, with most of their material needs satisfied, boomers place more value on new experiences than on recent purchases. In other words, they don't need more "stuff"—and more important, they told us they don't want it, either.

But that doesn't mean there aren't unmet needs. These needs now have to do with a desire to have more new experiences. However, to have those new experiences, boomers say, they need to have more time and less stress.

With that by way of context, let's consider three significant ways that baby boomers will shape the economy in the years ahead.

The Entrepreneurial Generation

One major reason baby boomers are feeling stress is that they are progressively behaving like entrepreneurs—making their own decisions and taking their own risks, instead of following bureaucratic corporate rules, in order to prosper.

In a way, this decision echoes the sentiment of "Do your own thing" that the boomers embraced thirty years ago. This isn't coincidental, and ironically it has taken our national character full circle.

After the devastation of the Great Depression and the inflationary trauma of World War II, typically fiercely independent Americans placed their faith in giant bureaucracies. They turned to the corporation that offered a job for life; or to unions that battled for better pay and job security; or to the U.S. military, which fought the Cold War and let you retire at half pay after just twenty years of service, and 75 percent of your last paycheck if you put in thirty years; or to a generous federal bureaucracy that sent out Social Security checks—checks that increased as the cost of living did—every month.

Many institutions lost their luster in the eyes of the American public during the late 1960s and 1970s. The war in Vietnam ended ignominiously. The War on Poverty failed, in essence creating programs that subsidized poverty instead of ending it, and an alliance between big corporations and big unions pushed inflation higher—and the standard of living lower—for most Americans.

We were wrenched away from big bureaucracies in the 1980s. Ronald Reagan, who was elected in large part by asking one simple question during the 1980 presidential campaign—"Are you better off than you were four years ago?"—reined in the federal bureaucracy, while corporations and unions were squeezed by both disinflation and foreign competition. S ud-denly the word "downsizing" entered our lexicon.

As a direct result of these changes, we saw the first tottering steps tov vard the entrepreneurial economy. For example, the percentage of workers em-ployed by firms with over one thousand employees dropped from 14.3; per-cent in 1980 to 13.1 percent in 1990 (and was only 12.9 percent in 199 5).

During the 1980s, entrepreneurship grew as many firms did leve;raged buyouts and venture capital boomed to provide financing to many o'f those who had left large corporations, some as part of corporate downsizin; g.

But the United States did not fully embrace an entrepreneurial aj)proach in the 1980s. Reaganomics was partially discredited by the huge fede ;ral bud-get deficit. And insider trader scandals, the S&L crisis, and the stoc k market crash of 1987 gave private enterprise a bad name. ("Greed," to par aphrase a widely quoted movie line of the time from *Wall Street,* "was 'no longer good.") In addition, the grinding recession of 1990–91, which di d not fully end for consumers until 1994, further discredited entrepreneurshi p. During a recession the idea of a steady paycheck becomes much more apf)ealing than going off on your own.

But the dramatic changes of the 1980s and early 1990s recast . not only the U.S. economy but the American psyche as well, and had the effe ;ct of moving us back toward a feeling that we must, once again, be self-re ;liant. We are

Union Membership as a Percentage of Wage and Sala)ry Workers

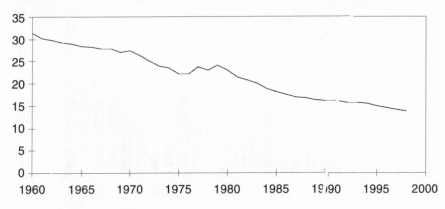

Source: Bureau of National Affairs

now more distrustful of large institutions, and we are being more entrepreneurial with both our careers and our capital. The chart describing union membership gives one quick example. Since 1960 the number of jobs that are unionized has been more than cut in half.

The new entrepreneurial ethic is likely to continue over the next decade because it is part and parcel of a dynamic, prosperous economy that is raising living standards more rapidly than at any time since the 1960s. Many people who have gone off on their own report they love it. Not only do they find the freedom from corporate bureaucracy appealing, but they are also discovering that they can make more money by letting the market dictate what their skills are worth.

The numbers tell the story of how the economy—and the workforce—has been evolving.

Firms with between twenty and ninety-nine employees account for 29 percent of all workers today. Another quarter of the workforce (25.7 percent) can be found in companies with less than twenty employees. And the percentage of people working at even smaller firms—including solo offices—has been increasing in recent years. Better and cheaper technology—including PCs, fax machines, multiple phone lines, cable modems,

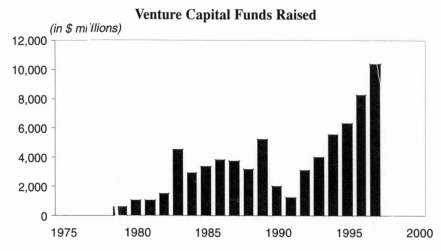

Venture Capital Funds Raised

Source: Venture Economics

e-mail, and the Internet—is making it increasingly feasible for us to set up small businesses in our homes. The amount of venture capital available to finance start-ups is booming, and so is the number of initial public offerings. As the preceding chart shows, venture capital funds raised have soared in the nineties, giving a great many fledgling companies the resources to bring their ideas to the market.

Also, as the initial-public-offering chart, below, shows, a host of new companies have gone public in the nineties, selling the shares to the public and gaining capital to expand and grow.

Employees in small, growing companies tend to be paid disproportionately with stock options rather than straight salary. Consequently, their fortunes are tied more directly to the success of the company they work for. Not surprisingly, they tend to work harder than those people who don't have a piece of the action.

Virtually no major corporation offers lifetime employment today. In fact, there are now two rules of thumb that have become commonplace within large companies:

1. When profits are squeezed, payrolls are reduced.
2. When corporations merge, redundant employees are cut.

Initial Public Offerings

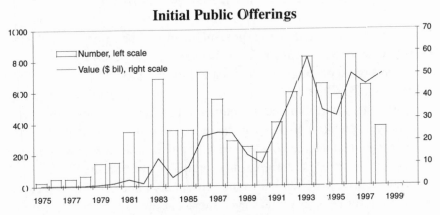

Sources: IPO Reporter; Securities Industry Association

The result? Every worker has to manage his or her own career (and increasingly, manage his own retirement as well).

Entrepreneurial Retirement

Up until the 1970s, corporations promised a "defined benefit," or pension—a specific amount of money they would pay each month to their employees who retired. But that promise proved to be too costly to keep once profit margins fell in the 1980s. As a result, companies have shifted to "defined contribution retirement plans," mainly 401(k)s, where the worker and employer pay in a specific amount each year and the worker is responsible for investing both contributions.

Today there are millions of us whose net worth and retirement prospects are directly tied to our own investment decisions. As a result, we are paying more attention to the daily doings on Wall Street and spending more of our time learning about investments.

This increased focus on asset management is positive for financial institutions that can meet the needs of both nouveau investors and those of us who now have had some experience managing our own retirement accounts.

Entrepreneurial Social Security

There is even a chance that entrepreneurialism will be extended to Social Security. One of the options being debated as a way of saving the Social Security system is privatizing at least part of the program.

Here's one way that could play out in practice. Each worker would deposit part of the payroll tax he is required to pay in his own investment account. Very much like a 401(k) plan, this account would be controlled by the worker, who could decide how to invest the funds. The worker would own the principal—and all the earnings it generated—once he retired.

Social Security privatization would profoundly affect American society. By tying the fortunes of retirees even more closely to the stock and bond market, it would increase the public's support for low inflation and a prosperous corporate sector, two key factors in promoting a healthy stock market. And of course, an increased flow of funds into the market would put upward pressure on stock prices as well. (We will be talking more about where Social Security fits into your overall financial planning in chapter 16, "Rethinking Retirement Planning.")

The debate on Social Security has just begun, however, and how it will proceed is impossible to predict.

The issue of Social Security raises a logical question: won't this entrepreneurial trend end once baby boomers start retiring, which will happen within the next ten years?

Our answer is no. We have surveyed baby boomers about their retirement plans (see chapter 16) and it turns out that many intend to keep working, although not necessarily at their current jobs, once they reach traditional retirement age. To borrow a phrase from Yankelovich Partners, boomers will not retire, they will retread. As they grow older they will restructure their lives so as to relieve stress. They will continue to work—on their own terms—be it with different hours than they have now or in a different job entirely. Only 15 percent plan on having a traditional retirement, where they stop working entirely.

That is not surprising. Unlike their parents, who grew up amid the hardships of the Depression and World War II, baby boomers today do not view a leisurely retirement as their reward for years of hard work and sacrifice. For many boomers, work is a career and a way of life, not a job; it provides a social network and a source of inner satisfaction in addition to being a way to pay the mortgage. Boomers have always been work centered and will remain so.

In reviewing the highlights of the cradle-to-grave entrepreneurial trend, there are two major points we should underscore. First, reflecting a continuation of the shift from relying on the big bureaucracies of the 1950s through the 1970s to the self-reliant economy of the 1990s, more and more Americans are being forced to behave like entrepreneurs in managing their careers and in planning for their retirement. The move toward defined contribution plans guaranteed that would happen. Second, given that we are living longer, many people are likely to choose the intellectual stimulation of work over the monotony of having nothing to do in retirement, even if they can afford to

stop working. (A significant number of people who have not planned sufficiently won't have that option. They will have to work.)

Time, Time, Time

We talked earlier of the time pressure baby boomers—and indeed everyone—feels today. You might suppose the cause is that more and more Americans are working longer hours. Actually, more people are indeed working,
thanks to the increased percentage of women who are employed, but the
workweek is actually getting shorter. (But don't tell that to the many professionals who find themselves working longer hours.)

The labor force participation rate for all adults has risen to a record level,
primarily because the number of working women has climbed, from 38 percent in 1960 to 60 percent in 1998. Although more people are working, the
workweek is not expanding. The amount of time the typical employed
American works has actually declined six hours per week for women, and
about seven hours a week for men, since 1965.

If Americans are working shorter hours, why are they so stressed out? In a
word, multitasking. Instead of doing just one thing at a time, we frequently
find ourselves doing two, three, or four things simultaneously.

Once upon a time, when radios were bulky appliances, the family sat
around the radio in the evening and listened to *The Shadow* or a Brooklyn
Dodgers game. By the 1950s they listened to the radio while driving. Today
we listen to the radio while driving and making phone calls. (This fact has
not gone unnoticed by the world's car makers, who now offer a cell phone as
an option on every car they sell and seem to be competing with one another
for the number of drink holders they can fit into their vehicles to make it easy
to consume a meal as we drive.)

Perhaps the ultimate multitasking appliance is a personal computer wired
to the Internet, which allows us to almost simultaneously write a report;
e-mail a friend; check stock prices, sport scores, and bank accounts; follow
the latest news headlines; and play a game of solitaire. No wonder even free
time may be stressful.

Intriguingly, the time/stress crunch elevates the power of well-established
brands. Brands save consumers time in two ways. When you buy a trusted

brand, you don't have to spend much time researching the purchase. And you have a high degree of confidence that you will like the product and not have to exchange it or get it repaired.

Yankelovich Partners' extensive research shows that consumers strongly want to be in control of the buying process. Purchasing established brands helps us do just that. Why take chances buying no-name khakis at a mom-and-pop clothing store when you can acquire a tried-and-true brand-name pair in a familiar, easy-to-shop environment?

Stressless Leisure

With both their leisure time and discretionary income rising, besieged consumers—especially baby boomers—are spending heavily on vacations and other leisure activities. That isn't surprising. Our surveys revealed something that you probably already suspected: baby boomers want not only less stress but also more fun in their lives. Certainly they want to escape the usual pressures of middle age. But to baby boomers, reducing stress means something more.

As boomers grow older, less stress typically means:

Less effort. According to a Yankelovich poll, the percentage of people who turn to physical exercise and sports as a way to relax fell from 30 percent in 1993 to 27 percent in 1997.

Less risk. Gratuitous risk taking is unappealing to stressed-out consumers. For many, risk taking would include foreign travel: they may not like the food, the culture, the people, the weather, or the problems getting from here to there.

Fewer projects. Most people think that a leisure activity that can be classified as a "project" is too much like work.

The lists on the next page tell the same story.

In short, consumers want leisure that comes easy. If it adds worry, or requires energy or effort, it is not worth it. Among the forms of leisure that do appeal to consumers, let's highlight three.

What Americans Want in a Vacation

"Comfortable"	94%
"Relaxing"	92%
"Adventurous, not too dangerous"	78%
"Physically challenging"	35%
"Slightly dangerous"	20%

Favorite Way to Express Yourself

Activity	1993	1997
Do-it-yourself projects	57%	47%
Home improvements	52%	41%
Gardening	47%	34%

Full-Service Leisure

When vacationing, stressed-out baby boomers don't want extra hassles or extra charges. Many prefer integrated, all-in-one packages, especially ones that have plenty of options for kids. An obvious example is cruise ships. They offer the convenience of going overseas without necessarily leaving the U.S. (or its territories); going out to dinner every night without the potential difficulty of finding a restaurant and getting a reservation; and high-quality entertainment available without the work of driving to a theater or nightclub, parking, and having to drive home after the show.

Time-Efficient Leisure

Reflecting the time drought that most of us—but baby boomers especially—feel, leisure activities that cram a lot into a limited amount of time are popular. Quick getaways—vacations that last five days or less—are increasingly popular. And a getaway does not even have to be a long weekend. The number of day spas in the United States has risen from 30 in 1987 to 600 in 1997, while the number of health clubs—which peaked at 14,000 in 1990—had fallen to 13,000 by 1997.

Controlled-Risk Leisure

This is an activity that offers a sense of adventure as an antidote to the dull routine of the everyday, but is not too risky or uncomfortable. Two examples from either end of the controlled-risk spectrum are going on safari—at an animal park—and gambling in casinos.

What are the investment implications of all of this? Companies that can offer one-stop shopping when it comes to entertaining baby boomers will do well in the years ahead.

The No-Service Full-Service Economy

Stressed-out, time-starved consumers demand good service, and this is particularly true of baby boomers who have become jaded after more than two decades of shopping and spending. But consumers are not satisfied with the service they are receiving. Some 90 percent of the people surveyed by Yankelovich Partners say, "The prices I pay entitle me to the best possible service," with 64 percent saying, "Service people don't care." But because of the tight labor market, it will become even harder for companies to meet consumers' high expectations in the years ahead. Hotels, restaurants, retailers, health care providers, and many other services will have a hard time hiring competent workers at reasonable wages, as workers gravitate toward high-wage jobs.

Here's a quick example of what employers are up against. While retailers were paying $8.67 an hour for help in 1998, manufacturers paid $13.44. That's 55 percent more. Computer and data processors were offering $20.82 an hour on average, a 140 percent premium to what you would be paid working for a retailer. Obviously, everything else being equal, that kind of disparity in pay means the best and the brightest are not going to head into retailing, which in turn means service will continue to suffer.

The shortage of workers is likely to cause a further split in the U.S. service sector. Expect to see highly automated do-it-yourself service on the one hand, and premium-quality traditional service on the other.

To provide automated service, successful retailers are beefing up their catalogue operations and/or moving to the Web. Currently catalogue apparel sales, for example, total $9 billion, or 5 percent of the total. That number is likely to increase.

There won't be a total migration to the Web, of course. Fashion-minded shoppers will continue to make daylong excursions to malls, where they can visit many department stores and specialty shops. And there will also be a certain percentage of people who will want to try items before they buy, and examine the goods firsthand. However, the key for retailers and other service providers will be to make sure that the shopping experience is enjoyable. That is not easy in a period of tight labor markets.

What are the investment implications of this? Companies in the middle of the retail market are in trouble. Retailers will have to be either upscale establishments, known for providing superior service, or efficient low-cost providers in order to thrive in the years ahead. Conversely, retailers at the low end can also prosper by providing more service than you would expect. Examples, of course, would include the superstores. The key to retailing success will be providing a combination of service, price, and quality that beats the competition and meets the customer's needs.

The New Drug Culture

Earlier we talked about the fact that people are living longer. A key reason is that they are staying healthier. But baby boomers, by and large, are not staying healthy simply by living better—exercising, eating well, and getting enough sleep. They are also doing it by fixing things when—or even before—something goes wrong.

Boomers are comfortable with this medical activism because they were born into a world awash with drugs (and I am talking about legal drugs here). Penicillin, available for widespread use in 1944, made many serious conditions, such as tuberculosis and venereal disease, distant memories overnight. New vaccines vanquished polio in the 1950s, and subsequently childhood diseases such as measles were reined in with massive inoculation programs.

There are other factors reinforcing this new drug culture as well.

- Since the laws regulating the advertisement of prescription drugs were relaxed in the 1980s, marketing promotions by pharmaceutical companies have soared. In 1997, manufacturers spent over $700 million on direct-to-consumer advertising, and as a result, more and more patients are asking their doctor to prescribe a particular drug.
- Many employers offer health care programs that include prescription drug plans.
- Many doctors in managed care systems are under pressure to see as many patients as possible. Prescribing a drug is often the quickest way to treat a patient.

With the heavy emphasis today on managing health care costs, in many instances drugs are the most cost-effective treatment for patients.

Reflecting this new drug culture, today's boomers are making trips to the doctor at an unprecedented rate.

And not only are boomers taking drugs to treat medical problems; they are also popping pills to fight the aging process.

Visits to the Doctor by People Aged 45–64

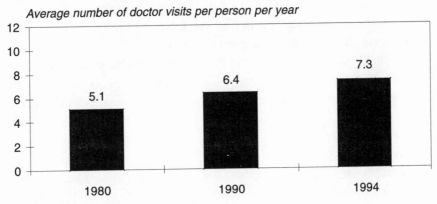

Average number of doctor visits per person per year

Source: U.S. Center for Health Statistics

Prescriptions Written per Person Annually

Total prescriptions issued divided by civilian population

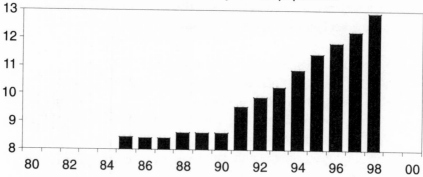

Source: IMS International

This generation considers itself, in the words of the Bob Dylan song, to be "forever young." Indeed, a Yankelovich survey revealed that boomers give 79 as the median age they consider "old," and countless other studies show that when asked how old they feel, baby boomers invariably give a number that is five to ten years less than their chronological age.

Not surprisingly, given what we have already seen about the boomers, they are looking for a stress-free road that will keep them healthy.

This sets up an interesting quandary. For boomers, feeling good means not feeling stressed. But worrying about your diet and fretting about getting enough exercise is stressful. How do you cope with this paradox? By taking the easiest road possible. There is a growing trend away from being thin and toward feeling well, regardless of how you look.

A second alternative is to use prescription drugs.

Desiring to stay healthy and young, but unwilling to take on the stress that comes with going on a diet or increasing their exercise program, many baby boomers are taking one or some of the following medications on a regular basis:

Propecia for hair loss
Dexatrim for weight loss
Zyban to stop smoking
Prozac for depression

Xanax for anxiety
Viagra for sexual dysfunction
Lipitor for high cholesterol
Norvasc for high blood pressure

And as boomers get older, they will likely take even more drugs to treat such health concerns as arthritis, prostate problems and osteoporosis.

Back in the late 1960s and early 1970s when boomers talked about "better living through chemistry"—echoing the DuPont advertising slogan at the time—they were talking about the use of illicit drugs. They have just recycled the idea of better living through chemistry and applied it to legal pharmaceuticals.

What are the investment implications of this? Not surprisingly, selected drug stocks should do well as the baby boom generation grows ever older.

Summing Up Theme 1

The baby boomers, due to their numbers, will shape the economy in the years ahead, just as they have throughout their entire lives. We expect them to continue to remain entrepreneurial—in everything from how they earn their paychecks to how they spend their time once they reach retirement age. And there is no reason to believe they will either lessen their search for stressless leisure or give up their reliance on pharmaceuticals that can make them feel and look better.

A Cautionary Note

Thematic investing obviously isn't simple, and health care is a good example of how complicated it can get. Health care is an obvious theme: an aging population consumes more health care, and in this era of medical miracles, there is ever more health care to consume, in the form of new drugs, new surgical applications, and new medical technologies, virtually assuring strong growth in this sector. Moreover, our drug and medical product health care industries are global leaders, with huge potential overseas markets for their products.

But herein lies the cautionary note. Despite these promising fundamentals, which have been in place for a number of years, in 1993 the drug industry lost over a third of its market value, with many other health-care-related stocks declining by like amounts, as President Clinton attempted to pass a national health care plan that included various forms of price controls.

Many of these stocks recovered and went on to post new highs, but the severe price decline they faced in light of President Clinton's proposal illustrates that even the best themes and ideas are subject to the realities of government actions and other vagaries of the economy. It also confirms the necessity of constantly assessing the theme and the relevant stocks in light of all developments.

With that caveat, let's move on to the second significant trend affecting the investment landscape in the years ahead: technology.

Theme 2:
The Information Revolution

The Internet represents phase two of the information revolution. Phase one consisted of the digitization of individual enterprises, which created networks of increasingly ubiquitous computers—mainframes in the 1950s and 1960s, mini computers in the 1970s and 1980s, and PCs in the 1980s and 1990s. Though extremely important, the process mainly sped up traditional ways of doing business. Executives might save time by creating a document on a PC rather than a typewriter, but then they dropped it in a mailbox as they always had. Phase one just made communication a bit faster.

Phase two makes it instantaneous. Once you finish typing the letter, you e-mail it, and the recipient has it in a few seconds, not a few days. We now take this rather amazing fact for granted. Overnight mail—something truly revolutionary twenty years ago—is now seen as much too slow. And phase two—where electronic devices of all kinds will be linked—is only now beginning.

The best way to appreciate the sweeping impact of the information revolution is to glance back at the two earlier revolutions that created the modern industrial economy.

The first industrial revolution erupted in England in the late eighteenth century and spread to the United States and elsewhere during the nineteenth century. The essence of the revolution was, in the phrase of Harvard historian David Landes, "the substitution of machines—rapid, regular, precise, tireless—for human skill and effort." The results were the mechanized factory, driven by water or steam; the coal-burning steam engine; the railroad; and the rise of a modern steel industry that permitted wholesale substitution of metal for wood.

Railroads did for the industrial revolution what the Internet is doing for the information economy—making it faster, and more efficient.

The results were dramatic. Railroads left few industries unaffected, as they carried the first industrial revolution across the continent. During the second half of the nineteenth century, manufacturing's share of the U.S. gross domestic product rose from 22 to 30 percent, while agriculture's share was cut in half, falling from 42 to 20 percent.

But this does not mean the U.S. suddenly became an industrial society. In 1899, fully 43 percent of American workers still labored in agriculture. (Presumably, farming's share of output fell faster than its share of workers because productivity growth lagged.)

In the second industrial revolution, which occurred between 1880 and 1930, the U.S. economy shifted from steam engines and water power to gasoline and electricity. As a consequence, mechanical power became ubiquitous in most dimensions of daily life, including communications (the telephone), lighting (the electric light replaced kerosene and coal oil), refrigeration (electric refrigerators replaced the icebox), entertainment (radio, phonographs, and motion pictures were responsible for killing vaudeville), and transportation (autos replaced horses in local transportation and began to supplant railroads in long-distance travel).

Factories gradually shifted from steam power to electricity, which increased flexibility and efficiency and led to the modern assembly line. As a consequence, there was a quantum leap in manufacturing productivity during the 1920s.

Lessons from the Previous Revolutions: What We Can Expect from the Next One

It will be bigger than anyone thought

It is easy to underestimate the potential magnitude of revolutions. Who would have guessed that by 1910, railroads would be hauling ninety-nine times as much freight as they did in 1860? Their business grew by about 10,000 percent in fifty years. (Their employee count increased by only a factor of 23 over that time.) Investors underestimated the popularity of autos as well, initially considered playthings of the upper class that would have limited economic impact. In 1908, the entire auto industry manufactured only sixty-five thousand cars. But Billy Durant, founder of General Motors, foresaw the revolution; he said the industry would be producing half a million cars within a few years. George W. Perkins, a senior partner at J. P. Morgan and Co., told Durant to stop making such preposterous projections if he wanted to get funding for his fledgling enterprise. Eight years later, the industry turned out 1.6 million cars, three times Durant's "preposterous" forecast.

Even revolutions take time

Railroads were introduced in the United States in 1826, but their full impact was not evident until the 1880s, some sixty years later. And although electricity was commercialized in the 1880s, the real payoff in terms of raising industrial productivity came in the 1920s. The information revolution fits this mold. Computers were widespread in the 1950s, but the most dramatic productivity improvement that evolved from them is the Internet, which did not become a major factor until the mid-1990s.

Unexpected Side Effects

The ultimate impact of industrial revolutions is remarkably pervasive. Who would have thought the introduction of the railroads would reshape Wall Street (which financed the revolution); give rise to Chicago's commodity futures market (which became possible thanks to relatively easy transportation and communication); change the nature of retailing (mail order became a possibility); and lead to the creation of four time zones in the United States?

Benign Deflation

It is no coincidence that inflation was remarkably low, or even negative, in the 1880s, 1920s, and 1990s, eras of remarkable change in the economy. In each period, the U.S. economy was the beneficiary of an industrial or information revolution that drove down prices. In the revolutionary industry itself, the unit price of a key product—overland transportation in the 1880s; electricity and roadway travel in the 1920s; computing power in the 1990s—plummeted thanks to increased productivity and rising demand, which allowed companies to spread their fixed costs over a wider base.

Bigger, Better Markets

Perhaps, most fundamentally, business revolutions reorder entire ways of life. For example, railroads transformed the U.S. economy by slashing transport times and expanding markets. That, in turn, created a host of business innovations ranging from mail-order retailing (the Sears, Roebuck catalogue) to long-distance trade in refrigerated meat (Swift Premium). The result? Business, and the way we live, were never the same again.

New Corporate Models

The railroad enabled manufacturers to accelerate the flow of raw materials into, and finished product out of, factories. That forced companies to cultivate a mass market that could absorb the torrent of goods. Shorter transport times cut inventory-to-sales ratios, which, of course, raised the return on capital. Entrepreneurs like Andrew Carnegie, who perfected this new model, could cut costs, boost market share, and in the process become rich.

The Information Revolution Creates a New Model

Like its predecessors, the information revolution will create a different and better economy. Instantaneous, low-cost digital communication will make markets much more efficient. More and more products will be made to order—as Dell now makes personal computers—reducing the need for manufacturers to guess what demand will be.

That will reduce inventory, and the World Wide Web will render whatever unsold inventory there is virtually obsolete. Goods that sell poorly—be they apparel products in a store or cabins on a cruise ship that is about to sail—will be auctioned over the Web to a global market; that will make an efficient capitalist market even more efficient.

Just as important will be the creation of more-efficient labor markets. As the Internet connects them with a global market, knowledge workers will be able to specialize in their area of expertise. (We are beginning to see glimmers of this today as people post their résumés on various electronic job-matching services and tell the world who they will and will not work for—and what they need in terms of salary and benefits.)

Consumers will be more efficient as well because they will easily be able to retrieve information, compare prices, and shop for the best deal just by using the Web.

From a company perspective, the information revolution will reconfigure corporate operations so that speed to market and customer responsiveness become paramount.

The likely result?

- a lower ratio of inventories to sales
- fewer earnings swings as inventory swings become less pronounced
- slightly more financial leverage, as a less cyclical economy renders debt less risky
- a higher ratio of sales to assets
- higher sales per employee
- lower profit margins as markets become more competitive

How does this new model play out in practice? It is still evolving, of course, but four trends are already clear.

Information Age Versus Industrial Age

Jack Welch, the outgoing CEO of General Electric, has said, "Product is dead." And while that is hyperbolic, it makes the point. The information revolution is pushing the economy full force into what is widely known as the Information Age, when capturing and effectively exploiting information become the keys to speed to market and improving customer service, the two factors that will govern corporate performance going forward. The best companies are shifting their product mix away from product and more toward information and information services, as GE has already done.

There will be "new industrials"

Like Carnegie Steel and Ford Motor Company in former times, these new companies will be built on the infrastructure of the day, creating opportunities not only in technology companies but in telecommunications as well.

Producer Versus Distributor

The Web increases the power of producers, making distributors vulnerable—or irrelevant. Dell's direct model has revolutionized the way PCs are sold, at the expense of retailers. Established manufacturers have set up their own e-tailing sites, as opposed to having their products sold exclusively through traditional merchants such as JCPenney and Sears. In the Information Age, being a middleman is a very perilous position to occupy.

Commoditized Information

If knowledge is power, consumers have a lot of muscle today. One of the reasons for going through a travel agent used to be that they had nearly exclusive access to key information, such as which airline flew to what airport at what time. Now all this information is easily available on the Web. In addition to disseminating information that previously was hard or impossible to find, the Web makes readily available—for free—huge quantities of information that consumers once had to pay for. Here's one quick example. Since 1990, sales of the *Encyclopædia Britannica*'s multivolume sets (which cost between $1,500 and $2,200) have plunged from around 350,000 to almost none in 1999, reflecting the abundance of data now freely available on the Web.

But consumers continue to be willing to pay for proprietary information, such as *The Wall Street Journal*'s coverage of financial markets. Similarly, large entertainment companies have a valuable franchise in their ability to create original content.

What do you do if the Web has commoditized the information you used to sell? To succeed you will have to offer insight and context as opposed to just information. That is especially true in the financial services business. You can already see signs that traditional investment and finance companies are making the transition, moving away from the concept of transactions—buying or selling a stock; writing an insurance policy—toward taking care of all of a customer's financial needs and positioning themselves as providers of all the information that their customers might need. They are trying to evolve from being transaction-oriented to being relationship-oriented.

The Challenge Facing Incumbents

Being entrenched can be a liability. The Internet threatens many existing companies because new business models can easily be created that attack their core positions efficiently. (Consider how on-line booksellers have undercut sales of traditional bookstores.) The Internet allows companies to move into new business channels easily. They can go directly to consumers, bypassing the need for distributors. And the World Wide Web eliminates geographic boundaries that used to keep competitors out of a market. An on-line retailer can serve the national marketplace with only a few warehouses. There is no need to have a store everywhere.

Historically, established companies have done a poor job of fending off the threat of new technology. For example, each phase of the development of the computer industry has been dominated by a different company—IBM for mainframes; Digital Equipment for mini computers; Compaq and Dell for PCs. It has been extremely difficult for the established market leader to make the transition into the next phase of the information revolution.

Similarly, since World War II, with each new generation of shoppers there has been a fundamental shift in retailing. Baby boomers' parents shopped on Main Street in the 1950s. The boomers themselves hung out in the malls in the 1970s. Boomers' teenage kids headed to superstores in the 1990s, while the category killers such as Staples and Bed Bath & Beyond took share from traditional retailers. Each time the business model changed, a new group of leaders emerged—and those who were slow to adapt were left behind. Woolworth never really escaped Main Street. Sears, for the most part, remains stuck in the mall. Kmart was blindsided by the emergence of the superstore. Toys R Us has had a hard time coping with the decision by retailers such as Wal-Mart to beef up their toy sections, and with the rise of toy stores that have taken up residence on the Web.

Of course, the Web won't replace traditional retailing, but it will raise customers' expectations about convenience, speed, price, and service. Retailers who fail to acknowledge the consumers' desire for the advantages e-tailing provides will suffer. And there is no quicker road to financial ruin than making customers unhappy.

What are the investment implications of this? Companies that fail to embrace the current revolution will be crippled or fail. And even if they embrace it, they may fail if they do not move fast enough. Those who benefit will either provide the infrastructure of the revolution—making personal computers, telephones, modems, routers, switches, and the like—or use it to their advantage.

Summing Up Theme 2

It is clear by now that we are in the midst of a technology revolution that will have an impact as great as—or perhaps even greater than—the industrial revolution that occurred more than a century ago. Everything—the way we work, communicate, live, and play—has already changed and will continue to do so thanks to advancements in technology, most notably the Internet.

Conclusion

The baby boomers have always had a disproportionate effect on the economy because of their sheer numbers, and that is not going to end anytime soon.

They expect to work longer, and that—coupled with the fact that they are living longer—is good news for both the economy and the stock market. In the past, investors were told that as they approached retirement age, they should skew their asset mix away from stocks and toward bonds and other conservative investments to make sure they would have sufficient income in their few remaining years. Today, knowing that they are going to live longer, the boomers understand that they need a heavier weighting in equities if they expect to retire and continue to live in the manner to which they have become accustomed.

Which stocks will do well in this new world? The ones that cater specifically to the boomers' decision to become more entrepreneurial while decreasing the stress in their lives. In particular, we would expect selected retail, drug and leisure stocks to thrive. An aging population consumes more health care, and the dramatic increase in new drugs available, with more in the pipeline, virtually ensures strong growth in drug sales. As boomers seek relaxing ways to spend their leisure hours, companies such as cruise lines that cater to them should win. And time-constrained boomers will seek re-tailers providing the right combination of service, quality, and value.

The baby boomers' continuing influence on the economy is the first major investment trend we see in the years ahead. The second theme, technology, is equally important.

Luddites aside, no one wants to go back to the days before computers. Having gotten a taste of instantaneous communication and the ease that comes with ordering and paying on-line, we are going to want more. Companies that can cater successfully to our desires will continue to do well.

Now let me state the obvious. A company must not only fit into the investment themes we have identified but also meet the same stringent criteria that any investment should—good management, a sound balance sheet, and a strong competitive position—before it is worth purchasing. And of course, even if you decide to buy, the stock must be constantly reevaluated to determine that it is still attractive as the theme develops (sometimes in unexpected ways, as the example with health care showed).

When looking for themes, I quickly learned that personal experience can be helpful. After all, I am a baby boomer. I also learned not to extrapolate my personal experiences to the population at large—New Yorkers are not a proxy for the rest of the United States. (Do I hear you heaving a sigh of relief?)

Thematic investing captures only a segment of the opportunities available in the market, and is not meant to be exhaustive of all the investment possi-bilities out there. At any given time there are a number of compelling themes operating, but many industries and sectors will not participate. Thematic in-vesting is simply a disciplined approach to investing that has shown superior returns over time. It is an ideal way for long-term investors to make their stock selections. Equally important, it turns the focus from *the market* to-ward investing in high-quality companies with superior prospects, the true means of building wealth.

9

Picking Stocks and Bonds:
The Efficient Way

One of my favorite features in *The Wall Street Journal* is the stock-picking contest that it runs periodically. The newspaper invites professionals to select their most promising stocks for the coming months, and then a group of *Journal* writers and editors tape the stock tables to a wall and throw darts at the listings. Whatever they hit becomes the portfolio that competes with the professionals' picks. While the professionals sometimes have an extended roll, frequently the dart throwers have the best performance.

The contest—professional advice versus random chance—is amusing when you know up front that the competition is designed to be a source of entertainment. It is less funny if throwing darts—or some other random method—is the way you have chosen to decide which stocks and bonds to include in your portfolio.

The dart throwers would feel right at home if they looked at what some investors own—a hodgepodge of today's hot stocks, yesterday's losers (hope springs eternal), and a few stocks bought years ago, although the investors cannot remember exactly why.

Investing at random is certainly one way to go. But it is probably not the best course.

There are roughly seven thousand publicly traded companies out there whose stocks you can buy, and approximately ten thousand fixed-income issues. If you think of the investing universe as a funnel, we are going to move from the top of the funnel—where all seventeen thousand stocks and debt instruments exist—down to the narrowest part, where we will identify the stock and fixed-income investments that are best for you.

Along the way we will be giving you a rationale you can apply in the future, to make selecting your investments easier and, hopefully, more rewarding. Before we begin, it is worth noting that over time, different types of stocks and fixed-income investments go in and out of favor. When that results from changing market conditions, as is often the case, investors must be prepared to reassess their strategy.

Winnowing Down the List: A Search for True Value Stocks

In chapter 7 we discussed the best ways of determining where specific types of investments fit into your portfolio. To oversimplify: If you are thinking long-term, stocks are the place to be. To offset the volatility that comes with investing in equities and to generate current income, long-term bonds with various maturities are a solid choice. For the short term, cash equivalents are probably your best option.

But which stocks? And which kinds of fixed-income investments? That's what we are going to concentrate on here. Let's start with stocks first. Where should you start looking if you are in search of equities?

I'd begin with companies that fit into the big ideas we talked about in chapter 8, "Tools for Success: Why Thematic Investing Can Give You an Edge." After all, you want to bring some concerted intelligence to the stocks you buy and hold, and that means you want to have a theme that explains your purchases. In chapter 8 we identified themes that can serve as an overarching guide to constructing your stock portfolio.

Can you winnow down that list even further? We think so. The way to do that is to search for the best values.

Please note that sentence. I said you want to look for the best values. I did not say, "Buy value stocks."

I am stressing that distinction for two specific reasons. First, the definitions of growth, value, and other stock categories now tend to vary greatly among market participants. A look at what stocks are held in mutual funds grouped in the same category, such as value funds, confirms the disparity. While most traditional value mutual funds hold primarily stocks with low price/earnings ratios, one of the most successful value managers owns Internet and technology companies because he finds they offer better value.

The second reason is that I think the traditional definition of value stocks is wrong.

Growth stocks continue to offer the best _value_ in the market.

Traditionally, value stocks are defined as equities selling at low prices relative to their earnings, hence they are perceived to offer value. These stocks may be accorded low price/earnings ratios because they are growing slowly, are in unattractive industries, or have other problems that result in Wall Street valuing them less highly than their peers. The buyer of a value stock believes that Wall Street has misunderstood the company's prospects and that its true value will be realized in a higher stock price down the road. But with many of these companies, you get what you pay for.

Yet even if these stocks are not flawed, there is still a problem. This traditional definition of value may, ironically, not provide the best value in the new, low-inflation environment in which we find ourselves.

We have long argued that growth stocks—those companies that are increasing their sales and earnings faster than their peers, and faster than the economy as a whole—offer the best true value in the marketplace today.

It has been a better strategy in the last decade to pay a higher price for the more rapidly increasing earnings that growth companies provide than to buy the so-called value stocks just because they appear to be cheap. When you study the numbers, you realize that growth stocks have significantly outperformed value stocks over the last decade. BARRA (a full-service provider of analytical products, investment data, trading services, consulting, and asset management) has maintained value and growth indexes based on the S&P 500 since 1975. In the ten-year period from 1989 to 1998, the S&P 500 BARRA growth index has had a compound annual growth rate of 21.3 percent, versus 16.7 percent for the S&P 500 BARRA value index. The chart below makes that clear.

It is often said that the solid performance of the S&P 500 over the past several years has been driven by the strong gains of the largest stocks in the index. This view is correct, but it is important to understand why it is correct.

The top tier of the S&P 500 is increasingly dominated by fast-growing "gorilla" stocks that "own" their industries. These are companies gaining market share and growing rapidly despite—or perhaps even because of—their large size. In 1998, of the top ten companies in the S&P 500, at least eight were high-growth stocks: Microsoft, GE, Intel, Wal-Mart, Merck, Coca-Cola, Pfizer, and Cisco. The expected annual earnings growth of the S&P 500 fell from 7.5 percent in 1988 to 6.5 percent in 1998, largely reflecting the steep drop in inflation. But the average expected growth rate of the top ten stocks, which was only 9 percent in 1988, rose to 15.5 percent at the end of the 1990s.

Think for a minute about what that means. Over that time, the inflation rate declined from 4.5 percent to a projected 2 percent. So, the average expected real earnings growth of the top ten stocks within the S&P 500 rose to

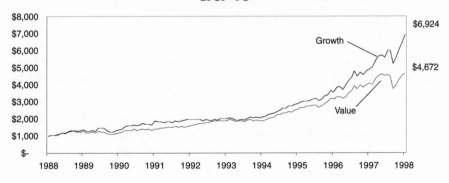

**Relative Performance of S&P 500 BARRA Growth Index
Versus S&P 500 BARRA Value Index
1989–98**

Source: Standard & Poor's

13.5 percent, versus 4.5 percent in 1988. No wonder the S&P 500 has performed so well.

But Which Growth Stocks Should You Buy?

The environment in the years ahead—one that will have low inflation, slow growth, and moderate interest rates—should continue to favor growth over value. So, clearly growth stocks are the way to go. And in trying to determine which ones have the greatest likelihood of success, we already have a head start. We have identified what we believe will be the major economic trends for at least the coming decade. Those were the themes we talked about in chapter 8—investment trends driven by technology and the aging baby boomers.

The Picture Becomes Clearer

So, here is where we have come so far in trying to winnow down the seven thousand publicly traded stocks to those we think have the most potential to be long-term winners. We began our search by looking for economic themes we see emerging in coming years, and then we tried to find stocks—regardless of their current cost—that have the best prospects of benefiting from those themes. That led us to concentrate on growth stocks.

But what kind of growth stocks? Large-cap stocks—with market capitalization of $5 billion or more? (Market capitalization, as you remember, is the product of the number of shares a company has outstanding, multiplied by its stock price.) Should we be concentrating our attention on mid-caps—those stocks with market capitalization between $1 billion and $5 billion? Maybe we should be searching the universe of small-caps—stocks with a market cap of $1 billion or less. Or we could go even smaller, looking at micro-caps, a subset of small-caps—companies with less than $100 million in market capitalization. (There are no firm definitions, by the way. These parameters are what I have found useful in defining these size categories.)

Where is the most efficient place to search when you are looking for long-term winners? In investing, just as in many parts of life, history tends to re-peat itself, so let's look at how these various classes of stocks have per-formed over time.

During the time frame from 1926 to 1998, small-caps outperformed large-caps, as represented by the S&P 500. According to the Ibbotson data, the compound annual growth rate (CAGR) of small-caps is 12.4 percent ver-sus 11.2 percent for the S&P 500.

But our search is not yet finished, as you can see from the chart on the next page. During the time frame from 1980 to 1998, large-caps outperformed the small-caps, and they have outperformed them with a vengeance since 1995. The CAGR of the S&P 500 since 1980 is 17.7 percent, versus 14.8 percent for small-caps. In the period since 1995, the CAGR of the S&P 500 is 30.5 percent, versus 15.5 percent for small-caps.

Over the last few years, there has been an extraordinary performance gap, with small-caps substantially underperforming large-cap stocks, particularly the Standard & Poor's 500. We expect the trend to continue.

Why? Primarily because large-caps are likely to continue to produce faster earnings growth than small-caps. And as we have seen, investors will pay a premium for that kind of performance.

Why don't we expect small-cap stocks to stage a comeback? There are a number of factors.

Accumulated Wealth of S&P 500 Versus Small-Cap Stocks: 1926–98 (1926 = $1)

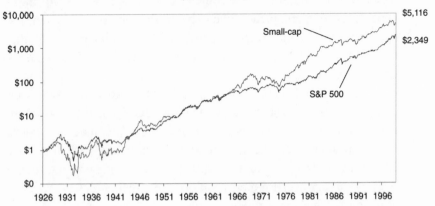

Source: Ibbotson Associates

Accumulated Wealth of S&P 500 Versus Small-Cap Stocks: 1980–98
(1980 = $1)

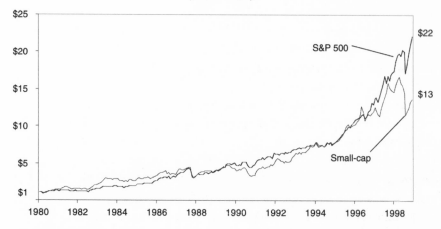

Source: Ibbotson Associates

- Large-cap companies made major investments in technology and telecommunications starting in the late 1980s, triggering productivity gains that continue today. These enormous up-front investments were difficult for small companies to match.
- Large-cap companies have much greater exposure to the global marketplace, which gives these companies access to markets growing more rapidly than our own. An estimated 42 percent of the earnings of the Standard & Poor's 500 Index comes from outside the United States, while the smaller companies tend to be much more limited in their foreign exposure. While overseas earnings can be vulnerable (as they proved to be in 1998), overall this international growth has enhanced large-cap earnings.
- Small-caps suffer from a lack of liquidity, which appeared to be worsening in the 1990s and has become a major issue for investors, resulting in both professional and individual investors' shunning the stocks. Small-cap stocks are more difficult to trade, particularly when the market is falling. Also, as mutual funds have gotten bigger they require greater liquidity because their positions are larger, and they are gravitating toward the large-caps as a result.

- Forces of supply and demand also favor the large-caps. As long as mutual fund index funds continue to funnel regular sums into the S&P 500, the large-capitalization stocks—which include those that make up the S&P 500—will benefit. Conversely, the flood of initial public offerings, including hot Internet issues, has increased the supply of small-cap stocks and siphoned demand from the existing pool of small-caps.
- Foreign money also favors large-caps. Foreign market turmoil benefits the U.S. stock market, which is seen as a safe haven. Foreign investors prize liquidity. They want to be able to get out of a stock quickly if they have to. And as we have seen, large-cap stocks are more liquid than their smaller counterparts.

As a result of all this, the large-cap stocks are likely to continue outperforming.

In the coming months and years we expect the small-cap stocks to experience brief rallies of limited duration and possible outperformance. After all, they can underperform for only so long, or go so far down, before offering compelling value. However, we don't believe that stock appreciation will match that of the large-caps over time.

A Quick Word About Mid-Caps and Preferreds

Mid-cap stocks present a very interesting alternative to both the small-cap and large-cap markets. Mid-caps can combine the liquidity of the large-cap market with the growth opportunity of the small-cap market, at times offering the best of both worlds. In fact, as the market leadership became narrower and narrower in the 1995–98 period, and the prices of the large-cap growth stocks were bid higher and higher, mid-caps offered investors growth at a cheaper price without incurring the liquidity risk of the small-caps. Because they are more seasoned companies, mid-caps also offer less fundamental risk than smaller companies that have not yet proven themselves.

Mid-caps were not given full recognition in the market until 1991, when the Frank Russell Company and Standard & Poor's both introduced mid-cap indexes. The measurable performance history of mid-caps is therefore limited, but in every year since 1991 with the exception of one, the annual returns of mid-caps have been between the returns of small-caps and large-caps, regardless of which group outperformed.

Preferred stock is also an interesting asset class because it combines features of both stocks and bonds. Like a bond, preferred stock pays a fixed rate of return, or dividend, on a quarterly basis. Unlike a bond, however, most preferred stocks have no maturity date, and in that regard are similar to common stock. In the past, the yield on preferred stock has generally been below that of the highest-grade corporate bonds. However, the introduction of a new class of preferred stock, one that is issued through special trusts set up just for this purpose, has changed all that. These trust preferred issues—often known by their acronyms MIPS, QIPS, and TOPrS—actually offer yields greater than corporate bonds. However, most of these issues are callable, that is, the issuer retains the right to call back an issue before maturity, and in the pecking order of claimants in the case of a corporate bankruptcy, preferred stockholders rank lower than bondholders (but higher than common stockholders do).

Owning preferred stock gives investors the ability to participate in some of the advantages of both common stock and bonds. The dividend yield on preferred stock is higher than it is for common stock—and in the case of the trust preferred shares, higher than corporate bonds as well.

Growth and value stocks, large-caps, mid-caps, small-caps, and preferred stocks all can be part of a diversified portfolio. The proportions will depend on objectives, time horizon, and risk tolerance. But given the fundamentals of the market and the growth rates likely in each of these categories, we believe large-cap growth stocks should be the central core of an investment portfolio.

Can You Become Even More Efficient?

If we know large-cap growth stocks should be at the heart of a diversified investment portfolio, then why not buy tomorrow's winners right now, some investors ask. The way to do that, they argue, is to go out and buy today's small aggressive growth stocks, firms that appear destined to become tomorrow's large-cap stars. By taking this approach, they maintain, you'll be buying tomorrow's winners at yesterday's prices. Who wouldn't want to have bought Dell Computer or Home Depot when they were small companies and were trading at a fraction of their current prices?

It is an intriguing argument, but it overlooks one major factor: risk.

There is just no guarantee that any of today's hot software companies, to pick an example, will become tomorrow's Microsoft. Maybe one or two of them just going public will, but the vast majority won't. They will flame out. And the earth can get scorched along the way as you are trying to sort the winners out from the losers. When Starbucks—an aggressive growth stock by any measure—told analysts during the summer of 1999 that its quarterly earnings would fall below expectations, the stock fell 28 percent. It lost more than a quarter of its market capitalization in one day. (For some Internet stocks this kind of volatility is nearly routine.)

Could you buy a group of small companies early on, and invest the way venture capitalists do? Sure, you can make a number of bets and hope that your winners will more than make up for the companies that don't do well. It is one approach, and for investors with a high level of risk tolerance, it may be reasonable. And of course, as part of an overall diversification strategy, there may be a role for selected small-capitalization issues in a portfolio. Understanding that these issues are more volatile than the market, and less liquid, investors who appreciate the risks can still find opportunities in small-caps. But as with all investments, do your homework. And even after you burn all that midnight oil, you probably don't want to be too heavily weighted in small-caps. As a group, we believe, large-cap growth stocks will outperform them by a wide margin.

When you select stocks for long-term growth, there are some other considerations.

First, you don't have to pick individual stocks to benefit from the belief that large-cap growth stocks will probably give you the best returns. You can find good mutual funds that buy and hold these stocks. (See chapter 10, where we explore mutual funds in detail.)

Second, don't ignore the international markets.

The International Conundrum

International companies can give investors exposure to markets growing more rapidly than our own. With an aging population and an extremely tight labor force, our economic growth—while still admirable—has been slower than that of many emerging markets, with their rapidly growing populations and rising levels of affluence. Not surprisingly, this has American investors looking overseas for opportunities. But if you are considering going global there are issues—some good, some bad—that must be weighed before investing in foreign companies.

First, the good. Many foreign companies have ADRs (American depository receipts) that are traded on U.S. stock exchanges. That makes it easy to buy and sell these stocks.

But now some of the bad news. Foreign companies are not subject to the same accounting rules and regulations that govern American public companies. Neither do they have the same reporting and disclosure requirements. This can make researching and evaluating these companies very difficult.

Moreover, many foreign companies do not have ADRs. If you want to buy their shares, you must do so on a foreign market, and that can be a nightmare for individuals. In addition to the currency exchange issues, you also have to worry about finding a broker who can handle these transactions—and explain what your confirmation statement, which will be written in the native language, means. Moreover, you'll have to live with the fact that some countries put restrictions on foreigners trying to buy their stock, sometimes limiting them to a particular type or class of shares.

And currency issues can wreak havoc with performance for U.S. investors. It is not unusual to see global performance rankings at year end distorted significantly when the results are translated into U.S. dollars.

Many investors opt for mutual funds to get exposure to foreign companies, and I think that the international funds do provide a good means of overcoming the problems of foreign investing. This is a case where buying professional management is particularly prudent, given the difficulty of researching foreign companies and understanding the complexities of each country's political, economic, and currency situation.

One quick reminder: if you are going to invest in foreign companies through mutual funds, make sure you buy an *international* fund and not a *global* fund.

International funds must buy shares of companies based outside their home country. So, a U.S.-based international fund cannot hold any American companies. A U.S.-based global fund can. The distinction is particularly important if you already own U.S. companies such as IBM that have a significant foreign presence. You don't want to distort your global asset allocation.

And that brings up an intriguing point. You may not need to buy either a global mutual fund or shares of foreign corporations at all. You may have international exposure in your portfolio and not realize it.

As we have said, about 42 percent of the earnings of the S&P 500 come from outside the United States, so a U.S. investor can have global diversification without owning any foreign companies. It surprises many people to learn that Procter & Gamble and Gillette—our quintessentially American companies—receive more than 50 percent of their earnings from overseas. The net effect? You might find all the international exposure you need by owning large-cap U.S. growth stocks. In fact, if you end up buying an international fund, it is possible that you will be duplicating what you already have.

A final point about equities. Large-cap growth stocks have been the best performers in this bull market, and going forward, they are likely to continue delivering superior returns. That is where I have the bulk of my personal portfolio. But the prudent investor understands the benefits of diversification. While large-cap growth stocks should be the core of a growth-oriented investment strategy, you should take advantage of other opportunities as well, as market conditions warrant.

A More Efficient Way of Selecting Bonds

As we enter a new decade, there has never been a better time to efficiently buy the right kind of fixed-income investments. For that you can thank the rise of technology and the fall of interest rates.

It used to be that an investor had a hard time learning what kinds of bonds were being offered by whom. There was no easily accessible source of information. You had to call your broker just to find out what was available.

Today, thanks to electronic data services such as Bloomberg and Telerate, you can instantly learn not only what is available but also its current price. In a few years the electronic trading of bonds should become as widespread as the on-line buying and selling of stocks are today. In fact a number of companies have already started to provide just this service.

But it is one thing to be able to easily buy bonds; it is quite another to know which bonds to buy. The answer to this question is particularly important during a period of relatively stable interest rates. In less than two decades, long-term Treasury yields have declined nearly 900 basis points, from a high near 15 percent in 1981 to somewhere around 6 percent as we go to press. (Basis points are an annoying way the bond market experts refer to interest rates: 100 basis points equals 1 percent. Why they can't use percentages is a mystery to me.)

Since interest rates have already fallen sharply and future declines are likely to be more modest (something we will discuss in detail in chapter 12, "Bonds: Getting the Most Out of Your Fixed Income Investments"), the prospect for further material price appreciation within the fixed-income market appears limited for the foreseeable future—unless we experience a significant change in economic or Federal Reserve policy (something we don't think will happen).

In the low-inflation environment we expect over the next several years, when most of the returns from bonds are likely to come from interest income and not from capital gains, there are four keys to investing efficiently.

1. Shift toward market-neutral durations in the bonds you buy

Instead of buying bonds in anticipation of falling interest rates—which, of course, drive bond prices higher—invest on the premise that interest rates are going to remain relatively stable. It would be great if you could buy a thirty-year bond yielding 6 percent and then watch as long-term rates fall to 4 percent, which would drive its price up, but we just don't think that is going to happen anytime soon. Therefore, maintaining an above-average market weighting (duration) is no longer appropriate. With more gradual incremental declines in rates more likely, a more neutral position is warranted. Simply put, try to time the duration of the bonds you buy to when you will need to have the principal repaid.

2. Concentrate on the interest coupon

This point follows the last. If the odds say you are going to get only moderate capital appreciation, it is important to focus on yield. Remember that in an environment of stable yields and limited capital gains opportunities, "he who clips the biggest coupon generally wins." This means placing greater emphasis on premium and par bonds (bonds that sell at $1,000) rather than those sold at a deep discount.

3. Take advantage of the spread whenever you can

Most investors adopt an overly literal definition of spread: it is the difference between what Treasury bonds, the safest long-term bonds, are yielding and the yields on other fixed-income instruments. Such investors look for an investment that offers a premium to whatever Treasuries are yielding at the moment. This typically means buying agency, corporate, high-yield, and mortgage bonds. However, we would extend the definition of spread to include taxable equivalent yields. When you factor in the tax rate, it is quite possible that for someone in the 28 percent tax rate or above, municipal bonds will be offering an after-tax yield that is greater than what you can get from Treasuries. After all, as you have always been told, when it comes to investing, it's not the income you get that counts, it's the income you get to keep.

4. You can answer the call

When interest rates were steadily declining, investors—not surprisingly—looked for bonds that had either no call provisions or ones that offered high levels of call protection. (Call provisions allow the issuer to recall the bonds from investors prior to maturity. For example, a company that issued bonds during a high-interest-rate environment would want to recall those bonds and reissue new ones at a lower rate to save borrowing costs.) Investors wanted investments that would pay the highest possible interest rate for the longest possible time. Today, call risk no longer looms quite as large, since the odds of a bond being called have decreased significantly. After all, an issuer typically calls a bond when he thinks he can get a better rate by refinancing. Since interest rates are not likely to decline much further in the future, there is little incentive to call in existing bonds. All other things being equal, you are now better off buying the bond with the higher yield, even if it is callable. If it is called, it will be fairly easy to find another fixed-income investment that is paying just as much.

Summing Up

When it comes to investing, your time is worth a lot. That is one reason you work with professionals. Not only should they be able to help you generate returns that more than cover their cost, but they also save you time.

If you focus your search for investments on the places we just discussed, concentrating primarily on large-cap growth stocks and bonds that provide for your current income needs, you will be able not only to save time but to generate substantial returns in the process as well.

10

Using Mutual Funds Strategically

Mutual funds are an increasingly popular and readily accessible tool for investors, both as basic investments and as part of a diversified portfolio. They provide individual investors with the ability to diversify their investments across a range of securities with a single investment. The array of choices is vast, with fund offerings to suit virtually any investment objective.

While mutual funds have been around since the 1930s, it was the advent of money market funds in the late 1970s that escalated their popularity. This led to the many types of funds available today—stock funds, bond funds, combinations, and index funds.

Individual stocks, of course, can offer greater potential for significant gains—provided, of course, that you select the right stocks. While it may be easier for a $20 stock to increase 50 percent in value than it is for a mutual fund that is trading at $20 a share to move to $30, the risk of investing in individual stocks is greater as well. While it is highly unusual for a mutual fund to lose 25 percent of its value in a given day, in today's trading environment, individual equities can fall precipitously in a short time.

But rapid gains should not be your main objective when you choose to invest in mutual funds. They can be an attractive means to achieve diversification as well as overall balance in your portfolio when used strategically.

They are an especially good way for investors who do not have the resources to purchase many individual stocks to achieve a balanced portfolio.

Let's take a look at the benefits of mutual funds before we talk about how you might want to use them as part of your portfolio.

The Advantages

Here's a quick summary of eight key advantages that a mutual fund offers.

Diversification

Mutual funds are an ideal way to gain diversification. By buying a single diversified stock fund, you may be able to invest in a broad range of companies across a number of industries. Or to gain broad diversification across the entire market, you can purchase an index fund, which replicates the companies in a given index, such as the S&P 500 Index or the Wilshire 5000 Index. Because of the many different kinds of mutual funds—diversified stock funds, nondiversified (or sector) funds, bond funds, municipals, and so forth—you can also own several different funds that can give you exposure to a broad base of investments, or a portfolio of funds. For example, instead of buying 100 shares of an oil stock, you could put the same amount of money into an energy sector fund, which limits its investments to a particular economic sector, and thereby own a number of energy-related equities. Or you could choose a fund category—such as growth and income or aggressive growth—that meets your investment objectives and risk tolerance and complements your other holdings.

Low Initial Investment

Most mutual funds today require a minimum initial investment of $1,000 and some require as little as $500. This is, of course, a great advantage for the individual investor who may have limited resources. These low minimums allow you to participate in a diversified portfolio and you can add to your holdings whenever you want. That's an advantage all investors, even the most experienced, can appreciate.

Professional Management

Every mutual fund is run by at least one professional portfolio or money manager, whose responsibility is to manage that fund in accordance with its investment objectives. The manager stays abreast of industry and company developments so he is always in touch with the markets.

Management can be active or passive

The choice is yours to make. You can choose the passive management of an index fund, which attempts to replicate the performance of a specific benchmark, such as the S&P 500, or you can choose an actively managed fund that will try to outperform its benchmark.

Liquidity

Mutual funds are easy to buy and sell. You can buy a no-load fund directly, or a load or no-load fund through a broker or financial planner. Purchases are usually handled quickly, and open-end mutual funds, by definition, will keep issuing shares to all that are interested (although some funds may close after they become too large to operate efficiently). Redemptions of shares are also relatively easy to transact because open-end funds buy back their shares as well. (Closed-end mutual funds, those that trade like a stock after a finite number of shares are issued, of course do not. You have to sell to a willing buyer, as you do when you sell a stock.)

Low Cost

There are three different ways to purchase mutual funds. You can buy them with a load, or up-front sales charge; with a back-end load, or exit fee, that generally declines over several years to zero; or with no load. Today, many firms offer a series of options to buy a fund, known as A, B, or C shares, so the investor can choose to pay the load up-front, or avoid it by paying a higher fee over time. In addition to sales charges, there may be administrative fees that are generally included in the net asset value of the fund. Net asset value (NAV), the stated value of each share, is determined by dividing the total net assets of the fund by the total number of shares outstanding. There are also management fees associated with running the fund. Management fees tend to be reasonable, although the investor should examine these fees in advance of buying a fund to be sure they are in line with industry standards. Fees vary depending on the complexity of management. For example, fees charged by international and global funds may be higher because of the expertise required in those areas; bond fund fees are often lower, and index funds tend to be among the lowest because the manager is tracking an index, rather than actively managing the fund. All of these fees and charges are disclosed in the prospectus.

Automatic Reinvestment

Most mutual fund companies offer you the option of having the dividends and capital gains you receive reinvested in the form of additional shares at net asset value, or with no additional sales charge. And many, if you instruct them to, will automatically withdraw money from your paycheck, or your checking account, on a regular basis to make purchasing additional shares easier. Both approaches not only make acquiring more shares relatively painless but also assure that your investment keeps building.

Switching within Fund Families

Most fund families offer the option of switching from one of their funds into another one they offer with very little or no cost. This can make managing your portfolio easier, while giving you the ability to take advantage of changing market conditions.

Having reviewed the basics, let's move on to discuss how mutual funds can fit into the portfolios of more sophisticated investors.

Strategic Investing

With all the time and attention spent on picking individual stocks, some people think investing through mutual funds is for novices. Nothing could be further from the truth, as many people, including sophisticated investors, have discovered. Mutual funds account for about 19 percent of the ownership of all publicly held U.S. equities and one-third of all municipal securities.

This pervasiveness is not hard to explain. First of all, many of us have no choice but to purchase mutual funds—frequently they are the only option available when we invest in our company-sponsored retirement plans. But perhaps more important, mutual funds can serve an important role in the portfolio of the sophisticated investor.

Let's consider three potential scenarios.

1. Mutual funds can be one of your primary investment vehicles

For some investors, choosing a mutual fund that meets their investment objectives can mean one initial decision and a minimum of time and effort later, other than monitoring performance. If the stock market appreciates at its historical 11 percent a year, on average, money in an index fund will double in a little less than seven years; money in other funds will reflect the performance of those funds. Investors concerned about having an all-stock portfolio might decide to use a balanced fund, one composed of both stocks and bonds, as their primary investment vehicle. A typical balanced fund might hold 60 percent stocks and 40 percent bonds. Assuming that you earn historical rates of returns—11 percent for stocks and 5.5 percent for bonds—that would give the fund an average return of 8.8 percent a year, once the returns of the stock and bond components are blended together. At that rate, your money would double in a little over eight years.

2. You can use funds to balance your portfolio

Many sophisticated investors use mutual funds to help round out their portfolios. For example, they may invest primarily in large-cap stocks, and then invest in a small-cap mutual fund and/or a bond fund, in whatever proportion they feel prudent. Or they might select from among a range of funds with specific complementary investment objectives. (Bond funds typically have no fixed interest rates or maturity dates as individual bonds do. They instead have a daily net asset value and current yield, which change as the market does.) Similarly, to offset an all-domestic portfolio, investors might invest in an international mutual fund, one that invests only in companies based outside of their home country. (That is in contrast to a global fund, which can invest in firms located anywhere in the world.) Given the difficulties of investing directly in many foreign stocks and markets, the professional management provided by either an international or a global mutual fund is often a good way for individuals to participate in foreign markets.

3. Funds are a way to make specialized investments

Emerging market funds, global funds, and sector funds give investors the benefits of a specific area of market concentration. Finding opportunities in these areas can be a daunting task for individuals. Unlike identifying solid, large-cap growth stocks, for example, locating potential winners off the beaten track is more difficult. Mutual funds can be an excellent alternative. Not only do you gain the specialized knowledge of the fund manager in locating the opportunity, but you also spread your risk among a number of stocks that make up the fund. A quick word of warning: if a particular sector, such as gold, falls out of favor, a gold fund is going to drop precipitously, no matter how many gold stocks you own. Remember, in this type of fund, you aren't diversifying—that is, you aren't spreading your risks among different types of stocks or asset classes—you are concentrating your bets by having all the stocks in the fund share a common characteristic.

Disadvantages

Mutual funds usually issue a statement when you buy or sell shares, as well as periodically—sometimes as often as once a month. Even though record keeping is important, all those statements can be a nuisance. A real disadvantage of mutual funds is that different categories of mutual fund returns are subject to different rates of taxation, and the mutual fund owner has no control over the timing of these taxes.

The IRS considers mutual funds a flow-through entity. In other words, they pay out all income and capital gains to investors each year. The fund itself pays no taxes. That means the tax burden falls to the investor. Distributions of income and realized short-term gains are taxed to investors as ordinary income. Distributions of long-term gains are taxed to investors at the lower capital gains rate.

The mutual fund companies have responded as investors have become more conscious of the taxes on their mutual fund investments. In answer to investors' concerns, there are now scores of tax-managed mutual funds that have the objective of maximizing long-term after-tax returns. Returns are shifted toward distributions of long-term gains and away from distributions of income (dividends) and short-term gains. Tax-free bond funds and tax-free money market funds are also available to minimize the tax bill.

The second potential disadvantage stems from the fees the funds charge.

Say you invest $10,000 every year in a stock mutual fund that earns the historical compound rate of 11 percent annually. The total in that account ten years from now will depend in large part on what kind of fees and expenses you have to pay. It is therefore imperative that you review these numbers before you invest.

If you were charged a 5 percent load, or commission, for investing $10,000 in that mutual fund, and 2 percent more per year in management fees, at the end of ten years you would have $154,661. With no commissions, and fees of only 1.3 percent, your investment would grow to $169,417, or about $15,000 more.

Does this argue for investing only in no-load index funds? Not necessarily. But let's talk about the advantages of index funds.

Index Funds

Index funds offer many advantages.

- An investor can buy a broadly diversified portfolio with one purchase.
- Because the fund mirrors an index, such as the S&P 500, requiring no active management, expenses tend to be very low.
- Because trading is minimal, generally done only when the composition of the index changes, few taxes are generated.

Besides these positive attributes, index funds have the advantage of outperforming the majority of money managers over time. According to Lipper Analytical Services, over 81 percent of active managers underperformed the S&P 500 index in the ten-year period ending December 1997.

In 1999, over $300 billion was invested in index funds. The most popular index is the S&P 500, but investors can also choose from the Wilshire 5000, which tracks most publicly held companies, or the Russell 2000, which tracks small-capitalization stocks, or several others.

Not surprisingly, with the strong growth and interest in indexing, the industry has responded with enhanced index funds, where small adjustments are made to the index to improve performance.

Index funds are an attractive alternative for investors seeking broad diversification and market-matching performance, either as a stand-alone investment or as part of a balanced portfolio. But there are some negatives.

1. Some funds do beat the benchmarks

Occasionally they do so by a wide margin. That is something to keep in mind before committing all of your mutual fund money to an index fund.

2. You have to be careful about which index you choose

In 1999, the NASDAQ index, with its heavy technology component, substantially outperformed the S&P 500. The Dow Jones Industrial Average also outperformed the popular S&P 500 Index. (It is now possible to buy a DJIA index fund.)

3. Limited Upside Potential

If you invest in an index fund, there is a cap on what your returns will be. If the Wilshire 5000 is up 6 percent in a given year, you will make only 6 percent. (Actually, it will be slightly less, since fund expenses are deducted from your returns.) By definition, you won't be able to do better than the average.

4. No Protection in a Down Market

Index funds will do only as well as the specific benchmark they are designed to mimic. Most people intuitively understand the upside of this approach: if the S&P 500 is up 10 percent, then their S&P Index fund will be up 10 percent as well (minus expenses). But many people forget about the downside. The index will track—on a percentage by percentage basis—any loss as well. So, if the S&P 500 is down 12 percent for the year, the index fund will also fall by that amount. That is a risk you take with a passively managed fund. An actively managed fund might give you some protection in a down market.

. . .

You may want to consider an actively managed fund if

- you find one that fits your objectives
- you have confidence in the managers running the fund, because they have a good record over time
- you believe that the fund's performance will more than offset the costs and fees it charges

Could you have both kinds of funds? Absolutely. Indeed, it may be a good strategy, depending on what you want to accomplish. You may decide, for example, that an S&P 500 Index fund should be at the heart of your equity holdings, but you will supplement it by using actively managed funds to search for international winners, emerging growth and small-cap stocks.

Conversely, you might want to spend your time searching among the large-cap universe, using a bond mutual fund and perhaps both actively and passively managed sector funds to help you achieve overall balance in your portfolio.

You can invest in a no-load, low-expense fund that you find on your own, or use the services of a financial adviser to help you select the fund that best meets your investment objectives. You may pay a load, or compensate that adviser in the form of fees, but his expertise can save you a great deal of time. Your financial adviser has experience with mutual funds and their portfolio managers and will monitor the fund you purchase through him to be sure performance is good and the fund remains aligned with your investment objectives.

A Final Word About Mutual Funds

Mutual funds can be a strategic part of your investment portfolio. Since they come in almost an infinite variety (load, no-load, index, sector, stock, bond, cash equivalent—such as money market—and so forth) and are easy to buy and sell, they can either make up your core investment holdings or serve as a useful tool to help balance what you already own.

That last point should not be overlooked. Many people tend to segregate their accounts. They think about the money they have in retirement accounts—much of which may be in mutual funds already—as being in one pot, and the money they are saving for shorter-term goals as being in another pot. You should look at what you have in total. If you do, and you find your portfolio is out of balance, you may want to use mutual funds as the tool that helps you make the necessary adjustments.

11

Working with a Manager, Doing It by Yourself: Creating the Best of Both Worlds

Part of my job involves traveling around the country, speaking to large and small groups of investors at various financial conferences and seminars. Although the travel is no longer as much fun as it once was—there probably isn't an airport in the country where I haven't been stranded for at least a couple of hours—I like meeting new people and I love the interaction.

The presentation generally includes an overview of the economy and the market, and a detailed discussion of current investment themes. Then I answer questions from the audience, and once the meeting is over, I talk to investors in a more informal setting.

I have been doing this for many years, and I have noticed that smart investors have changed in two subtle but significant ways.

The first shift deals with information. It is clear that the best investors now know much more about the inner workings of business and the economy. It is not unusual for me to get questions at nearly every stop about what I think the Federal Reserve is going to do about monetary policy and interest rates, both at its next Federal Open Markets Committee (FOMC) meeting and in the long term. And it seems I have been answering more questions about the global economy as well. Clearly, investors are trying to sort out and anticipate changes on the macro level that will affect their portfolios.

The second change, though, is perhaps more important. The best investors are now taking an increasingly active role in managing their money. I am not talking about the fact that they are investigating potential investments on-line, although a few of them are. More important, they are thinking differently about the best ways to manage their money. They are, in essence, acting like portfolio managers, and that is a healthy development.

It isn't hard to figure out why these changes have come about. There have been three major catalysts.

One is generational. With the baby boomers now in their forties and fifties, there are a huge number of people who have come of age in a bull market, and have spent much of their adult lives thinking about money and investments.

Second, and certainly as important, many of us have not had any choice but to become more actively involved in personal money management. As the companies we work for shifted from defined benefit retirement plans (where we knew up front the exact amount of the pensions we would receive each month once we retired from the firm) to defined contribution plans (where how much we have available for our retirement depends in large part on how well we invest our retirement assets) we were forced to take an active role.

The increasingly entrepreneurial nature of our economy is the third factor. As more and more people set up their own businesses, they quickly discover they are responsible for creating their own retirement plans as well. And not only do they have to create them, they must decide where to invest the money they put in their SEPs, IRAs, and Keoghs.

Consequently, people are taking more control of their finances and are thinking of all of their investments as a portfolio for which they are responsible. And acting like a portfolio manager—who frequently has stock and bond experts, tax experts, and the like to draw on—they, too, are calling on the expertise of professionals to help them make the best decisions possible.

Working with the Pros You Hire

In chapter 6 we explained how you can find people to help you manage your personal portfolio. Now let's see how you can work best with the people you have found.

The threshold question is, do you want to go with a variety of firms, each providing specialized services, or with a single company that provides all of the investment options you need? It is an important decision, and one that will govern all the other decisions you will have to make.

We live in an age of specialization. You can use one firm just to place buy and sell orders, another to provide investment research and professional advice, a third to provide actual money management, and even a fourth to deal with the first three. Or you can hire a firm that can do all of this—and more.

If you are going to invest in one field—say, commodities—or you simply want to do all your investing through mutual funds, then go with a firm that specializes in that area. But if you think your financial needs will run the gamut—from investing in stocks, bonds, and other instruments to retirement and estate planning—then you probably want to go with one firm that can provide access to all those services. You could find specialists within each of those fields, but the process of doing so would be extremely time consuming. You have to make a judgment call about which firm you want to go with in each individual area (stocks, retirement planning, and so forth). Also, by going with multiple firms, the process of keeping all the paperwork straight becomes more difficult.

There is a second, and frequently overlooked, reason for going with one firm if you are going to be investing in a number of areas. You need coordination, since all of your investments make up *one* portfolio. If you have stocks in one place, bonds in another, and retirement investments in yet a third, it becomes difficult to tell if your assets are properly allocated. Are you overweighted in bonds? Underweighted in stocks? You won't be able to tell at a glance. Every time you have a question, you'll have to sort through what will seem like reams of paper.

Moreover, if you are going to elect numerous investment choices, you are going to need someone to help you decide among them. How much of your assets should you put where? After all, specialists—whether experts in stocks, bonds, futures, commodities, real estate, or cash—are likely to argue that their option is best. Some objective advice in sorting out all of those conflicting recommendations can be helpful. And don't forget, a portfolio is never fixed in stone, but must respond to changing market conditions and changing life circumstances. This argues for an ongoing relationship with someone who understands your total financial picture. You may need help in knowing when to rebalance, as well as assistance in actually doing it.

To simplify matters, I would try to find an investment firm whose philosophy and approach is similar to mine and I would keep most, if not all, of my accounts there.

Within that firm, you want someone who can work with you as a partner in the truest sense of the word. While every financial adviser has his or her own style of working, and every firm has particular investments it likes to recommend, the best advisers put the interests of their clients first. They alter their approach and tailor their company's investment advice to the client's particular needs. They know it is the only way they can ensure a continuing long-term relationship with a client.

What You Want from a Broker

The best advisers understand that you are going to value three things from them:

- **Investments.** They know you want suggestions about the best stocks, bonds, mutual funds, and so forth for what you are trying to accomplish.
- **Life-stage planning.** They recognize that the financial concerns you have when your children are going off to college are different than when you are planning on retiring early, or trying to get your estate in order, and they guide you through your current situation.
- **You.** They help you leverage your strengths, offset your weaknesses, understand your risk tolerance, and respond to your needs, all in the context of helping you meet your objectives.

With the ability to trade through the Internet, transactions are no longer the reason to go to a broker or financial adviser. If all you want is to buy or sell something, you can go to the deepest discounter you can find. The reason to seek a broker's expertise is advice and counsel. The basis of the relationship is the value of that advice, not the ability to take an order. Technology has freed up much of the time brokers used to spend on paperwork. That allows the adviser to focus on the far more important aspects of the client's needs.

You should meet at least once a year with your financial adviser for a thorough discussion of your investments, their performance, and any changes in your personal, family, and economic situation. Of course, you may want to meet more often, and more frequent meetings will help develop the relationship. But no matter how often you meet, your spouse should be a regular participant.

Not surprisingly, to make this relationship work to its fullest requires a commitment on your part as well. The best thing you can bring to the table is candor. You have to tell the financial experts with whom you work what is really important to you. Many people have problems doing that face-to-face. If that describes you—or has described you in the past—be sure to fill out in complete detail the investment profile your adviser gives you during one of your first meetings.

If you are candid, the payoff can be enormous. And it goes beyond the typical services that most financial advisers provide—that of generating investment ideas and being an easy way of double-checking the ideas you come up with on your own. Clearly that is a huge part of the investment process, but a financial adviser can do that even if you are not particularly open with her. I am talking about creating a relationship that can be much deeper.

Investment options are now virtually unlimited. Not surprisingly, the information about those investment choices—especially the information aimed at financial professionals—is virtually unlimited as well.

An adviser with a full understanding of your goals and objectives can act as a filter so that you see only what is relevant to you. For example, if all you tell her is, "I am interested in stocks," you may receive calls on everything from start-up biotech-based agricultural companies to trucking firms that have been around for decades. After a full discussion of your goals and objectives, together you may determine that you are interested in large-cap growth stocks, investments that you plan to hold for the long term. If you make clear you are investing for current income, she won't send you too many research reports about micro-cap growth stocks or zero coupon bonds. The process becomes more personal and certainly much more efficient.

Despite all your experience in the market—and despite all your devotion to your long-term financial plan—let's suppose you've become smitten with a high-tech start-up that you are absolutely convinced will be a winner. You decide you want to take 20 percent of your money and buy as much of this company as you can. A good financial adviser, one who understands your goals and objectives, thanks to your candid discussions with her in the past, should be able to help you reconsider your decision simply by playing back to you all the things you told her you wanted your money to do for you. That, in turn, will help ensure that the decision you make is appropriate. And of course, your financial adviser can make sure you are remaining on course. If you have told her up front that you are expecting 8 percent growth on your investments, or that you need to generate $5,000 a month in income, she can help you monitor whether your goals are being met.

You will want to keep your advisers constantly updated about changes in your circumstances—and in your thinking. Do you have a private-school tuition bill coming up? A child getting married who you want to help with a down payment for a house? Are you now thinking of retiring early? Don't spring these facts on advisers at the last minute. With enough time, they can tailor your investments to meet your needs in a timely manner and can put you in touch with other people who can help as well. For example, a discussion of your retirement plans could lead to referrals to professionals in estate planning.

Working with Your Other Professionals

It does you little good if your professional advisers are not working with one another. Again, if you are thinking as a portfolio manager, someone who is ultimately responsible for all of the assets you own, it is your responsibility to ensure that there is sufficient interaction between your broker, accountant, and lawyer, as well as a money manager (if you have one) and anybody else you are employing to make certain that your money is invested as efficiently as possible and that your financial affairs are in order.

Some of that interaction will be inevitable. Your broker and accountant clearly should be in touch at least once a year, as part of completing your tax return, while you may call in your attorney only for specific tasks, such as changing your will or setting up a new trust.

And if you have a wrap account, where all your different investments with the brokerage firm are tied—or wrapped together—your financial adviser may be interacting with money managers and others to make sure the asset allocation you want is being maintained and the management of your money remains stable. But the person who ultimately must decide how much interaction there should be—and how that interaction should be structured with all of your advisers—is you.

Doing It on Your Own

The alternative to working with investment professionals is, of course, doing it yourself. With the proliferation of financial information, more than ever before investors have the tools to make investment decisions on their own. And the availability of discount brokers and the Internet make it easier than ever to buy and sell stocks easily and cheaply. I work for a full-service investment firm, and you may wish to discount what I have to say. Nonetheless, there are still at least four things to consider if you are going to handle investing on your own.

1. Major Time Commitment

It takes a great deal of time to stay up to date on the market, the economy, interest rates, and individual companies. Be prepared to spend a lot of your free time staying abreast. Selecting a good company includes analyzing the balance sheet and income statement, looking at the competition, suppliers, and customers.

2. Investing can be complicated

Just to give one example, there are tax issues and strategies that a novice may not be aware of; professional input can provide advantages. Be sure you know what you don't know to avoid costly mistakes or omissions. The rules on IRAs and retirement accounts can stymie even the experts. If you are committed to going it on your own, be sure to ask for help in the specialized areas where you need it.

3. Not all markets are bull markets

Investors who have managed their own investments since 1995 have had the wind at their backs during this unprecedented bull market. With gains of 20 and 30 percent each year, investing may have seemed easier than it in fact is. The strategies that worked in this bull market may be woefully inadequate if we return to the more normal returns of the past.

4. Investing is more than buying stocks

Investing early in life may be as simple as just buying good-quality companies. But as you get older, there are many more things to consider, such as funding college, building for retirement, and estate planning. Again, be sure you get the professional help you need along the way.

Few areas are as important as or have greater consequences than managing our finances properly. For the few who want to and can do it on their own, there are numerous tools available. But most of us use professional help in many other areas of our lives, everything from doctors to hairdressers to plumbers to architects, and not surprisingly, we may find we need it to invest as well.

The Best of Both Worlds

For many, the services of a trusted financial adviser will play an integral role in helping us achieve our financial goals. But is there a third alternative besides full service and no service? Fortunately for investors today, many firms have responded to the new technologies and new financial environment with an array of accounts that can meet the needs of virtually any investor. Instead of the traditional means of paying for advice through commissions, investors can now often choose the type of advice and service they want, and maintain responsibility for the aspects of investing with which they are comfortable.

An investor who wants to trade on-line with limited advice provided by an adviser can choose that type of no-frills account. An investor who wants more access but less than a full range of services can choose a different type of account that gives him exactly what he needs. Expect more of these variations from financial firms as technology allows more options. The end result? Clients are largely able to customize the account structure that works best for them.

12

Bonds:
Getting the Most Out of Your
Fixed-Income Investments

In the past, managing a bond portfolio typically meant clipping coupons, avoiding defaults, and reinvesting the proceeds once your bonds matured. Fixed-income holdings were viewed as a source of current income and a safe balance against the riskier, equity portion of your portfolio.

Perhaps more important for purposes of our discussion here, they were also viewed as something that didn't require much thought. You bought the bonds—after deciding whether you wanted taxables or tax-frees—made sure you clipped the interest coupon and took it to the bank on time, and basically did little else.

Times have changed. Fixed-income portfolios now must be managed much more aggressively, both to generate greater returns and to more effectively control the level of risk in a portfolio.

Frequent repositioning of assets along the yield curve, and/or shifting of funds between different sectors, has become standard practice for experienced investors as they try to grab every last potential basis point of return out of the relatively flat fixed-income market we find ourselves in.

Bonds: A Refresher Course

In talking to investors about their fixed-income selections, it often seems they are unaware of the many options available to them. That isn't surprising, given how much the market has changed in recent years. So, a quick review of some of these fixed-income options, and some of the basics, may be useful. Let's start with a concept that some investors—even experienced ones—find confusing: credit risk.

How Safe Are They?

When you invest in any bond, your primary concern should be the issuer's ability to meet its financial obligations. The issuer has promised to return your money to you with interest, and you want to be sure it is going to keep its word.

Issuers disclose details of their financial conditions through official statements, or offering circulars, which are available from your bank, brokerage firm, or local library. As always, you are urged to study these documents before you invest. And as always, most people don't. (And I sympathize. Couldn't these documents be written in comprehensible English?)

There is another way to evaluate an issuer's ability to repay the money it is borrowing, and that is by examining its credit rating. Many bonds are graded by agencies such as Moody's Investors Service, Standard & Poor's Corp., and Fitch Investors Service, Inc. A number of banks and brokerage firms have their own research departments, which also analyze and rate fixed-income securities.

Obviously, bond ratings are important because they reflect a professional assessment of the issuer's ability to repay the bond's face value at maturity.

Generally, bonds rated BBB by S&P or Baa or better by Fitch or Moody's are considered investment grade, or suitable for the preservation of capital.

The following table presents the various grades a bond can be assigned.

Credit ratings, however, should not be the sole basis for any investment decision. For example, the ratings do not take into account market trends.

Credit Ratings

Credit Risk	Moody's	S&P	Fitch
Prime	Aaa	AAA	AAA
Excellent	Aa	AA	AA
Upper medium	A	A	A
Lower medium	Baa	BBB	BBB
Speculative	Ba	BB	BB
Very speculative	B, Caa	B, CCC, CC	B, CCC, CC, C
Default	Ca, C	D	DDD, DD, D

Source: Moody's; S&P; Fitch

And of course, as with any fixed-income investment, the higher the yield, the higher the risk.

(Credit ratings are not infallible. Orange County, California, defaulted on its debt in 1994, yet at the time of the default, its bonds carried a rating of AA–. Neither the ratings agencies nor most of the people in Orange County were aware of the speculative investments being made by the investment group handling the county's finances, investments that spectacularly failed. However, credit rating failures of this kind are exceedingly rare.)

With that background established, let's move on to a quick review of specific types of bonds, starting with the ones you probably know best.

Municipal Bonds

Munis are among the most popular type of investments today, and for good reason. They offer a number of benefits:

- Attractive current income free from federal, and in most cases, state and local taxes. Your net yield with municipals is often greater than what you can get with a taxable alternative. Residents of high-tax locations such as New York City, who have to pay taxes to the city, their state, and the federal government, find the municipal market very attractive.

- A high degree of safety with regard to payment of interest and the repayment of principal. A government entity defaulting is an extremely rare occurrence (although the Orange County example shows it can happen).
- Dependable income.
- A wide range of choices to fit in with your investment objectives, with regard to investment quality, maturity, type of bond, geographic location.
- Marketability. In the event you must sell before the bond matures, you will find a liquid secondary market.

Types of Tax-Exempt and Taxable Municipal Bonds

Some general background, to jog your memory. Tax-free municipal securities consist of both long- and short-term issues. Short-term issues, which are frequently called notes, typically mature in a year or less. Generally the issuer sells the notes in anticipation of future revenues, such as taxes, or state or federal aid payments being received in the near future.

Bonds are the long-term version of notes, and usually mature in more than a year. They are generally sold to finance long-term capital projects.

Bond interest is usually paid twice a year. On notes, interest is typically paid at maturity.

There are two basic types of tax-free municipals:

- **General obligation bonds.** Principal and interest are secured by the full faith and credit of the issuer and are usually supported by the issuer's taxing power. General obligation bonds are voter approved.
- **Revenue bonds.** Principal and interest are secured by revenues derived from tolls, charges, or rents paid by users of the facility built with the proceeds of the bond issue. Public projects financed by revenue bonds include such things as highways, bridges, airports, water and sewage treatment facilities, and housing for the poor. (Many of these bonds are issued by special authorities created for this specific purpose.)

While general obligation and revenue bonds are usually tax-free, there are situations where municipal bonds pay taxable income. In fact, this is a rapidly growing part of the fixed-income market. It is easy to see both why taxable municipals exist and why they are so popular.

The reason a bond is tax-free is that the government has decided that the project it is being used to fund is for the public good. To make funding for the project easier to come by, the government decides to forgo the taxes it would otherwise receive on the interest paid to investors, in order to make the project more appealing to investors.

Taxable municipal bonds exist because the government will not subsidize the financing of activities that do not provide a significant benefit to the public at large. Investor-led housing, local sports facilities, and borrowing to replenish a municipality's underfunded pension plan are examples of bond issues that are federally taxable.

Taxable municipals offer yields more comparable to those of other taxable bonds, such as those issued by corporations or agencies. The growth of the taxable market in recent years has been astounding. Of the roughly $60 billion of outstanding taxable municipals, $40 billion have been issued since 1990.

Insured Municipal Bonds

Municipal bonds historically have been exceptionally safe as well as tax-favored investments. And they're even more attractive when they are insured—that is, when their scheduled interest and principal payments are guaranteed by triple-A-rated municipal bond insurers.

Municipal bond insurance protects investors primarily in two ways. Occasionally, cities or states that issue debt securities get into financial trouble. When that happens, of course, they may not be able to pay interest and principal on their debt as scheduled. Even if an issuer does not default, the rating agencies may lower their ranking of the issuer's securities if its financial condition deteriorates, causing the market value of its securities to decline.

Investors in bonds insured by triple-A-rated municipal bond insurers are insulated from these risks because they can depend on the insurer, whose claims-paying ability is itself rated triple-A, to make timely payments of principal and interest.

The strong demand for insured issues—almost half of all new issues are now insured—is due primarily to the following eight factors:

- **Investors' desire for security.** They want to know they will receive the interest they have been promised, and they also want to know that their principal will be returned as scheduled. Before an insurer agrees to guarantee a municipal security, its underwriters rigorously analyze the issuer and the specific issue. If a bond is 100 percent insured by a triple-A-rated municipal bond insurer, investors can be confident that experts have thoroughly researched every aspect of it.
- **Quality.** Insured bonds typically receive the highest rating available, triple-A, based on the triple-A claims-paying ability of the insurer.
- **Ratings strength.** Municipal bond insurers are highly regulated by state insurance departments and are closely monitored by the major ratings agencies, which historically have reaffirmed their triple-A ratings at least once a year. (The rating agencies don't want any surprises either.)
- **Liquidity.** Large volumes of triple-A-rated, 100 percent–insured securities are traded every day in the secondary market. Investors who wish to sell their insured bonds before maturity usually find a ready market for such highly rated securities. In addition, when an issuer faces financial difficulties, history has shown that insured bonds have more liquidity and greater price protection than uninsured bonds.
- **Yield.** In most cases, triple-A insured municipals offer slightly lower yields than uninsured triple-A securities.
- **Opportunity for even higher earnings.** There are certain types of municipals—revenue bonds and structured issues, for example—that pay higher yields than conventional general obligation bonds. However, many investors are unfamiliar with these securities. By guaranteeing timely payment of interest and principal, insurers enable investors to purchase them with confidence and enjoy their higher yields.
- **Surveillance.** The insurer monitors the performance of every insured issue to maturity. Surveillance teams make on-site visits to issuers and require a variety of financial reports, which are analyzed for any sign of credit deterioration.

- **Lower costs.** Issuers often prefer to offer their bonds with the highest ratings possible, in order to lower their borrowing costs. As we have seen, insured municipals typically pay less than uninsured bonds, reducing the issuer's financing costs.

How the Insurance Process Works

Insurance is good, but it is only as good as the insurance company offering it. The question then becomes: how reliable are the companies offering the municipal bond insurance that guarantees payment of interest and the return of principal? The answer is they are very reliable.

Monoline insurers—companies that are in the business of insuring only investment-grade securities—insure today's municipal bonds. They are not exposed to risks from any other lines of business (such as property, casualty, life). Moreover, every monoline bond insurer has received at least one triple-A rating from a nationally recognized rating agency, and every insured bond, in turn, receives a triple-A rating based on the insurer's own capital and claims-paying sources. Among the key indicators the rating agencies examine before they assign a triple-A rating to an issuer of bond insurance are the quality of the insured portfolio, financial performance, operating efficiency, risk management, liquidity of assets, reinsurance, ownership, and the skill and experience of management.

In addition, they subject each insurer's portfolio to what is called a depression analysis. This exercise is designed to show how well the insurer would withstand the economic stresses of a simulated four- or five-year worldwide depression. If the conclusion is that the company could not continue to meet all its obligations as a going concern, should such a global economic collapse occur, then it usually does not get the triple-A rating.

Two other factors contribute to the strength of a bond insurer's triple-A rating. The first is government regulation. State insurance departments—particularly those in New York and California—exercise rigorous oversight of the municipal bond insurance industry.

Finally, bond insurers cannot be required to pay interest and principal ahead of schedule, should a default occur. The insurer is obligated to make payments only as originally scheduled. This preserves capital and protects the bond insurer against a run on its capital.

In recent years, when many financial institutions have experienced difficulties, bond insurers posted record performances. They added considerably to their claims-paying ability and to the strength of their triple-A ratings. In general, they have been successful because they guarantee only bonds that meet their high quality standards, and because the bond insurers themselves limit their own investments to the most conservative liquid securities.

HOW MUCH DOES BOND INSURANCE COST?

For the investor, there are no direct charges for bond insurance. The issuer of the bonds, or the investment banks and securities dealers that sell them, pays the premium. But that cost is, of course, passed along. In exchange for the extra security of guaranteed payment, and the accompanying triple-A rating, investors ultimately give up about $5 in interest per year for the average $1,000 bond that is insured. That is why uninsured bonds will yield slightly more.

How do these companies choose what to insure? To begin with, they work only with issuers that have stable, investment-grade credit profiles. And more important, they insure only bonds that would be investment-grade quality even without insurance. "Investment grade," as you'll remember, refers to those issues that would be rated Baa/BBB or higher by Moody's, S&P, Fitch, or other rating agencies. (See the table earlier in the chapter.)

Having limited themselves to guaranteeing investment-grade bonds, these insurers go through a very thorough underwriting (that is, risk-assessment) process. They each have a sizable staff—including credit analysts, attorneys, and economists—who review each bond issue in great detail, looking at such factors as the issuer's financial condition, tax base, regional economy, existing debt, expected future borrowing and spending requirements. Analyzing the quality of municipal bonds is all that these people do.

Obviously the goal of this analysis is to weed out any issuers who have financial problems and to do business only with issuers who meet the insurers' standards. In fact, one such standard is what is known as zero loss underwriting. This means confirming that the issuer is so strong—or is providing such ironclad protections in the bond issue—that the insurer believes it will sustain no losses from issuing the insurance.

Before we talk about how to invest in this new environment, let us review one other type of fixed-income investment that you may not have thought about recently.

Zero Coupon Bonds

You don't hear much about this popular investment anymore, but they made quite a stir when they were introduced in 1982. A lot of people had problems understanding exactly what this investment was, but sophisticated investors got the concept right away: zero coupon bonds work exactly the way U.S. savings bonds do.

Just like saving bonds, zeros are sold at a substantial discount to their face amount. When the bond matures, the investor receives the full face amount. The difference between what you pay and what you receive at maturity is interest.

Let's say you buy a twenty-year zero coupon bond yielding 5.5 percent. You'd pay $6,757 today and receive $20,000 twenty years from now. That future payment would be made up of the return of your initial investment—$6,757—plus $13,243 interest.

The three most common types of zeros are zero coupon Treasury bonds, zero coupon corporate bonds, and zero coupon municipals.

Zero coupon Treasuries are generally considered the safest zero coupon bond, since they are backed by the full faith and credit of the U.S. government. There are a limited number of corporate zero coupon bonds as well. Zero coupon corporates offer a potentially higher rate of return than zero coupon Treasuries, commensurate with additional credit risk. Of the three, only zero coupon municipals earn interest that compounds free from federal income tax, and in many cases, free of state and local taxes as well. In contrast, the two other types of zero coupon bonds require you to pay tax each year on the amount of interest that has accrued for that year, even though you don't actually receive the interest.

The same situation holds true with zero coupon corporate bonds and Treasury STRIPS (Separate Trading of Registered Interest and Principal of Securities), a form of U.S. Treasury bonds. The investor is responsible for paying taxes on the phantom income. Since no dividend income is actually received until maturity, the investor is in a negative cash flow situation throughout the life of the zero coupon bond or STRIPS. These types of securities are best suited for IRAs, Keogh plans, pension funds, and gifts to children.

There is one other variation of zeros we should touch on quickly.

Convertible zero coupon municipals start out as traditional zeros. But then, generally after eight to fifteen years, they convert into interest-paying bonds. They are ideally suited for individuals planning for retirement. During your working years, you can accumulate capital—tax-free—so it is ready for you when you retire. Then, once you stop working, you can receive the income stream you need to help pay for living expenses.

Why Zeros?

Zero coupons, especially zero coupon municipals, have a number of advantages.

Low Minimum Investment

Zeros are typically sold in denominations of $5,000 face amounts. But because they are sold at a substantial discount from what they pay at maturity, you can purchase more zero coupon bonds for your money than other types of bonds. (And of course, the greater the number of years a zero coupon has to maturity, the less you have to pay for it initially.) So, zeros allow you to put aside a modest amount of money today, while letting you know exactly how much money you will receive on a specific date in the future.

Protection from Reinvestment Risk

Zero coupons allow you to lock in a particular rate of return without worrying that the bonds can be called.

Wide Choice

There are zeros available in maturities ranging from six months to forty years. The majority of the bonds offered have maturities of eight to twenty years.

Quality

The majority of zero coupons being offered are rated A or better by the three major ratings services. However, there are lower-grade zero coupon bonds available. They have a higher yield, but of course carry more risk.

Liquidity

Should you have to sell your zero before it matures, you'll find there is a generally active secondary market that will usually allow you to find a buyer who will pay the prevailing market price.

Tax Advantages

Because zero coupon municipal bonds offer the benefit of compound interest free of federal income taxes, they provide returns that are often much higher on a net (that is, after-tax) basis than comparable taxable securities. Further, tax-exempt zero coupon municipals earn interest that in many cases is also free of state and local taxes. (Certain out-of-state municipal bonds may be taxable at the state level.)

What Do We Do Now?

Since simple coupon clipping is no longer sufficient, the question becomes: how should one approach this new market?

No one of sound mind would consider building a house without a detailed plan. Yet investors often plunge into the municipal bond market, for example—investing amounts many times above the value of their own homes in the process—with little thought to the structure or design of the investment vehicle. If you build a house with bargain construction materials, it might not survive the test of time. Likewise, a fixed-income portfolio built exclusively by opportunistic buying might not fulfill your specific objectives.

You need to establish a clearly defined set of guidelines for managing your fixed-income holdings. These guidelines should spell out your long-term objectives, of course, but they should also

- be consistent with your overall investment objectives
- be achievable within the current credit market environment

Before we talk about the future—and how to maximize the positive effect bonds can have on your portfolio—it is important to take a quick glance backward, if for no other reason than to underscore why everyone's thinking about fixed-income investments needs to change.

Ah, the Good Old Days

For more than fifteen years, we were in a bull market for bonds. In the early 1980s, bond yields were hovering around 14 percent, and from then until the mid-1990s, fixed-income investments were outstanding performers. For one thing, investors locked in higher yields, and received that increased income on a regular basis—and if that income was tax-free, so much the better. For another, you had the chance for capital appreciation, as interest rates declined throughout the period. (An environment where interest rates are falling is good for bonds. It makes the interest that those bonds pays more valuable. To oversimplify, when a new bond is issued that provides a 5 percent yield, an older bond with a 6 percent yield is more desirable. That's how capital gains are created.)

And bond prices did rise. Bonds provided annual returns of only about 3.1 percent between 1926 and 1981, but produced returns of 14.2 percent annually between 1982 and 1998.

Real returns—or what you were actually left with after inflation was factored out—were essentially flat from 1926 to 1981, a period when Treasury bonds yielded just slightly more than 3 percent. Real returns averaged 10.8 percent between 1982 and 1998.

The upshot was that if you held on to your fixed-income investments

Average Nominal Annual Returns

	S&P 500	Treasury Bonds	Return Differential
1982–98	18.89%	14.15%	4.74%
1926–81	11.40%	3.13%	8.27%

Source: Ibbotson Associates; Bureau of Labor

Average Real Annual Returns

	S&P 500	Treasury Bonds	Return Differential
1982–98	15.55%	10.81%	4.74%
1926–81	8.27%	0.0%	8.27%

Source: Ibbotson Associates; Bureau of Labor

throughout that decade and a half, you consistently received a high yield, and since interest rates were steadily declining, if you sold your bonds, you probably made a profit on top of those abnormally high yields.

If that was not good enough, you had a third factor in your favor as a fixed-income investor. Yields in the short-term markets were also very high in the early to mid-1980s, which meant that rolling over CDs and three-month Treasury bills was an astute strategy. With short-term instruments at times yielding 17–18% in the early eighties, investors rightly took advantage.

For fixed income investors it just doesn't get much better than a situation where

a. long-term rates are declining, which means you are getting more interest income from your existing bonds than you could from a new one
b. you can sell your bond and receive a capital gain
c. if you sell, you can put your money in a CD or Treasury bill and still stay substantially ahead of inflation

Unfortunately, when it comes to the double-digit returns we saw in the fixed-income market during much of the 1980s and 1990s, the good times are over for the foreseeable future. While we believe rates will go lower, we don't think that they will decline much below where they are today. We anticipate that the interest rate on thirty-year Treasuries will decline very modestly over the next few years (although certainly not in a straight line). With inflation in check and expected to remain so, there is no reason that bond yields should be much higher than they are now; indeed, we expect yields to stay in the 4.5 to 6.5 percent range for at least the next five years.

The days of double-digit returns in the bond market—an aberration to begin with—are over. We have to reorient ourselves to a future that looks a lot like the more distant past. Bond yields are going to return to the days when they were only 2 percent to 3 percent greater than inflation.

We have talked throughout this book about the need to be in stocks. Does that fact, coupled with the low-inflation environment that we are currently in, mean that you should banish all thoughts about bonds being in your portfolio? Hardly. But it does mean you should not expect your fixed-income investments to turn in the double-digit total returns you enjoyed in the last decade and a half. In short, you still may want to invest in bonds, but where and how is more of a strategic decision than ever before.

The Benefit of Bonds

The remarkable returns that fixed-income investments have produced since the early 1980s has obscured the reason that sophisticated investors have traditionally used bonds as part of their overall portfolio. A quick review may be helpful.

Diversification

Bonds typically don't correlate well with stocks, and that provides advantages. As you know, the best way to assure consistency in the overall return of your portfolio is to reduce any potential deviations. The easiest way to do that is by creating a blend of asset classes that do not move in tandem. Many people find the result of adding bonds to their equity holdings appealing, especially given the volatility that seems to be inherent in the current bull market. And should this remarkable bull market slow, or falter, even today's more modest bond yields may look very appealing and will underscore the importance of diversification. Of course, you can diversify further by adding different types of bonds to your portfolio. For example, most experienced investors consider it prudent to blend general obligation bonds, revenue bonds, and municipal bonds to protect their portfolio from the risks that come by being in one sector or being invested in one particular type of bond.

Safety

With high-quality bonds, the odds are extremely low that you will lose your principal. Bonds are really nothing more than IOUs issued by government entities or corporations. When the Ford Motor Co. or the federal or local government borrows money from you and promises to pay it back, there is an excellent chance they will. Default rates on corporate bonds have historically been low—generally ranging from 0 to 2 percent per year since 1900. There have been a couple of periods when the rate has spiked higher. The first was during the Depression of the 1930s. The second time default rates increased substantially was during the recession of 1990–91, which, not surprisingly, was exacerbated by the speculative corporate borrowing excesses in the 1980s. Since 1993, however, the corporate bond default rate has remained in the 0–2 percent range. And as you know, many municipal bonds are backed by insurance, which has been added to reduce investment risk even further. In the unlikely event of default of one of these types of bonds, the insurance company that guaranteed payment would pay you both the interest and principal you are owed when they became due. Bond insurance is now commonplace. In fact, in 1998, over half of new municipal bond issues were rated triple-A, thanks to the insurance they carried.

Current Income

This is becoming progressively harder to obtain if you invest solely in stocks. As stock prices climb, their dividend yield falls by definition. We have been in a bull market for quite a while now, and that means yields have been steadily declining. In addition, companies in recent years have decreased the emphasis they had placed on steadily increasing dividends, figuring their shareholders would be happier if that money were invested in ways that would boost the underlying stock price. (Not only are dividends taxed as corporate earnings, but when you, the shareholder, receive them they are taxed again, this time as ordinary income. Stock appreciation—if you've held the stock for at least a year—is subjected to the normally less harsh capital gains rate.) Whatever the reason, the result of both trends is that you'd be hard pressed to find many stocks—even in the utility industry—that yield 5 percent today, a yield that used to be commonplace without an undue level of risk.

Reducing the Overall Risk Within Your Portfolio

This is obviously another part of the diversification argument, but it is worth some discussion, because risk is a concept that most people—including sophisticated investors—don't completely understand.

Let's start with the most basic idea. When you invest in a stock, there is absolutely no guarantee that you are ever going to get any of your money back. And there is also no guarantee that your investment is going to be worth at least what you paid for it, when you sell.

Bonds—especially Treasuries, blue-chip corporates, and insured municipals—have an excellent record in both instances. They may fluctuate in value while you own them, depending on what happens with current interest rates, but if you hold one of these bonds to maturity, you can typically count on getting your money back, plus all the interest you are owed.

What About the Downside?

But, people ask, what about the risk of rising interest rates? Well, it is true that if (for example) you sell your Treasury bond that has a 6 percent coupon at a time when interest rates have risen beyond that point, you won't get your full principal back. But if you hold the bond to maturity, you will. And to frame the question that way is to miss half the argument.

We typically talk of bonds and discuss the risk that comes with holding them as interest rates rise. But what if interest rates fall? If you don't already have bonds within your portfolio, the amount of current income you receive will be cut.

And if you go and buy bonds in periods of falling interest rates, you will find their yields will be declining in tandem with interest rates overall. (Certificates of deposit and other cash equivalents also will be paying less.)

This point leads to two others.

Utilities

Sometimes people invest in utility stocks, thinking of them as bond surrogates, or perhaps more accurately believing them to be the equivalent of a preferred stock—something that provides a relatively high yield, while at the same time giving investors some equity participation in the market.

There was a time when that thinking was sound. Back when all utilities were heavily regulated, you could count on your shares in the phone company or your local power concern to climb steadily as their (regulated) earnings did. And as the stock price increased, the dividends paid out also rose, as the utilities rewarded their shareholders. In fact, those dividend yields frequently reached the level of a good-grade corporate bond. (Hence the thinking that utility stocks were bond surrogates.)

Those days are gone. First, deregulation opened up home markets to competition—leading to lower prices. As a result, many utilities are not earning what they once did. That can make dividend increases—and in some cases dividends themselves—difficult to come by.

Second, in this deregulated market, utilities are diversifying, sometimes geographically, and often into new businesses, and they are using the money they once would have paid out as dividends to fund their expansion plans.

Third, when you buy a utility stock there is no guarantee that if you hold on to it for a certain length of time you are going to get your principal back. That is something people who have invested in utility companies that have not done well in a deregulated environment have learned the hard way.

When you put all these factors together you can understand why the notion of utility stocks as bond surrogates has been outdated for some time.

Cash

Some investors think they can get around the potential risks that come from investing in bonds by using cash—and cash alone—to offset the equity portion of their portfolio. For example, where a typical portfolio might have 70 percent of its assets allocated to stocks, 25 percent in bonds, and 5 percent in cash, people who wanted to avoid bonds would go with a mixture of 70 percent stocks and 30 percent cash, figuring that by eliminating the bond component of their portfolio, they have decreased their risk.

Actually, they may have increased it.

Why? Because by eliminating bonds they have taken, in essence, a fairly aggressive interest rate position. They are betting that interest rates are going to rise. That is the only way they would benefit by being in cash, instead of bonds.

Here's why. If interest rates remain where they are, investors would be better off in longer-term bonds, because traditionally bonds tend to yield about 2 to 3 percent more than investments in cash equivalents such as money market funds. (Obviously there are exceptions, such as when a bank offers a special promotional rate on a CD. But those kinds of exceptions are short-term aberrations. Bonds almost always yield more than cash equivalents.)

And if interest rates fall, investors would be substantially better off being in bonds. They would lock in the higher yields that bonds provide without having to frequently roll them over at progressively lower rates (a problem known as reinvestment risk). Also, they would have the potential for capital appreciation as well, if they sell while interest rates are declining.

As you can see, moving to an all-stock-and-cash portfolio—from one that contains stocks, bonds, and cash—can actually increase your risk.

How to Play a Neutral Market

Because we don't think long-term interest rates are going to go much lower, it is likely that stocks will outperform bonds in the years ahead. Bond investors will have to deal with a more neutral market.

How should you react to this interest-rate environment? Well, we certainly don't advocate dumping your bonds wholesale and putting the proceeds into cash. Nor do we suggest abandoning those positions you have established over the past several years to fund long-term liabilities. Instead, we recommend you change your thinking. Don't think about bonds being the potential capital gains vehicles they have been in recent years. Return to thinking about them in a more traditional way, as a defensive part of your portfolio, one that can generate income.

But you have to do more than change your thinking. You have to change your actions as well. Specifically, that means

1. shortening the duration or maturity of the bonds you hold
2. trying to increase current income
3. increasing your exposure to callable paper

Let's take them one at a time.

Shortening Duration

It is now time to begin to liquidate your speculative bond positions because, as we have seen, the chances of generating significant long-term capital gains from fixed-income investments are pretty small going forward. In fact, barring a significant change in U.S. economic policy, or radical changes by the Federal Reserve, our projections show that bond yields are likely to remain largely within the $4\frac{1}{2}$ to $6\frac{1}{2}$ percent fair value range right through the middle of the first decade of the twenty-first century. In the coming years we foresee a combination of moderating global inflation pressures and shrinking government borrowing that should help to keep bond prices in line.

First consider the background. Inflation pressures have continued to decelerate in the United States in recent years, despite significant economic growth and the tightest labor markets in three decades. While bouts of deflation overseas in the late 1990s were partly responsible for the surprisingly benign price pressures that we experienced in the United States in the late 1990s, that is not the real explanation. Technology driven improvements in productivity, the vigilance of the Federal Reserve, and an increasingly competitive global economic environment are what have been chiefly responsible for holding inflation in check. As the chart on inflation shows, in sharp contrast to the mid-seventies and early eighties, inflation, as measured by the Consumer Price Index (or CPI), declined sharply.

The progress we have made on inflation, therefore, is not a cyclical phenomenon that is likely to reverse once global economic activity picks up again. Rather, relatively benign inflation shows all the signs of being a trend that will be with us for some time. This is one key reason bond prices will probably remain relatively stable.

A decrease in government borrowing is another significant reason. One pleasant by-product of the shift from federal deficits to federal surpluses is that Uncle Sam is using that excess cash to whittle down the government's debt for the first time in a generation. The $70 billion budget surplus for fiscal year 1998 was the first one since 1969 and marks the beginning of what is likely to become a string of such surpluses.

The chart on page 184 shows that the federal budget started running a surplus in the late 1990s, and also makes clear that the Congressional Budget Office (CBO) expects that surplus will increase in the years ahead.

Less borrowing means, of course, less upward pressure on bond yields. With the prospects for additional significant declines in bond prices having diminished, going long, or buying bonds that mature many years out, in the hopes of picking up capital gains, doesn't seem to make much sense.

Inflation: Year-to-Year Change in Consumer Price Index

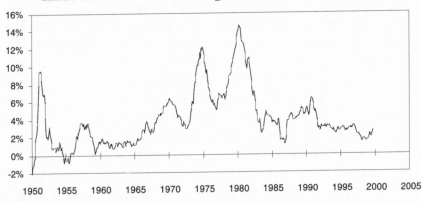

Source: Bureau of Labor Statistics

Federal Budget Balance

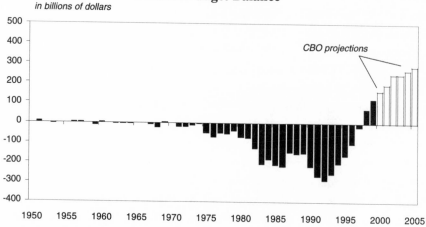

Source: Bureau of Economic Analysis; Congressional Budget Office

The best plan going forward will be to match bond maturities to when you are going to need to have your principal returned.

Trying to Increase Future Income

As we have seen, the interest-rate environment for the immediate future is likely to be one in which the bulk of returns for bonds comes in the form of coupon income, and not capital appreciation. Therefore, it only makes sense to look for the highest yields, consistent with acceptable risk.

If you have invested only in government Treasuries up until now, you might want to broaden your horizons a bit and purchase high-quality fixed-income products that have a slightly greater yield. You can get a bit more interest by investing in bonds backed by Freddie Mac, Fannie Mae, or other government agencies, as well as from bonds offered by blue-chip corporations.

But trying to get the most income you can does not begin and end with simply going after the highest-quality bonds with the highest yields. For most people in the higher tax brackets, sacrificing the higher coupon of a taxable investment for the *seemingly* lower tax-exempt income that comes from a municipal bond is still the best decision they can make. After all, taxes—

unfortunately—must be taken into account, and from an after-tax point of view, municipals are often the best investment.

And that brings up an intriguing point. When experienced investors discuss income maximization, they sometimes talk about searching for spread product. That is a term used by bond traders to describe a fixed-income investment that has a greater yield than a Treasury security. But most investors—even sophisticated ones—use an overly literal definition of spread products. To them, if the interest being paid by the fixed-income investment in question isn't greater than the current yield on a Treasury, it is not a spread product—and they stop considering it as a potential purchase. But if you do the math, you'll discover that this kind of thinking is a mistake. Tax-free municipals are very often a spread product.

Let's assume you are in the 36 percent tax bracket, have $30,000 to invest, and are considering two investment choices: a tax-exempt municipal bond yielding 4.5 percent and a taxable corporate bond yielding 6.5 percent. Which is a better investment?

With the thirty-year Treasury bond hovering around a 6 percent yield, investors looking for a traditional spread product wouldn't consider the municipal bond at all. They would zero in on the corporate bond because its yield is a full 200 basis points higher than the municipal's yield.

They'd be making a mistake.

If you invested your money in the municipal bond, you'd earn $1,350 in interest (a 4.5 percent yield) and pay no federal income taxes. On the other hand, the taxable corporate bond investment would provide you with $1,950 (the 6.5 percent pretax yield), *but only $1,248 after taxes.* So, where the municipal bond gave you a net yield of 4.5 percent, the taxable bond's yield, *after taxes,* provided just a 4.16 percent return.

The municipal bond would provide the best yield after taxes are taken into account, despite the fact that you might not have initially thought of it as being a spread product. Moreover, the tax-exempt security could be an even better investment if you accounted for state and local taxes by buying a state- or city-issued bond. In most states, interest income issued by governmental units within the state is exempt from state and local taxes.

For high net worth individuals, then, the inclusion of municipal bonds as a spread-product alternative is not only appropriate, it is essential.

Effect of Federal Income Taxes on Yield of
Tax-Exempt and Taxable Instruments

	4.5% Tax-Exempt Bond	6.5% Taxable Bond
Cash investment	$30,000	$30,000
Interest	$1,350	$1,950
Federal income tax due for someone in the 36% marginal bracket	$0	$702
Net return	$1,350	$1,248
Yield on investment (after taxes)	4.5%	4.16%

Source: PaineWebber

The way to determine the yield you need from a taxable investment in order to equal the yield from a tax-exempt security is easy. You just subtract your tax bracket from 100 percent (for example, 100 percent minus 36 percent equals 64 percent), then multiply the result by the taxable yield (6.5 percent) to find it's tax-free equivalent (4.16 percent).

Or you can simply use the table opposite.

Increasing Your Exposure to Callable Paper

In a period of steadily falling interest rates, you know it is a good idea to make sure that the bonds you are buying are not callable. When interest rates are on their way down, you want to be sure that you are going to receive the relatively high yields the issuer promised until the bonds mature. You don't want to worry that the issuer is going to call the bonds in early for redemption, leaving you to scramble to try to find a comparable source of income elsewhere.

Locking in a rate is obviously less important today, since yields are rela-

Tax-Exempt/Taxable Yield Equivalents

Tax Bracket:	15%	28%	31%	36%	39.6%	41%
Tax-Exempt Yield	Taxable Equivalent Yields (%)					
2.0%	2.35%	2.78%	2.90%	3.12%	3.31%	3.39%
2.5	2.94	3.47	3.62	3.91	4.14	4.24
3.0	3.53	4.17	4.35	4.69	4.97	5.08
3.5	4.12	4.86	5.07	5.47	5.79	5.93
4.0	4.71	5.56	5.80	6.25	6.62	6.78
4.5	5.29	6.25	6.52	7.03	7.45	7.63
5.0	5.88	6.94	7.25	7.81	8.28	8.47
5.5	6.47	7.64	7.97	8.59	9.11	9.32
6.0	7.06	8.33	8.70	9.37	9.93	10.17
6.5	7.65	9.03	9.42	10.16	10.76	11.02
7.0	8.24	9.72	10.14	10.94	11.59	11.86
7.5	8.82	10.42	10.87	11.72	12.42	12.71
8.0	9.41	11.11	11.59	12.50	13.25	13.56

Source: PaineWebber

tively more stable. In this environment, go with the bond that yields a bit more, even if it has a call provision. There are several reasons to do so, but most important, there is no certainty that the bond will be called.

Issuers often redeem a bond early when they believe they can float new bonds at a lower interest rate. (The analogy would be a home owner who refinances her mortgage when she can get a lower rate.) Since rates are not declining significantly, it is unlikely that the issuer will be able to save a lot of money by redeeming early its outstanding bonds and issuing new ones.

But even if the bond is called, odds are it will be easier than in times past to find a replacement with a comparable yield, since interest rates are unlikely to decline markedly in the foreseeable future.

For both of these reasons, go with the bond offering the higher yield, even if it has a call provision.

How to Invest: Bond Laddering

Interest-rate volatility is a serious concern to many bond investors, especially those who have amassed a portfolio of fixed-income investments highly concentrated with bonds that all mature around the same time. If yields are lower when all those bonds come due, you are faced with the problem of reinvesting your money at a lower rate.

One strategy investors have used to limit their exposure to interest-rate volatility is bond laddering. Laddering is a defensive strategy that involves purchasing bonds in successive maturities. A typical bond ladder consists of equal sums of money invested in bonds with maturities scheduled every two, three, or five years. Each group of bonds represents a rung on the investment-maturity ladder.

This approach allows the investor to have a flexible portfolio with funds becoming available at regular intervals—that is, when each rung on the ladder matures—for an unexpected use, or reinvestment, or a specific financial goal. (Of course, there is nothing about this strategy that would stop you from selling any of the bonds before they come due. But as with all fixed-income investments, you would be subject to gains or losses on your principal depending on what market conditions are when you sell.)

An evenly laddered bond portfolio provides access to your money (as the bonds mature) and allows you to participate in varying market environments. If interest rates rise, a portion of your portfolio will be available to reinvest at higher rates. Conversely, if interest rates fall, a portion of the portfolio will be locked away earning the higher rate.

The following chart can serve as an illustration of how laddering works. It is, however, *only an illustration, not a recommendation* of the particular types of bonds to buy.

Sample Laddered Municipal Bond Portfolio

Rating & Insurance	Par Amount	Name (Call Features)	Coupon	Maturity	Price per Bond	Yield
Ass/AAA MBIA	$50,000	Illinois State General Obligation (noncallable)	4.5%	6/1/04	$101.821	4.15%
Aaa/AAA MBIA	$50,000	Franklin Co. Ohio Hospital Revs (callable: 6/1/08 @ 101)	5.0%	6/1/09	$103.841	4.55%
Aaa/AAA FSA	$50,000	Carlsbad CA Unified School District (callable: 9/1/08 @ 102; 9/1/10 @ 100)	4.80%	9/1/14	$100	4.80%
Aaa/AAA Ambac	$50,000	Tampa Sports Authority Revenue (callable: 10/1/06 @ 101)	5.0%	10/1/18	$100	5.0%
Aaa/AAA FSA	$50,000	Long Island Power Authority, N.Y. (callable: 6/1/08 @ 101; 6/1/10 @ 100)	5.125%	12/1/22	$100	5.125%

Total and Averages

Credit Quality	Par Amount	Average Weighted Coupon	Projected Annual Income	Average Weighted Maturity	Average Weighted Yield	Taxable Equivalent Yield
100% triple-A	$250,000	4.885%	$12,212.50	15.56 years	4.725%	7.82%

Source: PaineWebber

Building Your Ladder

The crux of the laddering strategy is to always be invested. However, like Rome, a well-constructed ladder need not be built in a day. A methodical and systematic approach over time will build the most suitable portfolio to meet your needs.

When funds are available for investment, a quick portfolio review should uncover any missing rungs in your ladder, or places where you could create rungs that are closer together. For example, the sample portfolio that we constructed above is evenly laddered. But new money—or money that you want to reinvest—could be dedicated to 2006, 2011, 2016, and 2020 maturities to fill in that existing ladder. It would have the effect of increasing the number of rungs—that is, it would push the maturities closer together.

A reminder: in assembling or adding to your ladder, be sure to research the call features of the bonds you choose. Noncallable bonds, of course, are among the best choices to guard against lower rates and reinvestment risks, but as you know they are not always available. Bonds with eight- to ten-year call protections are a good second choice. Obviously, review the call protection of your ladder as a whole to make sure you don't have too many bonds that are susceptible to being called at one time. This is no longer the concern it was when interest rates were steadily falling, but it does remain an issue.

Laddering has a great deal of merit whether your bond portfolio consists of $50,000 or $500,000 or $5 million. While laddering may not produce as much income initially as buying the highest-yielding bonds, it is one of the safest ways to increase the overall yield of your bond portfolio. A ladder with staggered maturities minimizes interest-rate risk by allowing for reinvestment of principal at varied intervals. Since your portfolio is not weighted in one maturity, there may be opportunities for you to benefit from changes in rates and market strategies.

In addition to laddering maturities, consider a ladder designed to produce a steady stream of income. It is fairly easy to do. If you have monthly or quarterly fixed-income needs, identify bonds with semiannual interest payment dates spread throughout the year. If your ladder's coupon payments will be made in June/December, March/September, and April/October, three additions to this ladder with semiannual interest payments in the missing months (January/July, February/August, and May/November) could create a check-a-month portfolio to guarantee a steady stream of income.

A Concluding Thought

There can be no doubt that the fixed-income market has changed and that the days of merely clipping coupons are long gone. If you don't recognize that—and change your investment approach accordingly—the results can be devastating.

I received a blunt education on just how devastating that can be back in the early 1970s when reviewing portfolios put together in the 1950s, an era, similar to our own, when there was low inflation and low interest rates. Bonds yielded 1–3 percent in the fifties, and investing in bonds was considered a conservative and safe way to protect assets and get reasonable returns.

Unfortunately, by the mid-seventies, with inflation running at 10 percent, not only had the value of the bonds dropped precipitously (a bond that sold for $1,000 in 1955 was worth $500 by 1975), but the paltry income, $150 a year, had less than half the purchasing power it had in 1955. These conservative investors had made a disastrous investment.

This was my first lesson that bonds must be actively managed so investors can respond to changing economic environments. The reversal of fortune that comes to bond investors when rates are rising can be devastating.

Today, once again, there has been a significant change in the interest-rate environment that you may have become used to. But while the interest-rate environment has changed, the moral has remained the same: you must actively manage your fixed-income investments.

In summary, bonds can make up an important part of your portfolio. They provide safety, diversification, and current income. It may require more work on your part to obtain those benefits, but the payoff—should you want to maximize current income and/or offset the volatility in the stock market—is clearly worth it.

13

Rounding Out Your Portfolio: Other Investments That Can Help You Achieve Your Goals

A further way to achieve diversification is the use of more complicated investing strategies such as puts, calls, futures, and hedging in all of their various forms. While it is clearly beyond the scope of this book to talk about these strategies in detail—after all, we called the book *Beyond the Basics,* not *Complicated Investing Strategies*—it is certainly worth pausing a moment to discuss how these investment options could fit strategically into your portfolio.

Let's deal with futures first.

A futures contract is nothing more than an obligation to buy or sell a specific quantity of a commodity (such as gold) or a financial instrument (such as a Treasury bond) at a fixed price at some specific future point. You put up 5 or 10 percent of the price of the underlying contract and control a commodity or financial instrument that is worth ten to twenty times your investment. For example, if you were to buy 100 ounces of gold at $325 an ounce, you would need to pay $32,500. However, it is possible to buy a futures contract for those same 100 ounces of gold for $1,625—just 5 percent of the value of that precious metal.

By putting a small amount of money up—a deposit known as margin—you have the opportunity to make (or lose) large amounts of money very quickly. As the price of the underlying commodity—gold, in our example—

rises, the value of your contract climbs. As the underlying value of the gold drops—that is, the actual value of gold on the open market falls—the value of your contract falls.

Let's show how this works in practice. If the price of gold rose from $325 to $350 an ounce, the value of your contract would climb to $35,000. Your profit would be $2,500, because the $32,500 contract you bought would now be worth $35,000.

However, if the price of gold fell to $300, the value of your contract would drop to $30,000—a loss of $2,500. Your initial investment of $1,625 would be wiped out, and your broker would give you a call to put up an additional $875 to maintain your position, since the value of your contract had fallen by $2,500 and you had put up only $1,625 to begin with. If you didn't pledge the additional money, your market position would be liquidated immediately.

In our example, you were betting that the price of gold was going to *rise*. Just as with stocks, that decision is described as *going long*.

But as with stocks, you can sell a futures contract short, or take a *short position*. If you go this route, your hope is to make money when the value of the commodity *falls*.

Let's use an example from the National Futures Association to show how this works. Suppose it's August, and you expect the overall level of stock prices to decline by the end of the year. The S&P 500 Index in our example is trading at 1,200. To take advantage of the expected decline, you deposit an initial margin of $15,000 (to cover the cost of the contract) and sell one December S&P 500 futures contract at 1,200. Each one point change in the index results in a $250 per contract profit or loss. A decline of 100 points by November would thus yield a profit, before transaction costs, of $25,000. In other words, if the market went up, your contract would expire worthless (and you would lose what you paid to purchase it), but every point decline means you can fulfill your contract at a cheaper price, increasing your profit.

With this background out of the way, let's consider where futures might fit into your diversified portfolio. The first thing to note is that the performance of the futures markets does not correlate with the performance of stocks, bonds, or cash; they don't move in any way that relates directly to how traditional investments perform. Sometimes futures will rise when stocks fall, sometimes they will fall when stocks fall, and sometimes they will remain unchanged, whether stocks rise or fall. Having investments that don't move in tandem is one way that you gain diversification.

Another reason why you gain diversification by using futures is that they are not interest-rate sensitive. Bonds, stocks, and real estate can all be affected by a change in interest rates. (A rise in interest rates makes existing, or lower, bond yields less appealing, so the underlying price of the bond falls. Similarly, an increase in interest rates generally means higher corporate operating costs, which decreases earnings; that in turn decreases the stock price. And obviously the value of real estate—and real-estate-related investments such as real estate investment trusts, or REITs—rises and falls as interest rates climb or drop.)

While you certainly can buy futures on your own, most people don't. They invest their money through professionals. They can invest in what are called managed futures accounts, and if you go that route, investing in futures may offer diversification as well as portfolio hedging, thanks to the way those accounts are managed. While most investment strategies depend on a certain level of subjectivity—you (or your adviser) like long-term growth stocks; you don't like foreign stocks—almost all managed futures investment strategies are quantitatively driven. The subjectivity is taken out.

Most professionals in futures trading make their decisions based on computer-driven investment models that search out patterns that occurred in the past. If the pattern reveals that when X occurred, the value of the underlying commodity usually fell, the model sends out a *sell* signal. If the pattern produced new highs in the past, a *buy* signal is triggered. There is no human element in the decision-making process. The "black box" governs the investment strategy. The computer determines whether you buy or sell.

This investment approach is different from the one that most of us use to buy more traditional investments, and so it is a different way of gaining diversification.

Options Contracts

While options are also speculative, they have one big advantage over investing in futures: the amount of money you can lose is limited to what you paid for the option. If you are investing in futures and the value of your investment falls, you may be subjected to a margin call and be required to put up additional money. That doesn't happen with options. Your absolute exposure is limited to the price of the option.

Options come in two varieties, calls and puts.

When you buy a *call option,* you acquire the right (but not the obligation) to purchase an asset at a specific price for a fixed period of time, usually a few months. For example, let's say Intel is trading at $75 a share. You might buy a call option that would let you buy 100 shares of Intel stock at $70 a share anytime over the next three months. You get that right by giving the person selling the call what is called a premium, which in this case might be $6 a share.

If Intel stock climbs, the value of your call option will increase as well. You can then either exercise your right to buy Intel at $70 or sell your call at a profit. (Most people sell the calls.) Should the price of Intel's stock remain unchanged, or fall, your call option would expire, worth nothing, and you would lose your entire premium.

When you buy a *put option,* the transaction works the other way; a put gives you the right, but not the obligation, to sell the asset at a specified lower price, or to go short. Let's say you expect Intel, which is trading at $75, to fall in price in the near future. To try to benefit, you could buy an Intel put option. That would give you the right to sell Intel at $70 at any time over the next few months. Since Intel is trading at $75, that put won't cost you very much, perhaps only $.50 per share, or $50. (Puts, like calls, are sold in lots of 100.)

If Intel does indeed fall in price, the value of your put will climb, and it will climb substantially should the share price fall below $70. At that point you could exercise your option by selling Intel shares at $70, and then buying them back on the open market for less (pocketing the difference). Or you could simply sell your put option contract.

Investing in options and futures gives you the opportunity to make a lot of money in a short period of time. It also gives you the opportunity to lose money fast. As part of an overall diversified portfolio, these investments can make sense if

- all your other bases are covered
- you truly understand every aspect of the potential transaction, *and/or*

Mutual Funds Versus Hedge Funds

	Mutual Funds	Hedge Funds
Who invests	Nearly 63 million Americans own mutual funds. The only qualification for investing is to have a minimum investment of $1,000—often less.	Only sophisticated, high-net-worth investors are eligible to invest. The typical investor is a wealthy individual or an institution. A minimum of $1 million—or more—is usually required.
Fees	Mutual fund shareholders on average pay expenses that are about 1.25% of net assets. Sales charges and other expenses are subject to regulatory limits.	Typically, hedge fund investors pay a fee of 1% or 2% of net assets annually, plus 20% or more of a fund's profits. There is no limit on what can be charged.
Investment practices	Securities law restricts a mutual fund's ability to leverage (i.e., borrow against) the value of securities in its portfolio. Funds that use option futures, forward contracts, and short selling must cover their positions with cash reserves or other liquid securities. Investment policies must be fully disclosed to investors.	Leveraging strategies are hallmarks of hedge funds. Investment policies do not have to be disclosed, not even to investors in the fund.
Pricing and liquidity	Mutual funds must value their portfolio securities and compute their share prices daily. They generally must also allow shareholders to redeem shares on at least a daily basis.	There are no specific rules on either valuation or pricing. As a result, hedge fund investors may be unable to determine the value of their investment at any given time. In addition, new investors generally must pledge to keep their money in a hedge fund for at least a year.

Source: Investment Company Institute

- you are working with an experienced professional who has a solid track record

With that said, let's discuss one other kind of investment.

Hedge Funds

People sometimes consider hedge funds to be mutual funds for the extremely wealthy. But while that belief is understandable, the analogy really doesn't hold.

It is true that hedge funds are private investment pools, so in that sense they are like mutual funds. But it is there that the similarities end. Unlike U.S.-based mutual funds, hedge funds do not have to register with the Securities and Exchange Commission (SEC). Hedge fund investors are viewed as being sophisticated enough that they do not need government protection.

The preceding table, prepared by the Investment Company Institute, underscores the rest of the key differences between hedge and mutual funds.

Hedge funds vary widely in size and trading philosophies. While some pursue classic buy-and-hold strategies, others trade aggressively, often using extreme degrees of leverage to try to boost their returns. If you have the financial wherewithal to use hedge funds as part of your overall portfolio, you probably already have the necessary skills to research where they might fit as part of your portfolio.

A Final Thought

Your investment choices increase proportionally with the size of your portfolio. The more money you have to invest, the more choices you have.

Once you have all your bases covered, you may very well want to engage in more speculative investments. That's fine if you are comfortable with the risks as well as the potential rewards. But as always, long-term holdings should be at the heart of your portfolio.

14

Women and Investing: A Discussion for Everyone

As investors, women face many special hurdles, but let's begin with two women who have managed to vault them.

Linda Biagioni, 49, Vice President for Environmental Affairs, The Black & Decker Corporation. Married. No Children

Of all the early influences that prepared Linda Biagioni to be a steady, disciplined investor, the most important was her grandmother, a woman who came to the United States from Russia when she was 15 and never learned to read or write in any language. She did, however, raise eight children through the Depression, build two houses, and run a store.

"My grandmother never spoke about money specifically," Biagioni recalls. "Nevertheless, she taught her thirty grandchildren, especially the girls, to be assertive and believe we could do just about anything."

By the time Biagioni had finished graduate school (she funded her own education) she was already banking money. She began investing through a 401(k) almost twenty years ago, and soon realized the impact of steady, incremental investing.

"When I starting getting my quarterly statements," says Biagioni, "I would invariably say, 'This is money I don't even miss, it's not in my paycheck, and look how quickly it's adding up!' I was astonished when I looked at the projections for what my IRA would be worth twenty-five years later, if I kept contributing and it just matched overall market returns."

The habit of saving has never left her. Biagioni has been a regular recipient of bonuses and stock options, which have been folded into her portfolio. She has also continued to make uninterrupted paycheck contributions to her 401(k) and IRA accounts. Perhaps drawing on the discipline she learned from her grandmother, she has never withdrawn funds from her portfolio assets.

Biagioni's investing style is based on setting ambitious goals, then working toward them daily. She and her husband, both mathematically oriented and engineers by training, are heavy users of graphs—they enjoy creating charts that show their daily progress points against big goals, and frequently call up graphs that show the price patterns for a particular stock they are interested in. While they have invested in bonds for tax reasons, and occasionally in options, Biagioni and her husband have used individual equity investments in sectors they understand as the primary vehicles for portfolio growth.

Biagioni's approach works. In 1990, she and her husband set a goal to double the value of their investment portfolio in seven years. They far exceeded that goal in only six. They have since raised their sights—something Biagioni believes everyone should do.

"For young investors, the most important advice I can give is to set a stretch goal for a specific time period, then set daily milestones toward it, and pay attention. You will be surprised, as I was, how simple it is to achieve the smaller goals and how quickly they add up to your overall goal."

Jeannette Hobson, 54, Principal, Gateway Consulting Group, Inc. Married. No Children

When Jeannette Hobson realized she wanted to run her own business, she was 27 and working as a human resources professional for a commercial bank. Hobson wasn't certain what her company would do, only that she would need start-up capital, "a war chest," to get it under way.

In order to acquire that war chest, she reasoned, she would need to understand how money worked and how people acquire, raise, and manage it.

"In retrospect," says Hobson, "it was the goal of having my own company that drove everything I did and that led me to becoming a successful investor. There was a long-term reason that I was saving and then investing my money."

Hobson set her career sights on asset management, to which she had been exposed through a number of HR rotations at her bank. Within a year after graduating from Columbia University's Executive MBA program, she was a portfolio manager. By the time Hobson left the bank in 1989, she directed a staff of twenty-five and was responsible for the sales and marketing of the bank's investment management capabilities.

Hobson's new profession exposed her to asset-allocation theory, and stamped her permanently as an asset allocator by style and temperament. To her it is the best—and most efficient—way of investing. "Once you know how your money in each asset class will be invested, you don't need to look at a portfolio every day," said Hobson. "I believe in day-to-day information gathering, but not day-to-day tinkering with what I own."

By the way, Hobson did build her war chest. After an initial focus on building a joint retirement portfolio with her husband, she set a goal to fund one year's worth of operations for her company. Within three years, she made the goal, left the bank, and founded Gateway Consulting. After ten years, the company has six professionals on staff and a network of contract consultants, providing general strategic consulting services to companies in all industries.

Even given how well she has done accomplishing her initial objective of starting her own company, Hobson remains focused on distant goals. "Strategically, I'm a long-term player, not a trader," she says. "My measure of the success of a fiscal year is how much money it enables me to put into my retirement plans."

These Women Are Not Unique

The two women you just met—along with the two you will meet at the end of the chapter—are representative of the growing sophistication women are gaining as investors.

Indeed, our research—which has been confirmed repeatedly elsewhere—

shows that many of the traditional beliefs about women investors are simply wrong, or at least outdated. Consider three that are commonly heard.

Myth 1: Women come late to the party where investing is concerned. They don't get involved until late in life

Reality: There does not appear to be much difference in age between female and male investors. About one of every three female investors (32 percent) is 40 years of age or younger, compared with 29 percent of male investors. Similarly, 22 percent of female investors are retired, compared with 24 percent of their male counterparts.

Myth 2: "Women don't have any interest in this stuff"

Reality: While conventional wisdom suggests that women become investors because they inherit money from a spouse or relative—leading many to question whether such women take an active interest in managing their finances—women investors of all ages dispute these assertions. Some 93 percent say they have control of their financial and investment decision making, and more than 75 percent say their primary reason for investing is to achieve financial independence. (See the chart on page 202.) This desire is apparent among women investors of all ages and assets, including 80 percent of women aged 54 or older; 73 percent of women with a net worth of $500,000 or more; and 81 percent of women with a net worth between $200,000 and $500,000. What's more, two-thirds of women polled maintain investment accounts separate from their spouses. This is true for women across a range of assets and net worths, including 61 percent whose net worth is less than $100,000 and 72 percent with at least $500,000 in assets. Further, 76 percent of women say the money they are investing comes from their salaries, including 87 percent of younger investors; 81 percent of women 40 to 53; and 77 percent with a net worth of $500,000.

Reasons Women Have Taken Control of Investment Decision Making

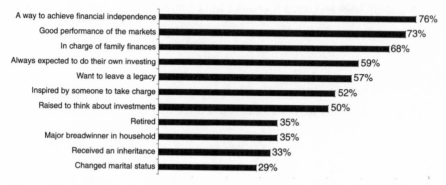

A way to achieve financial independence	76%
Good performance of the markets	73%
In charge of family finances	68%
Always expected to do their own investing	59%
Want to leave a legacy	57%
Inspired by someone to take charge	52%
Raised to think about investments	50%
Retired	35%
Major breadwinner in household	35%
Received an inheritance	33%
Changed marital status	29%

Source: PaineWebber

Myth 3: Everyone knows that women would rather spend money than save it

Reality: On average, women investors save about one-fifth (19.5 percent) of their household's total income, according to our research. Perhaps these women save a larger portion of their incomes because they know they will earn less than men do over the course of their lifetimes.

It is clear that women are taking a growing interest in, and more control of, their finances. Like the two women who lead off this chapter, they are gaining this knowledge on the job, or through formal education, or by learning on their own—and sometimes through seminars that I put on exclusively for women.

Invariably, the first thing I'm asked when someone finds out that I give seminars for women is, "Is that really necessary? Is investing different for women?" I wondered the same thing the first time I was asked to do a seminar exclusively for women, nearly fifteen years ago.

And on one level, of course, the answer is no. Price/earnings ratios, yields, and options are gender neutral. And on this level, the advice is the same as well: women should invest in the same good stocks that men do.

However, when it comes to how long women are likely to live, what they are likely to earn, and what resources they will have available to them at retirement, women *are* different from men, and their planning needs to take those differences into account.

There are sobering statistics that show just how different men and women are when it comes to finances:

- *Among the elderly poor, 75 percent are women, 80 percent of whom were not poor before they were widowed.*
- *One in four women over age 65 relies on Social Security for at least 90 percent of her income.*
- *The median pension for women is half that for men.*

Given that women's pensions are not as big, it isn't surprising that the U.S. General Accounting Office noted, in a study of 401(k) plans, that "women tend to invest their pension funds in safer and lower-yield assets than men." Since their retirement assets are relatively small, their first reaction is to be as careful with them as possible.

But while that attitude isn't surprising, it is wrong. Women need to take exactly the opposite tack when it comes to how they invest their retirement money. They need to begin saving earlier, and to invest those savings more aggressively to avoid outliving their assets—every retiree's nightmare.

Investing in low-risk assets—such as savings accounts or certificates of deposit that barely beat inflation and are fully taxed as ordinary income—is not the way for anyone to achieve long-term financial goals. That's especially true for women, who typically start with fewer assets.

Before we examine in detail what women need to do, let's provide some context, using an issue that affects all of us.

How Women Got in This Position

One of the major changes that occurred in the 1990s was a shift in responsibility from the corporation to individuals to provide for their own security in retirement. As you will remember, back in the 1950s and 1960s there was an unspoken contract between employer and employee. If the employee was loyal to the company, the company would, in return, provide reasonable job security, a secure pension, and possibly lifetime health care benefits for the employee and the employee's spouse.

But corporations have gotten out of the business of providing that security, and as the chart shows, the percentage of pension assets in defined benefit plans has been steadily declining in favor of 401(k) plans.

For corporations, 401(k) plans have many advantages, particularly when it comes to providing benefits to their younger employees. One major advantage is they don't require the company to provide a guaranteed check every month as pensions do.

Corporations are also getting out of the business of providing health care benefits to retirees, in response to the rapidly rising costs of health care and new accounting rules that require them to show—and make allowances

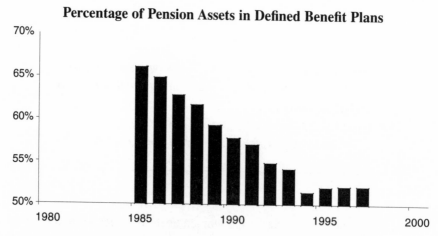

Percentage of Pension Assets in Defined Benefit Plans

Source: Employee Benefit Research Institute

for—future health care costs on their balance sheets. They are shifting the responsibility to the individual.

At the same time, the government—which provides a strong safety net to today's retirees in the form of Social Security and Medicare—is also likely to rein in its largess. As we look forward, it is virtually certain that retirees will not enjoy the same level of security from the federal government. The math almost ensures that. In 1960 there were more than five workers for every retiree. Today it is three, on its way to two in the middle of the next century, after the last baby boomer has retired.

What this means is that individuals have to be very astute; and they have to begin planning as soon as possible. That's especially true of women because of the special issues they face.

While it is fortunate for women that they live longer by several years than men, that also means that they will be supporting themselves much longer in retirement than men will. And they may be retired for a very long time. While the life expectancy today for women is nearly 80 years, if you live to be age 65, the actuarial tables predict you will live for another nineteen years.

Dealing with Reality

If you are going to live longer, you are going to need more money. And here women are at a distinct disadvantage, because they generally retire with far fewer benefits than men do.

A key reason for that is our responsibilities to our families—both to our children and to our older relatives—which tend to keep women out of the labor force for a portion of their working lives. Figures compiled by the Department of Labor tell the story. The typical woman spends 11.5 years away from her job, compared to just one year for the average man.

When you're in and out of the labor force, you don't build the same level of benefits as someone who stays on the job full-time. As a result, you end up with a smaller pension, 401(k), and Social Security check.

That would be daunting enough, but the situation for women gets even worse. The average woman over 25 changes jobs every 4.8 years, compared to 6.6 for the average man, probably because of tailoring her career to meet family responsibilities. This is a problem because many companies require employees to complete five years before becoming fully vested in a retirement plan.

Finally, because of family responsibilities, women far outnumber men in part-time jobs and consulting assignments—positions that don't normally offer benefits, particularly retirement benefits, which may not seem very important when you are in your twenties and thirties but take on enormous importance when you're facing your sixties.

The point is simple: women must deal with certain economic and demographic realities. They earn less than men, and because of their family responsibilities will probably enter retirement with fewer resources as well. We need to acknowledge these facts and understand how they affect our ability to meet our short-term and long-term goals.

But It Is Different for Married Women, Isn't It?

At this point in the seminar I often notice a group of women in the audience who don't appear to be at all concerned with these problems. Invariably they believe they won't be affected by the shortfalls we've just discussed. The reason? They are convinced they will benefit from their husband's financial planning.

Some of them are bound to be disappointed.

While there certainly are a small group of women who have—or will have—the luxury of financial security provided by a husband, the numbers show that about 80 to 90 percent of women will be solely responsible for their finances at some point in their lives—because they remained single, or became widowed, or got divorced. (In fact, there are currently between 10 and 11 million divorced women in this country, and only 28 percent are legally entitled to financial support. Only one of three receives that money.)

Another surprising statistic is that the average age of widowhood in the United States is 56. And as we noted earlier, 75 percent of the elderly poor are women. About 80 percent of them were not poor before they were widowed. Again, this is a strong argument for married women becoming very involved in financial planning. They must protect themselves in the event that they are widowed or divorced.

The average net worth of a single woman is only $58,900, compared to a couple's $130,000, according to the Census Bureau. Despite the fact that women run 38 percent of businesses in the United States and hold 45 percent of administrative, executive, and management jobs, their marital status remains the single most reliable predictor of their wealth and, consequently, their financial health at retirement. Since women outlive men by an average of seven years, their dollar—especially when it comes to planning for their retirement—needs to go further.

While women may understand this intuitively, so far they have not been acting on this knowledge.

PaineWebber regularly does a poll in conjunction with the Gallup organization (the Index of Investor Optimism) asking women investors where they are putting their money, and what we have learned is disconcerting. Despite a strong need for women to take control of their financial futures, only a small number do, typically women investors with assets over $100,000. Many other women tend to be so risk averse that it actually hurts their ability to invest astutely. This is true of all women, even baby boomers. Some 90 percent of the women investors polled have savings accounts, but less than 30 percent own stocks or mutual funds that invest in stocks. That is a great mistake because savings accounts can actually cost you money, once you account for inflation and taxes.

So, the first problem is inflation; the second is taxes. CDs and money market funds immediately require you to pay ordinary income taxes on what you earn. Compare that to how earnings are treated within certain retirement accounts: within 401(k)s, 403(b)s, and traditional IRAs, the earnings grow tax-deferred. You don't have to pay taxes on what you earned until you withdraw the money. And with a Roth IRA, there may be no tax due at all.

When you start at a disadvantage—as most women do, given that they still earn less than men and enter retirement with smaller pensions—you have to make your assets work harder. Putting those assets into extremely conservative investments is counterproductive.

Of course, I am not advocating extremely speculative investments for the typical investor, but rather a prudent level of investment risk appropriate for someone who is thinking long-term. And if you are thinking long-term, you want an investment that historically has produced greater returns than a CD. Otherwise, as our example shows, you are destined to fall further and further behind as you try to reach your goals.

The Tide Is Turning

There are substantial signs, however, that things are improving.

The boom in investing that we talked about earlier in the book has been particularly noticeable among women, perhaps because of their expanding role in the workplace, an increased desire for financial independence, and the recognition that government and corporations can no longer guarantee an individual's long-term financial security.

Indeed, not long ago, investing was often seen as the sole province of the man of the house. This is no longer the case. While men most frequently execute investment decisions, the pendulum has clearly begun to swing the other way. The Investment Company Institute reports that women are the primary financial decision makers in 32 percent of households that own mutual funds, an increase of 13 percent during the past four years.

That change shows no sign of slowing. For example, 35 percent of all first-time buyers of financial products are women, according to Oppenheimer Funds Inc., which adds that women's first-time fund purchases are 1.5 times the size of men's.

When you have a trend like this, it picks up momentum. The National Association of Securities Dealers (NASD) reports that 47 percent of all Americans who own mutual funds or individual stocks are women.

And apparently those investments are paying off. The U.S. Department of Labor reports that 47 percent of all wealthy Americans (those having assets over $500,000) are female.

Married female executives at the most senior levels of Fortune 1000 companies generate 66 percent of their family income, according to Korn Ferry

International, the executive recruiting firm. Women's role as key contributors to the household's finances is firmly established.

While There Is Reason for Optimism . . .

While there are a lot of reasons to be encouraged, we have also seen that women have been slower than men to invest in stocks, which historically have been the best way to make up a shortfall in earnings over the long term.

Part of the problem, it would seem, is a lack of education about finances. Our research bears that out. Less than half (46 percent) of all female investors with more than $100,000 in assets say they are "comfortable" or "very comfortable" with their ability to understand investment products and opportunities, versus 66 percent of men who hold this view.

One reason women lack confidence about investing is the way we were brought up. For many women in their late fifties and older, money was rarely discussed at home. Finance was a foreign language. But baby boomers are becoming better informed, and as a result the next generation should be even more enlightened.

But even before we get to the children of the boomers, there are hopeful signs. Women in their twenties and thirties, exposed much earlier to 401(k) plans and to far more business programming in the media, seem to be taking an earlier interest in their finances. This is particularly fortuitous because at those relatively young ages, not only can they take advantage of the power of compounding, but they can also benefit from allocating more of their investment dollars to common stock, given how far off their retirement is likely to be.

Clearly, women need to learn more through self-education or the advice of financial professionals. The more you know about a subject, the more comfortable you are discussing it. And of course, the more you know about investing, the greater the likelihood of success.

One place to begin that learning process is with a thorough understanding of what you already own. Specifically, women need to take stock of their assets and liabilities, do an income statement, and analyze how their investments are doing. This seems very basic but it is crucial. The next step is to set up a budget that includes a savings component. Understand all your future benefits. Married women need to find out now the provisions of their husbands' pensions, insurance, and retiree health care benefits, if any, so they can plan effectively. Many women think that when their husband dies they will continue to receive his pension. This is not always the case. Some pensions do not have survivor's benefits, and even if they are available, sometimes men opt to take a higher pension at retirement, giving up any survivor's benefits, rather than take a lower pension that would cover a surviving spouse. Learning *what you have* and *what you are entitled to* is a good place to start when it comes to your own as well as your husband's benefits.

Next, all women should be sure they are taking advantage of all the benefits being offered by their employer (or their spouse's), such as by maximizing their contribution to their 401(k) to benefit from tax savings. Look at plans that offer stock at a discount to employees. In addition, make sure you are benefiting from those retirement plans that offer to match all or part of the contribution you make to your retirement accounts. Not taking advantage of those plans that match your contribution or give you the ability to contribute pretax dollars is the equivalent of throwing money away.

Unfortunately, many companies do not do a good job of educating employees about the options they have to save and invest. The sad result is missed opportunities that might have made a significant difference in retirement. For example, the power of compounding is lost if you don't start early enough.

I am constantly reminded of a close friend who holds a Ph.D. and a tenured position at a prestigious university that offers excellent retirement options. When beginning there in her mid-twenties, she declined opting into the retirement program because it required that she contribute from her paycheck. Although the university generously matched contributions, my friend—having just completed graduate school, with education loans to repay and limited resources on hand—chose to keep all of her income. Belatedly she came to understand what a costly choice that was, as she began retirement planning in her mid-forties, having already missed twelve years of the bull market.

If you participate in a 401(k) or similar, self-directed plan, take time to review your investment options. Select the fund or funds that fit into your long-term goals, taking care not to be too conservative. View the 401(k) as part of your overall financial assets and allocate the rest of your assets accordingly.

Be sure to look at what is available outside your retirement plans. Are you eligible for an IRA, Roth IRA, or one of the education savings options? It is not the purpose of this book to explore all these alternatives in detail, but there are a number of ways to build retirement savings.

It is never too early to start building those savings. While earlier is better, later is always better than never.

Although most stereotypes about women are not reflective of today's women investors, one does hold true: they are savers. Recognizing that they often earn less than men do, women historically have saved more aggressively. This suggests that as women's salaries grow, their investing will continue to increase, and in the end, women may realize much stronger positions financially. It is this new status that will come to define women as the investors of tomorrow.

Summing Up

Now more than ever, women—especially baby boomer women—need to increase their investments in order to secure their retirement. Women can no longer depend on government programs like Social Security and Medicare for their retirement, or the largess of private employers. And because they are in and out of the labor force, any pensions they will receive are likely to be smaller. Therefore, they must rely on their own initiatives to secure a comfortable retirement.

Saving enough to secure their future will be a difficult task, since many women are faced with tuition and parental health care, child rearing, and other costs at precisely the time they are starting to think about retirement. In order for women to care for themselves after retirement, they will need to move away from traditional savings plans toward more growth-oriented investment portfolios.

There are encouraging signs that women understand this reality:

- Some 61 percent of women with investable assets of $100,000 or more say they have a plan for achieving their goals.
- Ninety-three percent of these investors say they have control of their financial and investment decision making.
- About half (49 percent) say they feel successful because they have reached specific net worth targets and have attained their retirement goals.

Many women investors today have embraced investing with great success, in part because of their desire for financial independence and their willingness to educate themselves about investing. (They are also influential investors, because they consider their knowledge about investing to be a legacy—much like an inheritance—that should be shared with future generations.)

Despite these hopeful signs, there is still more to be done.

Finally . . .

We began the chapter with profiles of two women who have learned to take control of their personal financial lives. Let's end it the same way.

Laura Thiem, 39, Portfolio Manager, Cisco Systems, Inc. Married. Two Children

As Laura Thiem sees it, her development as a successful personal investor is almost inseparable from her professional development as an institutional money manager. Ten years ago, Thiem moved into the corporate treasury arena from an earlier career in corporate finance positions. During that same period, her personal investing portfolio increased in value by many multiples. The common thread: daily immersion in financial markets and investment strategy issues. "I am a heavy user of financial information, and watch the markets constantly," said Thiem. "I also use financial advisers on a daily basis, both professionally and personally."

Since 1994, Thiem has worked in the treasury area at Cisco Systems, one of the country's fastest-growing companies. Her primary responsibility is managing Cisco's cash and investment portfolio, now valued at more than $8.5 billion. She also oversees daily a dozen outside investment managers who manage portions of the portfolio, and personally handles in-house trading and accounting for a $1 billion-plus portfolio that the company draws on for working capital, taxes, and acquisitions. Thiem understands performance—portfolio earnings account for 12 percent of Cisco's total earnings per share. "I like my work, have a lot of responsibility and visibility, and am well compensated," said Thiem.

A Bloomberg terminal sits on her desk, and she uses highly sophisticated computer modeling to support her professional trading activities. Nevertheless, Thiem is also a strong believer in the value of personal relationships. The investment management business, she points out, is still one based on "a handshake, a fax machine, and a phone call." "When my company has $50 million to spend," said Thiem, "I may use my Bloomberg screen to help me investigate prices or determine relative value, but I will always call an adviser to discuss the findings and actually execute a transaction."

Since her professional investment work involves only fixed-income products, Thiem makes it a point to keep her personal investments entirely in individual equity holdings. She regularly uses personal investment advisers, swapping stock tips daily. She is a strong advocate of asset allocation. "After ten years of professional and personal trading," said Thiem, "I am convinced that 97 percent of returns come from asset allocation. I have never once accurately picked the high or low of a given cycle—it doesn't happen. So select an asset allocation model wisely, and then don't touch it."

Thiem's other crucial piece of personal investing advice: trust your instincts. She learned that lesson herself during the mid-1980s, when she decided to learn about agricultural commodities trading. After enrolling in graduate business school courses and using computer-based trading simulation programs, Thiem realized she had no stomach for commodities trading. She also realized her instincts were nearly always right. "The issue with commodities trading was the incredibly short time horizons for trades, not my judgment calls," said Thiem. "So the experience really taught me to say 'trust yourself.' It is one of the hardest things to do when your own money is at stake."

Cheryl Watson, 38, Senior Vice President, USAGroup Secondary Market Services, Inc. Married. One Child

Cheryl Watson had a traditional start—a small rural town upbringing and marriage to her high school sweetheart. But convention stopped when she became the primary income earner in her household, a role she always knew she would fill. While an aptitude for numbers and a drive for financial security helped her choose accounting as her career, she joined her current company because it offered her the advancement prospects that only a start-up can provide.

When it came to her personal investments, she was—initially—more risk averse than many individual investors. But she has parlayed an increased understanding of risk into impressive portfolio growth.

"By nature, I'm a very conservative person," Watson says. "But I also have an instinct for opportunity."

Watson is head of secondary marketing services for USAGroup, which repackages various debt products into asset-backed securities. She joined the company's education assets group when it was launched with a $20 million portfolio and a $40 million line of credit. Eleven years later, Watson presides over a $6 billion debt portfolio. Her daily responsibilities include sourcing, analyzing, and acquiring the low-cost capital her company uses to purchase student loan pools for securitization.

"I chose this particular company because it had experienced significant growth in earlier endeavors," said Watson. "I was looking for opportunity."

As part of her job, Watson works with sophisticated computer modeling and must pay daily attention to financial markets. That has gradually transformed her personal investing style. When she began investing, all of her holdings were in extremely secure, low-risk instruments. Today, with an increased appreciation for risk strategy and eye on growth, her portfolio consists of 60 percent equities, 10 percent bonds, and 30 percent blended vehicles such as balanced mutual funds. Over the past decade, the value of that portfolio has increased by many multiples, an achievement even more impressive given that her company is a not-for-profit firm that cannot grant stock options.

"I believe in asset allocation," Watson says. "I also believe a strategy has to be long-term, and once it is in place, I may make a change twice a year, but that's it."

She began investing for the first time through her 401(k), motivated by her company's matching plan. At the time, she said, she thought of the matching component as "an opportunity to earn free money." Today, Watson's company matches 401(k) contributions dollar for dollar up to 6 percent.

She has never touched the funds. Watson believes matching plans are one of the soundest methods of getting a portfolio started—provided, of course, that the investor has the discipline to leave the funds alone. Few things disturb Watson more than accepting penalties or loss of matching contributions for short-term reasons. "Leave your retirement funds alone," Watson says simply. "It is not there for now. It is there for later."

Part III

Managing Your Investments for Tomorrow

15

Investing for Your Children:
Possibilities and Pitfalls

I believe in introducing children to investing early. In part that's because I have made my career in the investment world, but it is more than that. I have seen how sensible investment strategies have made a big difference in people's lives. My parents, for example, not only were able to put six children through college; they had a wonderful and financially secure retirement because of the investment choices they made. And countless other people have benefited as well. Conversely, I have seen what has happened to people who didn't start investing early enough. Their lives were less full than they might have been.

I don't want that to happen to my children. I want them to understand investing and to profit from it. Simply knowing about the power of compounding, and maximizing the benefit of it by starting to invest early, has the potential of making a huge difference in their lives later on.

But I want them to learn more than that. I also want them to understand how capitalism has succeeded in providing them—and the rest of us—with the highest living standard in the history of the world. I want them to know that democracy, since the day this country was founded, has fostered entrepreneurial activity that has given opportunity to countless millions of people (including their four immigrant great-grandparents) and has created enough jobs to absorb most workers.

Having grown up in New York City, my children are painfully aware that our system of democracy and capitalism is not perfect. They have seen first-hand the evidence that all do not participate equally. Still, it is without a doubt, the best system man has created so far.

It remains popular to bash Wall Street and corporate America, but on some level I still find it amazing that anyone with the money can become a part owner of IBM, or Microsoft, or any other publicly held company, and as an owner, participate in the future earnings and dividends.

Many of the strategies that you'll want to employ to help your children—or your grandchildren—are identical to the ones you have been following all along: invest heavily in stocks for the long term; maximize your returns by minimizing taxes; match bond maturities with current income needs; and so forth.

However, there are certain things you can do when you are investing for your children—such as being 100 percent invested in stocks for extended periods of time—that would give you pause if you were investing for yourself.

The actual strategies you employ will differ, of course, depending on the child's age, so let's discuss your options at each phase of your child's life.

From Newborn to Ages 12 to 14

I don't know what it was like at your house when your children came home from the hospital a few days after they were born, but I remember what my apartment was like. It looked as if someone had combined a Toys R Us superstore with the corner florist and decided to jam the complete inventory of both into my home, which was none too big to start. There were flowers, balloons, educational toys, and stuffed animals everywhere.

It was exciting, thrilling, and it reinforced the wonder I had felt when I looked down at the little girl—and a couple of years later, the little boy—I was holding. I wouldn't have traded a single gift for anything. And I would certainly never have thought of writing, on the bottom of the birth announcement, "Instead of gifts, please send Kaitlin (and later Steve) shares of your favorite growth stock fund."

But it would have made sense.

Long-term, the benefit of giving a newborn shares in a growth stock mutual fund or in large-cap growth stocks will be greater than any silver spoon, teddy bear, or other gift you can offer them. The reason: they will be able to exchange that gift later on for the greatest gift of all—education.

Education is the best investment there is. As the granddaughter of four Irish immigrants who believed passionately in education and sacrificed greatly so their sons could go to college—it wasn't until my parents' generation that many families were able to send their daughters to college as well— I saw firsthand what education can mean in terms of opportunities, choices, and quality of life.

As part of my commitment to education, I serve on the Board of Trustees of New York University, the Board of Overseers of NYU's Stern School of Business, and on the investment committees of NYU, and my son's school. (In addition I have lectured at both my children's schools and enjoyed greatly educating these bright young minds about how the market works, and the role of stock in a capitalistic system.)

Education has become increasingly important in a world that is changing rapidly because of technology. With little loyalty between employer and employee in this era of lean and mean, employees are likely to hold many different jobs over the course of their working lifetime. The best insurance for this new environment is to start with a good education and build from there, constantly upgrading your knowledge and skills throughout your career.

The era when opportunities were plentiful for unskilled high school graduates is over. Even many factory jobs today require advanced math skills because technology has made machines much more complicated. The old secretarial jobs, which required only basic typing and shorthand, have been transformed into jobs requiring a high level of computer sophistication. And we can expect technology to foster further change—and the need for even more education—in the years ahead.

Where a college degree used to be a ticket to the better jobs and enhanced lifetime income, increasingly graduate school is a requirement for many high-skilled jobs. Of course, Bill Gates is a college dropout, and he has done just fine, but he's the exception. Only a firm grounding in a good education will prepare today's students for tomorrow.

Education is costly, and the earlier it is planned for, the more you can take advantage of the power of compounding to help pay for it. Buying a mutual fund—or a handful of good stocks—for a child at birth and adding regularly to your gift can go a long way to making tuition bills less painful.

For many parents, those tuition bills hit at precisely the time they are trying to plan for retirement, and at a time when their elderly parents may need some help, too. It's tough to stretch your resources to cover all those costs, so implementing education planning as early as possible is essential. With annual bills at many private colleges now substantially exceeding $30,000 a year, few parents can simply write a check out of current income.

Grandparents, take note. Not only is starting an investment account or buying a mutual fund for a newborn grandchild a gift that can pay off handsomely at tuition time, it's a good way to take advantage of the $10,000 annual gift allowance. A $10,000 fund that appreciates 10 percent a year is worth $55,600 when the child turns 18. Appreciation of 12 percent a year would result in $76,900. If you add $1,000 at each birthday, that $10,000 becomes $100,200 at 10 percent, or $131,650 with 12 percent appreciation when the child turns 18.

It Doesn't Get Any Easier Than This

Investing for the first dozen years of your child's life is, well, child's play. Buy good-quality growth stocks or mutual funds, and relax. You can make the initial process of saving for your child harder than this, but there is no reason to. Of course, you have to monitor your choices. There is little need for diversification here if you start investing for the child shortly after they are born and you will not touch the money until tuition is due 18 years later.

When you have an investment time horizon that is more than a decade long, you can afford the risks that come from putting all your eggs in the equity basket. Of course, the market will bounce around while the child is growing up. It will surely suffer many corrections. Maybe even a crash. But that shouldn't matter to you in the long run. This is money that you (or the child) won't need for more than a decade, so short-term volatility isn't a real concern. In fact, anything that you try to do to reduce volatility can be counterproductive.

Stocks have traditionally returned 11 percent a year over time, and bonds somewhere around 5.5 percent. Suppose you are worried about the potential volatility of having an all-stock portfolio to fund a college education that is at least fifteen years off. To hedge your bets, you decide to make bonds a quarter of the college fund. If history holds, that decision will reduce the overall return of your child's college portfolio to 9.6 percent.

There simply is no reason to do that. When you are investing for a small child, the long-term horizon makes stocks the appropriate choice. As college approaches, you can then diversify into safer vehicles such as fixed-income investments.

I would also argue alternatives to using zero coupon bonds to fund the child's education initially. I know there are a lot of people who believe zeros are great for financing college. And they are. You can buy a zero that will yield $20,000 some twenty years from now for about $6,750 today. That's a pretty good deal. (It may pay for only about a half year of tuition at a state school by then, but that is another matter.) And there certainly is something to be said for knowing that your future college costs have been taken care of today. Once you buy the bonds, you don't have to worry about them, except for possibly having to pay taxes on the imputed interest.

But the security of investing in fixed-income vehicles comes at a price.

That zero coupon bond you are buying for $6,750 today is yielding only 5.5 percent, even if it is possible to get that rate tax-free. If you put that same amount of money—$6,757.04, to be exact—in stocks, or an all-equity mutual fund, and it earns the 11 percent a year that stocks have traditionally returned over time, you'd have better than $54,000 ($54,477.34, to be precise) twenty years from now. That's about two and a half times the amount of money from a zero. And even if you kept those stocks in your name and paid the tax—something we will argue against later in the chapter—you'd still be substantially ahead of the game.

Zeros may be a little bit easier to invest in than stocks, and they are certainly more of a sure thing. If you buy an insured zero, you know that $20,000 is going to be waiting for you in twenty years. But stocks are more than likely to be the better choice. Save buying the zeros until the child reaches age 14. (We explain more about zeros later in the chapter.)

Education IRAs

Another way of saving for college is through an education IRA. Like the Roth IRA, which we will also discuss, this is a relatively new wrinkle.

Contributions to education IRAs are nondeductible, that is, you contribute to the account with after-tax dollars, and withdrawals of your contributions—plus whatever interest, dividends, or capital gains those contributions have earned—are tax free, if the money is used for qualified higher-education expenses. To be eligible to contribute, you must have an adjusted gross income of less than $95,000 for a single filer, or under $150,000 if you file jointly. If your adjusted gross income is between $95,000 and 110,000, single, or $150,000 and 160,000, filing jointly, you may make a partial contribution. Contributions are limited to $500 per child per year. You can keep putting money into the account until the child is age 18.

The money—your contributions along with what they have earned—must be used for higher education, or transferred to another sibling, before the child is 30. If that doesn't happen, or the money is withdrawn from the account and not used for higher education, a 10 percent tax penalty is imposed. Incidentally, education IRAs cannot be used for elementary or secondary schooling.

Despite their name, education IRAs have nothing to do with individual retirement accounts, and do not affect in any way what you can contribute to your traditional or Roth IRA, or any other retirement fund. So, if you're married, you and your spouse can contribute a combined $4,000 to your retirement IRA accounts, and still invest $500 for each child in an education IRA account.

Give Them a Head Start

While you are getting this saving program under way, try to involve the children you are saving for. If you can, get them interested in what is going on with "their" money.

Now, there is no guarantee that they are going to be interested and will start turning to the business section on Sunday before the comics. But talking to them about what you are doing will give them a head start in understanding a subject—investing—that will become important to them later on.

When my children were young, I let each of them choose a stock to buy. I got them research reports and copies of what the business press had written about the companies they thought had the best opportunity for success. They had more background than most 7- and 10-year-olds, having been to Mom's office regularly and seen me on TV several times (although I made for very poor competition with their favorite shows).

They pored over the annual reports. Stephen selected Pepsi, impressed that they also owned Frito-Lay and Pizza Hut (subsequently spun off with KFC, Taco Bell, and the rest of their restaurants). Kaitlin, a more sophisticated investor at the time—she was 10, after all—chose Corning because of their fiber optic cable business, recognizing that the world was being wired.

I think selecting "their stock" gave them both a sense of participating, and some fun too as we explored the ups and downs of what happened to their companies over the years. They both also own mutual funds, which is another good way to expose children to the market.

While I haven't noticed a payoff from all this in a high level of voluntary saving of their summer job money, I know they keep track of their accounts, and I hope they will be committed savers/investors once they start working full-time. I insist that a portion of their summer earnings be saved and invested, and have agreed to continue their allowances so that those summer earnings can be put into Roth IRAs.

You don't have to go this route. Give your children shares in something like Disney or Viacom, which owns Nickelodeon and MTV. Buy them a large-cap growth fund that contains nothing but household names like GE, Microsoft, and Coca-Cola. Obviously the stocks you actually select will be ones that are suitable at the time of purchase, not necessarily these examples.

Once they own individual shares or a mutual fund, they are bound to pay some attention to how "their investments" are doing.

But you probably want to do more than just buy them a stock or mutual fund. Talk to them about the importance of saving and investing. The more children learn early on, the less frightening or confusing these subjects will seem when they become older. That will make them better savers—and investors—when they have money of their own they can put to work.

One reason people are reluctant investors is the very newness of the task at hand. One of the things you may have forgotten is how daunting investing could be when you were just getting started. The language is confusing (who came up with terms like "basis points" and "disintermediation," anyway?), and the number of options in the marketplace that a neophyte is faced with (stocks, bonds, mutual funds, options, futures, puts, calls, going long, going short, hedging) can seem overwhelming. No wonder many people put off investing for as long as they can. Talking to your children about investing—in their terms, of course—when they are young could go a long way toward making the subject less daunting later on.

From Age 14 to 21 or So

As your child approaches college age, your investment choices diverge a bit. If you don't need the money to pay for college, leave it invested in growth stocks and give the money—or the portfolio itself—to the child later on, perhaps when he or she starts working and can use it to fund an IRA. Just let the money continue to compound in the interim. As we have seen, if stocks continue their traditional 11 percent a year growth, the value of the portfolio will double in seven years, even if you don't add to it.

But if you are going to need the money to pay for college, you'll want to take a different route. When the child is 13 or 14, start thinking about shifting some of the money you have in stocks into fixed-income investments—either zeros or short-term instruments such as Treasuries or CDs, depending on the prevailing interest-rate environment. You want to make sure that you'll have enough money on hand when you need it. You can't afford a severe market drop the day before the tuition check is due.

But even though you'll want to be shifting money over to conservative investments once the child becomes a teenager, *you do not need to move the money out of stocks all at once.* Fortunately, colleges don't charge you up front for the full four years. You'll still have three years from the time you pay for freshman tuition until you write the check for senior year. That allows you to shift the money out of stocks into more conservative investments in stages.

To be safe, you might want to make sure you have money for a given year's tuition in fixed-income investments at least a full year before the tuition is due. That will also allow you to be more aggressive with the rest of the money you have put aside to pay for college. Let's see how this strategy might work if you decide to start shifting out of stocks and into zero coupon bonds once the child becomes a teenager.

Zero Coupon Bonds for College Funding

If you wish to be conservative, a good way to assure that funds for college are available when needed is by purchasing zero coupon bonds that mature in each of the four years when tuition is due. In today's lower-interest-rate environment, zeros are not as advantageous as in the early 1980s, when for a surprisingly small amount of money you could purchase a zero with a 14 percent coupon that would easily fund an Ivy League education eighteen to twenty-one years later. Unfortunately, those days are gone.

But even today, zeros can provide security and peace of mind. Here's probably the best way to use them. Invest in stocks when the child is young. When the child is about 14 or so, take 25 percent of the money you have in the college fund and buy a zero that has a face value equal to what freshman year tuition is likely to cost. Keep the rest of the college tuition money where it is. When the child is 15, buy a zero equal to what sophomore tuition is likely to cost, and so on.

That would be a fairly aggressive position to take.

If you are uncomfortable with putting money earmarked for college potentially at risk, you are not alone. If you would prefer to know that college is taken care of earlier on, here's a more conservative approach. Once the child reaches age 14, buy four separate zero coupon bonds. Take 25 percent of the money that you have saved for college and buy a zero that will mature in four years, for freshman year tuition. Take another 25 percent and buy a zero maturing in five years, for sophomore year. Buy a zero maturing six years out for junior year, and one maturing in seven years to take care of senior year.

By using zeros this way you will achieve the best of both worlds. Hopefully, stocks will have returned superior returns during the first fourteen years you saved for college. Then you can gain the peace of mind knowing that college is paid for, by shifting out of stocks and into bonds.

Two reminders, if you choose this route:

- Zero coupons don't pay interest until maturity. (The difference between what you pay for a zero and what you receive at maturity is your interest.) But you will have to pay taxes on the imputed interest you receive each year, if you have not purchased a zero municipal.
- Don't forget to factor in inflation when anticipating the cost of college two decades out.

From Age 21 to 30

Here you may want to think about gifting money—if you haven't used it all for college—but you may want to give your children something more valuable: sound financial advice.

As the mother of two teenagers I have learned that your children don't always heed your advice when they are young, no matter how sound it is and no matter how sincerely it is offered. But somewhere in their twenties, children will slowly discover that you have gotten a lot smarter, and they may be willing to take some advice. When they are ready, try to give them the benefit of what you have learned about investing over the years. For what it is worth, here are the four things I am going to try to get across to my son and daughter.

1. Debt is bad

My message here is extremely simple: with the exception of student loans and having a mortgage, there is absolutely no reason to have debt of any kind. I know this is an extreme position. And I know that there are the rare occasions when it may make sense to take out something like a margin loan to take advantage of a wonderful opportunity. However, to be candid, I don't care. I am going to tell my children people can get into serious financial trouble when they make a habit of buying things with money they don't have. Over the years I have come to believe that having any kind of nondeductible debt, other than student loans, is generally a bad idea. If my children grow up to be serious investors who learn how to use leverage as a resource, well, good for them. But they are going to hear Mom's voice about the perils of debt in the back of their head, nagging them at every step of the way.

2. Save, save, save, and save some more

I am fairly optimistic that my children—and yours—will actually heed this advice. It is unfair to making sweeping generalizations about millions of people, but it does seem to me that Generation X is better at saving than the baby boomer generation that preceded it. Gen Xers have a fairly good idea that retirement will come sooner than they think—and that it will cost more—and they have a healthy suspicion that the government will not be as helpful to them in their old age as it has been to previous generations. Given all this, I don't think it is going to be too hard to get my kids to save. Here are two specific suggestions I am going to give them: to try to save 10 percent of every check they receive, and if they end up working for a company, to have that money taken out of their paycheck before they even see it.

3. Take advantage of corporate savings plans

There is no doubt that corporate retirement plans can qualify as free money—especially if they offer any kind of matching. The first thing I am going to stress to my children is that contributing will reduce their tax burden. If they are making $50,000 a year and put $3,000 into a company 401(k), they will pay taxes on only $47,000 of income. And of course, any earnings or capital gains they earn in their 401(k) will grow tax-deferred.

This is good, but where it gets great is when the company offers matching in any form. I'll tell them that if their company matches their contribution, the return on their money will soar. For example, if the firm adds $1 for every $2 they put in, they'll have a 50 percent return on their contribution right from the start. That leverage can be enormous, as a simple example shows. Say they put $1,000 into a company-sponsored retirement plan on January 2, and their firm matches $1 for every $2 they contribute. At the close of business on January 2, their account is up to $1,500, giving the 50 percent return we talked about. If the account grows by 11 percent during the year—as, historically, the market has over the last seventy years—they'd end up with $1,665. That's a 66.5 percent return on their initial investment.

4. Be aggressive

No, I am not going to advocate that they invest only in IPOs and Internet stocks. But I will point out to them that it will be a long time until they retire, so they can afford to try for higher returns wherever possible. If they do, the effects of compounding can lead to dramatic results. Just look at the following table. If one of my children put $3,000 away each year for retirement, what would happen to that money at different rates of return? The differences are stunning. The difference between 6 percent on your money and 8 percent doesn't sound like much, but as the table shows, over thirty years there is a difference of $121,461. That is 48 percent more! At 10 percent, the results are more than double the 6 percent return.

The moral is simple. You want to get your children to invest aggressively for retirement. The payoff can be worth it. But you can do more than preach. You can help your children get a serious saving program under way. Here's one idea I particularly like: Help make sure that they fund their IRAs to the maximum. When the child starts working, offer to match on some basis (one-for-one, two-for-one, whatever) the contribution that they are able to make to an individual retirement account.

How Much Would $3,000 Contributed Annually to a
Retirement Plan Be Worth?
Annual Rate of Return

At the end of year	6%	8%	10%
5	$17,443	$18,369	$19,359
10	$40,970	$45,737	$51,211
15	$72,705	$86,510	$103,618
20	$115,510	$147,255	$189,842
25	$173,248	$237,757	$531,708
30	$251,129	$372,590	$565,122
40	$497,873	$872,752	$1,581,020

Source: PaineWebber

Which IRA should they open? Unless they are really not making a lot of money and they truly need the tax deductibility that can come with traditional IRA contributions, I would have them open a Roth.

Contributions to a Roth IRA cannot be deducted from current income—as is sometimes the case with "traditional" IRAs—but earnings grow tax-deferred in this new account as they do with a regular IRA. But here's the real kicker: with the Roth IRA the earnings on contributions can be withdrawn tax-free in retirement, or after the child is age 59½, if the account has been in place for at least five years. No matter how much their investments earn inside this account, the money will not be taxed when it is withdrawn. In almost every case, that more than makes up for the fact that the contributions are not deductible. We are of course relying on the government not to renege on this future promise.

At some point your child may be earning too much money to contribute to a Roth IRA. Currently someone who is single cannot have more than $110,000 in adjusted gross income a year (for couples the limit is $160,000 in adjusted gross income).

There are a couple of other minor benefits that come with the Roth IRA. You (or the child) can contribute to it forever. With a traditional IRA, you can't add any more money once the account holder reaches age 70½. In fact, the traditional IRA mandates that you start withdrawing money once you reach that age. There is no withdrawal requirement with a Roth IRA.

With existing IRAs, as we said, earnings grow tax-deferred, but are taxed upon withdrawal.

This brings up an intriguing point, which makes retirement planning complicated. Because IRA contributions are deductible for many taxpayers and compound tax-deferred, they are a great advantage for retirement saving. But note the "tax-deferred," meaning they are taxed at ordinary income when you retire, or conceivably as high as a 40 percent or higher rate in some jurisdictions. If you invested the money outside an IRA, it would not be deductible, but it would be taxed at the far more advantageous capital gains rate when sold in the future. What does this mean? If you are unlikely to trade much, it could prove more advantageous to take advantage of the lower capital gains rate in the future. There are so many uncertainties when you make decisions with implications decades down the road, such as what the future capital gains rate will be, what personal income tax rates will be, and what your tax rate will be when you need the money. Also, there is no guarantee that Congress will keep the non-taxability of Roth IRAs. With these uncertainties, I think it is fair to say that the deductible IRA is a good option for most. Those whose income is too high to allow the deduction should think about their options.

Obviously, this new Roth IRA is a wonderful tool. After all, who wouldn't want the earnings on their retirement savings to grow tax-free? Since it is such a good opportunity, you may want to help your children open an account as soon as possible. If parents or grandparents are able, they can subsidize teenage workers through allowances or gifts, so that even teenagers can begin their retirement savings by using their earnings for Roth IRA contributions. (Anyone can open a Roth IRA, as long as they have earned income.) That's why I have continued my children's allowances. The allowance lets them save the money they earned from their summer jobs and still have money to buy CDs and the like.

Where should your children invest the money they put inside a Roth IRA? That's an easy question. Simply have them invest their contributions in a growth-oriented mutual fund or even an index fund, and let the compounding begin. I promise they will thank you when they retire in forty-five years.

The Question of Trusts

Obviously, one way to invest for your children is through the use of trusts. The most common one goes by the name of the law that created it, the Uniform Gift to Minors Act. This type of account allows an adult to act as a custodian for a minor, who is actually the owner of the account. Assets in the account become the minor's to do with as he wishes once he reaches the age of majority, which is 18 in most states. The fact that the minor owns the trust sets up a potential problem that we will note in a minute. But first, let's discuss the primary benefit of the UGMA.

There can be significant tax advantages to UGMA accounts. The primary one is that initially earnings in the UGMA are taxed at the child's tax rate. For children under 14, the first $650 of earnings each year in an UGMA are not taxed, and the next $650 are taxed at the minor's tax rate of 15 percent. (Earnings over $1,300, however, are taxed at the adult's tax rate. For children over 14, all earnings are taxed at the child's tax rate of 15 percent.) Since the child's tax rate is usually lower than an adult's, there can be tax savings if you create an UGMA.

An UGMA can contain any kind of security. There are no limitations. However, there are two points I want to stress.

1. Gifts from an adult to a minor that exceed more than $10,000 per year are considered taxable and could be subject to gift tax, which would be paid by the person making the gift.
2. Once you place the asset into the account you have made an irrevocable gift. You may not take it back. (The gift may be returned to the donor once the minor reaches the age of majority, which differs by state, if that is what he or she chooses to do. Potential gift taxes, would, of course, apply.)

Until the minor reaches the age of majority, the custodian has full control over the UGMA and is charged with fiduciary responsibilities in managing it. At maturity, the child gains control of the account—and therein lies the problem.

You might have planned that the money be used for college, but your child may have other ideas. Unfortunately, if she decides she would rather have a Porsche than an undergraduate degree, she may very well end up with one. By definition it's her money once she becomes of age, and she can do with it as she pleases.

One way to get around the problem of having the child take control of the assets at age 18 is to create what is known as a minor's trust. It is similar to an UGMA, but assets are not turned over to the beneficiary until age 21.

A better option is to set up an irrevocable trust for the benefit of the child. We will discuss in detail how irrevocable trusts work in chapter 17, "Wealth Preservation: Strategies That Work," but let's touch on the highlights here.

The first thing to stress is the word "irrevocable." Once you place assets into the trust, they are no longer yours. And unlike in some trusts, here you *cannot* name yourself a trustee. However, just because you cannot be the trustee doesn't mean you don't have a say in how the assets are going to be handled. You do. In fact, you can allocate them just about any way you want.

You can give the child a certain percentage of the assets at specific intervals—20 percent when she turns 25, another 20 percent at 30, another 20 percent at 35, and so on. Or you can stipulate that she gets 100 percent of the assets at a specific point, say when she turns 35. You can give her the interest portion of the portfolio only, if you wish, leaving the assets to someone else at her death. You can even grant total discretion to the trustee to do what he thinks is in the best interest of the child. There is basically no limit on how the trust can be structured.

Aside from the obvious point that you are going to need professional help, there are three specific factors you should be aware of if you want to create a trust:

- **It makes sense only if you have significant assets.** The reason for that is the cost involved. Attorneys' fees to establish the trust can cost as much as $5,000.
- **Determine how the income within the trust is going to be taxed.** Once the assets in the trust have generated more than $8,250 in income, the trust is taxed at a rate of 39.6 percent. Taxes might be substantially less if the assets were kept outside of a trust.
- **There will be ongoing costs to keep the trust operating.** Federal, state, and local (if applicable) tax returns will have to be filed each year.

In Summary

You have gained a significant amount of knowledge about investing over the years. Passing along what you have learned to a child or grandchild can be as important as giving him a financial leg up in life. While the money you can give him—in whatever form you choose to give it—certainly can help, giving him the foundation that will allow him to handle his own finances successfully in coming years could prove to be invaluable.

16

Rethinking Retirement Planning: All the Rules Have Changed

As my mother became increasingly ill over the last few years of her life, my father was helpless to prevent her decline. But I know it gave him great comfort that he could at least retain control of the quality of her care, the benefit of a lifetime of saving and investing. As her needs increased—from ever more at-home care to day care and ultimately to assisted living—he was still able to provide the best care possible. Isn't this ultimately the goal of us all: to provide security in retirement, with a cushion for the unexpected; to be able to take care of our loved ones?

Even if we know what we want in retirement, getting from here to there can be challenging, if not downright daunting. Traditional retirement planning may not be up to the task, given how much has changed in our economy and society in the last few decades. To determine the best strategies for today, we talked directly to people about their futures.

A funny thing happened when we started asking people about their plans for retirement. Almost no one said they wanted to retire. And when PaineWebber, in conjunction with the Gallup Organization, surveyed investors about retirement, we received a similar response. An overwhelming number of the people interviewed indicated that they fully expect to continue working once they reach retirement age. Only 15 percent of the investors polled said they plan to travel, pursue leisure activities, "enjoy life," and not work.

And that was true of just about everyone talked to, regardless of his or her current age or income. Of the 986 investors with employment income surveyed, some 566 were "average" investors, with investable assets of $10,000 to $100,000. The remaining 420 were "substantial" investors, with investable assets of more than $100,000. Of course, since this survey included only investors, the results are not applicable to all of society. But even among this relatively sophisticated group, many are not realistic about what it will take to retire comfortably.

The accompanying table, organized by age and gender of respondent, summarizes the results of the survey.

As the table shows, five distinct groups emerged from the survey. The first were those people who fully expect that they will continue working in their current job until they are no longer able to perform in a satisfactory way. Those people represented 15 percent of the overall group.

Investors' Plans for Retirement

Activities	Overall* %	18–34 Male	35–49 Male	50–64 Male	18–34 Female	35–49 Female	50–64 Female
Work as long as I can	15%	12%	16%	19%	8%	12%	22%
Become an entrepreneur	26%	44%	27%	18%	23%	23%	22%
Seek a new job	34%	28%	36%	37%	32%	34%	30%
Seek work/life balance	10%	4%	12%	18%	6%	9%	9%
Enjoy a traditional retirement	15%	12%	10%	8%	31%	22%	16%

Source: PaineWebber's Index of Investor Optimism

The largest number of responders said that they intend to change careers. Most of the people who answered this way said they plan to become an entrepreneur and start their own business (26 percent), or seek a new job (34 percent). For many, that will mean taking a hobby, such as photography, and turning it into some type of a moneymaking venture.

Another group indicated that they would like to continue to work, but at a much reduced pace. They want to continue their employment (perhaps not at their current job, but by doing something else) *and* spend time with their families and enjoy leisure activities. They were looking forward to finding a greater balance in their lives.

And that brings us to the remaining 15 percent, who said that they wanted to enjoy what we would call a traditional retirement. They said they planned to leave the workforce and spend their time pursuing leisure activities and "enjoying life."

Can They Afford to Do This?

We were amazed at how confident these investors were in their assumption that they would live very comfortably once they moved into retirement, no matter how they defined it. Some 92 percent felt that they would have more than enough money to support their new way of life.

They gave two distinct reasons for their optimism: One, they fully expected that their largest expenses, such as putting their children through college and paying the mortgage each month, would be behind them. Two, they felt the majority of their retirement income would be derived from their own savings and investments.

To their credit, they said they did not expect to rely on the government, Social Security, or defined benefit plans such as corporate pensions—which, as we have seen, have been steadily declining in favor of defined contribution plans like 401(k)s. However, it appears they may not have thought through how much money they are going to need in the future.

Consider, for instance, their belief that most of the funds they will draw on will come from personal savings and investments. That certainly might happen, but it hasn't been the historical norm. For people over 65 who have stopped working, the combination of Social Security and corporate pensions accounts for 63 percent of income.

That percentage falls, but not dramatically, for people over 65 whose annual income is over $50,000 a year. Pensions (28 percent) and Social Security (21 percent) still make up nearly half of their retirement income.

In fact, in 1995 the median value of families' retirement income generated from savings and investments was just $15,600, according to the Federal Reserve.

Most investors are very comfortable with the idea that they will have enough money to retire the way they want. Unfortunately, the reality is they may have substantially underestimated how much money they are going to need.

As people retire in the future, more and more of the income that they'll need will have to come from their investments and/or some form of continued employment. This is a fact that most people have not yet come to grips with. Consider:

- Few—only a third of the people surveyed—have really set up a plan to focus on how much they are going to need when they do retire.
- Another 38 percent said that they had considered their retirement needs a "moderate amount."
- The remaining investors (29 percent) told us they have given it "little or no thought."

This means that two out of three people have yet to give retirement planning serious attention. Perhaps even worse, studies have shown that when they do start to plan, they underestimate by as much as two-thirds how much money they are going to need.

These numbers can lead to only one sobering conclusion: the majority of people really don't know how they are going to achieve the financial freedom that defines a successful retirement. They need to plan more in order to be able to define a successful retirement on their own terms.

Given that the old way of thinking about retirement has produced these potential shortfalls, a new way of considering the issue is called for. While everyone's description of what retirement is going to look like is different, the desire for financial freedom and flexibility remains universal. You want to make sure you will have all the money you need, and to consider strategies that might allow that to happen.

Here's How to Rethink Retirement

Here's a thought that should shape your planning as you go about rethinking your retirement planning: the odds are you are going to be retired for longer than you think. People are retiring from full employment earlier. The average investor today is planning on leaving his or her job at age 62, and younger workers (those 18–34) are thinking of quitting even earlier. They say they'll retire at age 58.

At the same time, people are living longer. The average life expectancy in America, according to the Bureau of the Census, is expected to climb to 81 by the year 2010.

The combination of retiring earlier—at somewhere around age 60—and a longer life span means that you should plan on funding a retirement that could last *at least* twenty to twenty-five years. (And you could be retired for a lot longer. People over 80 are one of the fastest-growing segments of the population.)

Obviously, if you live longer, you will need more money. Unfortunately, the traditional sources of retirement funds are becoming harder to find.

- Corporations have switched from providing pensions—which would guarantee you a certain amount of income each month once you retired—to defined contribution plans, where the amount of money you receive will be determined by how much you (and in some cases your company) contribute to the plan and how much those contributions appreciate or earn by the time you retire. Defined contribution plans have many advantages, but a secure monthly check for life is not one of them.

- Social Security will probably not be as big a part of your retirement funds as it was for previous generations. It alone will be inadequate to fund the kind of retirement most of us want, but that should not come as a surprise. Social Security was never meant to be more than a supplement to the rest of your retirement income.
- There is the problem of inflation. Even if it stays benign, it will cut into the money you have available. At a 3.1 percent inflation rate, which is what inflation has historically averaged in recent times, something that costs you $1 today will cost $1.84 twenty years from now. You need to build that 84 percent (or more) increase in prices into your retirement planning.

But there are more than these three macroeconomic forces that will be draining your retirement funds. There are personal issues as well.

If you are one of the people thinking of starting a new business once you "retire," you are going to need start-up capital. While you certainly could borrow the money or raise it from investors, knowing that you have what you need in your own accounts (or at least a significant portion of what you need to get started) can make the start-up process less stressful. And there is the question of how you want to live once you retire. You may not want to cut back.

The conventional wisdom is that you will need 70 to 80 percent of your current income once you retire. The thinking goes that you can get by on less than you do now because certain expenses—such as commuting—vanish once you retire. But many people will continue working once they reach traditional retirement age, so employment-related expenses are unlikely to decrease—and others, such as health care, are bound to increase. In addition, I have yet to meet anyone who wanted to cut back on his or her standard of living at any time. That argues for having as much money as possible in retirement.

When you realize how long you may be retired, the idea of shifting completely—or even substantially—into fixed-income investments once you reach traditional retirement age may no longer make much sense.

In this new kind of retirement—one that will start earlier and last longer than it has in the past—people must think differently.

One conventional asset allocation of stocks used to be: "Subtract your age from 100." So, the "right answer" for someone 65 years old would be to have 35 percent of their money in stocks, with the rest of the money allocated to bonds and/or cash equivalents. If you followed this formula—and many people did—then the older you got, the smaller the percentage of stocks in your portfolio got. And the percentage of fixed-income holdings rose.

That formula may no longer work, given longer life expectancies and the fact that fixed-income investments now offer moderate returns at best. People who are 65 years old today run a substantial risk that their investments won't grow fast enough to support the lifestyle they want, if they have only 35 percent of their portfolio in stocks.

If you are looking at a retirement investment time horizon of several decades, you may need more growth than fixed-income vehicles can provide. We have said throughout that when you are investing for the long term, equities should make up the majority of your portfolio—and that is true even for people who plan on retiring in their sixties. After all, it is not your age that should dictate your investment choices, but your financial goals.

Obviously, each individual has to make choices based on his or her assets and goals, but in this new environment it will make sense for many retirees to continue to have stocks as the mainstay of their portfolios. After all, if you are going to need the money for twenty years, you are going to need it to grow.

Today, many people in their sixties should be thinking of themselves as long-term investors. That means they should have a significant portion of their portfolio invested in stocks.

How to Think About Retirement Today

The traditional way of thinking about retirement—as a time you take it easy and reap the rewards of a lifetime of hard work—is giving way to a new definition. The odds are that you are going to work, in one form or another, longer than you think, and that this new form of retirement is going to last a long time. If you are going to live longer, you are going to need more money, and even if you are in your sixties or early seventies, you should be thinking like a long-term investor.

The biggest advantage that you have as you go about planning your retirement is time, for nowhere is the power of compounding more important than when it comes to retirement planning.

Consider saving for retirement as rewarding yourself for working. In effect, you are paying yourself first and building a solid foundation for enjoying the time in your life when work won't be the first priority.

As your money starts to grow, the power of compounding will help your savings to increase more rapidly. By now, this is familiar territory. Early Starter starts saving $2,000 a year, every year, when he is 25, and Late Starter, who is the same age as Early Starter, also saves $2,000 a year, but he doesn't get started until age 35. Both save until they reach age 60, and they both earn 8% a year on their investments. (And to make life easy we won't take charges, commissions, fees or expenses into consideration as we do the math.) When they reach age 60, Late Starter has $157,909, but Early Starter, who saved for an extra 10 years, has more than double that, $372,204 to be exact. In fact, Early Starter could have stopped contributing the same year that Late Starter began and he still would have come out ahead. He would have ended up with $214,296 to Late Starter's $157,909. (See chart on pages 244 and 245.)

By now this should be your mantra: *start saving as much as you can as early as you can.*

Also, remember that tax deferral is one of the most important tools in retirement planning. "Try not to pay a tax today that you can put off until tomorrow!" is good advice because, over the long term, you will retain the use of Uncle Sam's money and your nest egg can potentially grow faster. The

Starting Early to Save

Age	Early Starter		Late Starter		Early Starter (stops contributing after 10 years)
	Jan. 1	Dec. 31	Jan. 1	Dec. 31	Dec. 31
25	$2,000	$2,160			
26	$4,160	$4,493			
27	$6,493	$7,012			
28	$9,012	$9,733			
29	$11,733	$12,672			
30	$14,672	$15,846			
31	$17,846	$19,273			
32	$21,273	$22,975			
33	$24,975	$26,973			
34	$28,973	$31,291			$31,291
35	$33,291	$35,954	$2,000	$2,160	$33,794
36	$37,954	$40,991	$4,160	$4,493	$36,498
37	$42,991	$46,430	$6,493	$7,012	$39,418
38	$48,430	$52,304	$9,012	$9,733	$42,571
39	$54,304	$58,649	$11,733	$12,672	$45,977
40	$60,649	$65,500	$14,672	$15,846	$49,655
41	$67,500	$72,900	$17,846	$19,273	$53,627
42	$74,900	$80,893	$21,273	$22,975	$57,917
43	$82,893	$89,524	$24,975	$26,973	$62,551
44	$91,524	$98,846	$28,973	$31,291	$67,555
45	$100,846	$108,914	$33,291	$35,954	$72,959
46	$110,914	$119,787	$37,954	$40,991	$78,796
47	$121,787	$131,530	$42,991	$46,430	$85,100
48	$133,530	$144,212	$48,430	$52,304	$91,908
49	$146,212	$157,909	$54,304	$58,649	$99,260
50	$159,909	$172,702	$60,649	$65,500	$107,201
51	$174,702	$188,678	$67,500	$72,900	$115,777
52	$190,678	$205,932	$74,900	$80,893	$125,039

Age	Early Starter		Late Starter		Early Starter (stops contributing after 10 years)
	Jan. 1	**Dec. 31**	**Jan. 1**	**Dec. 31**	**Dec. 31**
53	$207,932	$224,566	$82,893	$89,524	$135,042
54	$226,566	$244,692	$91,524	$98,846	$145,846
55	$246,692	$266,427	$100,846	$108,914	$157,514
56	$268,427	$289,901	$110,914	$119,787	$170,115
57	$291,901	$315,253	$121,787	$131,530	$183,724
58	$317,253	$342,634	$133,530	$144,212	$198,422
59	$344,634	**$372,204**	$146,212	**$157,909**	**$214,295**

Source: PaineWebber

fact that you have to pay the tax at some point down the line is less important, because you will be taking advantage of compound interest growth on all of your assets.

The chart on page 246 illustrates how a stream of $2,000 investments per year for twenty-five years at 8 percent growth with a 31 percent tax rate fares over the planning horizon. The third bar shows the value of the account on a pretax basis ($157,900). Assuming the account is liquidated after twenty-five years, and taxes are paid, the remaining amount is about $109,000. Had taxes been paid each year on the growth, the account would have been worth only about $74,700.

And of course, you need to factor inflation into your planning. That's a formidable challenge, because the many economic, political, and social factors that impact its rise and fall make projecting an inflation rate tricky. What we know for sure is that a high rate of inflation can have a dramatic impact on your purchasing power over time.

But we also know there is a very definite trade-off between risk and return. The so-called risk-free investments, such as bank accounts and Treasury bills, carry risk because they are adversely impacted by inflation. The

interest you earn on these instruments is often very close to the rate of inflation, which can have the effect of stagnating the growth of your assets. The
challenge, then, is to balance the various risks and develop a portfolio designed to meet your retirement objectives.

A Four-Step Plan

Getting started may be one of the biggest challenges you face. Even if you
are already under way, you probably want to check your progress against the
following four-step process. Each step can make your retirement planning
easier, and the result more enjoyable.

Step 1. Determine where you are and what resources you are likely to have in the future

Assessing your current financial situation and determining a retirement income goal give a snapshot of where you are now and where you want to be.
It will also enable you to decide which savings tools to employ to help you
meet your retirement income goal.

A $2,000 per Year Investment After 25 Years

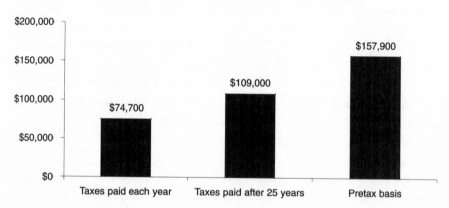

Source: *PaineWebber*

To get a realistic idea of how much money you are going to need in retirement, you need to answer three questions:

- **When will you retire?** This question will govern every other decision you make. Many people in their twenties, thirties, and forties are tempted to answer, "When I am in my mid-fifties." And that is a perfectly acceptable response—if you can afford to do it. But that may be more difficult than it sounds. If you retire early, you make funding your retirement three times as hard.

  First, you reduce the amount of money you can save, since you will be leaving the workforce early.

  Second, your retirement money will have to last longer. Someone with a life expectancy of 81 who retires at 65 needs her money to last sixteen years. That same person, retiring at 55, needs it to last twenty-six years—and she has denied herself a chance to earn retirement money between the ages of 55 and 65, because she has already left the workforce.

  Third, you reduce the amount of Social Security you'll receive. Even if you leave the workforce early, you cannot apply for Social Security until you are 62. Since your Social Security benefits are based on your forty quarters of highest earnings, you may be reducing the amount of benefits you receive by leaving the workforce early. And by taking those benefits early, you certainly are. For example, someone born after 1960 who takes Social Security at age 62 will receive just 70 percent of what she would receive if she waited until "full retirement age"—which for her is 67.

- **How much money will you need?** My advice is to estimate on the high side. Traditionally, experts say that you will need about 75 percent of what you earned in the last year on the job to maintain your standard of living in retirement. It could be less than that if you are planning to move to a place with a lower cost of living once you retire. However, to be on the safe side—and to make sure that you can do everything in retirement you've dreamed of—you might budget as if you need 100 percent of your current income.

- **How long will you need it?** Obviously you'll want the money you have saved to last as long as your projected life expectancy. But again you might want to budget on the high side, for two reasons: first, you may live longer than the actuarial tables predict, and second, you'll definitely want to budget higher if you are planning on leaving any assets to your heirs.

That's how you determine what your retirement goals should be. To strategize, you need to assess your current situation.

- **What is your current financial situation?** What do you currently have saved for retirement? How much, realistically, is that likely to grow between now and when you will need the money? (Be sure to include not only how much you plan to save but also what you truly expect to earn on all the money you have saved for retirement.) What do you have in savings, outside of your retirement accounts? How much is it likely to grow? Will you be getting a pension? How much will it be? Is it indexed for inflation? Will you be working? How much do you expect to make? Will there be other income coming in? How much do you expect to receive from Social Security? (The Social Security Administration can tell you.)

As you know, Social Security will provide only a percentage of your pre-retirement income once you stop working, and your employer may not sponsor a pension plan. As a result, you will want to identify the income sources you now have and the ones you will have, and set a realistic goal for what you will need. These are important questions to answer before moving forward in the retirement planning process.

Step 2. Develop your savings strategy

Once you have gathered the relevant information about where you currently are financially and have projected where you would like to be, you can begin to do some computations. How much will you have to save, and how much will those savings have to grow, for you to meet your retirement goals? There are numerous software packages that could help, and so could your financial advisers.

Once you have determined the shortfall, you have, in essence, created your plan. Eliminating this shortfall becomes your savings goal.

Step 3. Implement your strategy

Now that you have determined how much to save, you can begin to execute a strategy that will help you meet your goals. Of course, you are going to draw on all the tools and resources at your disposal, but give special emphasis to whatever tax-deferred and tax-free savings vehicles are available to you. Also, remember to allocate *all* the assets in your portfolio among different types of investments in order to balance risk against potential rewards.

Step 4. Assess your progress regularly

Up until this point in the process, you have determined your goals, defined how you are going to achieve them, and have begun to save and invest. The last step is to periodically review how well you are doing. Specifically, you want to check that you have done everything that you were supposed to do (hit your saving targets; use all available tax-advantaged investments, and so forth). And you have to determine if your investments are performing the way you would like, and if any changes in your strategy are called for.

This review should take place at least annually. Expectations, assumptions, and economic realities often change—and your plan needs to reflect these changes. Perhaps last year's optimistic goal of retiring at age 50 does not seem realistic in light of your daughter's decision to pursue an Ivy League Ph.D.

As you can see, planning for retirement is a daunting task. It is easy to put it off until later, but earlier is better than later, and later is infinitely better than never.

Now let's review some other ideas you might consider regarding the future. Let's start with a way you can increase the amount of money you have available in retirement.

- The 401(k) today is one of the best ways to build wealth. Many companies have 401(k) plans. They offer tax-deductible contributions, tax-deferred growth, and usually a wide variety of investment choices. If your company matches your contribution, your return soars. For example, if your firm adds $1 for every $2 you put in, you have a 50 percent return on your money even before you decide where to invest. That leverage can be enormous.
- For individuals who are self-employed or who work for a company but have additional sources of income—perhaps consulting work—there are advantages to setting up a business retirement program. There are programs that are flexible and that don't require a lot of administration. And it's, again, another way to put away money for retirement.
- Finally, IRAs are a great savings vehicle. You should supplement whatever savings program you've set for yourself using the IRA.

The 1 Percent Solution

If you don't think you can fund your company retirement plan to the maximum immediately, there is a strategy that you might consider. We call it the 1 percent solution. It's an easy, systematic way to increase your retirement plan contributions by 1 percent each year, until you reach the maximum allowable amount.

Consider two people just starting out in the workforce. Both John and Sally make $25,000 a year and contribute 6 percent, ($1,500 a year) into their 401(k) plans the first year they are eligible. John decides to implement the 1 percent solution and increases his contribution by 1 percent annually for the next nine years, until he reaches the maximum annual rate of 15 percent allowed by his plan, and then he maintains his contribution at that level. Sally does not.

If both John and Sally earn a hypothetical 8 percent on the money they put into the plan, at the end of thirty years John would accumulate $307,387. Sally would have just $152,496 in her plan—in other words, half the amount.

The suggested course of action is clear: if you can't fund your retirement plan to the maximum right away, try to increase what you put in over time.

Making the Most of Your IRAs

There are a couple of aspects of individual retirement accounts (IRAs) that even sophisticated investors get wrong.

Perhaps the biggest mistake they make is ignoring them. Yes, you can contribute "only" $2,000 a year, and yes, that contribution is no longer deductible for many people; but even so, earnings, dividends, and capital gains grow *tax-deferred* in traditional IRA accounts, and *tax-free* in Roth IRAs (although eligibility is limited by income—currently you cannot have more than $110,000 in adjusted gross income if you are single, or $160,000 if you are a couple filing jointly, to invest through a Roth IRA).

Investors should also consider consolidating their IRAs. Over the years, you may have opened one IRA at your brokerage firm, another where you bank and a third—or fourth, or fifth—somewhere else.

If you combine your IRA accounts, life is much simpler. Not only will you cut down on the number of IRA statements you receive, but you'll be able to see at a glance everything that you own in your IRAs. That makes it easier to fit your IRA investments into your overall asset allocation. Finally, having one IRA account makes handling required minimum distributions easier. It is a relatively small point, but an important one. Investors should consider funding their IRAs to the maximum and try to keep those funds in one account, if possible.

Social Security

Social Security benefits are useful but hardly constitute government largesse. (The Social Security Administration will give you a written estimate of what your benefits could be at retirement. All you have to do is ask, and that's a good idea no matter what your age.) A 44-year-old baby boomer who retires at age 66—the age that she can receive full Social Security benefits—will be entitled to a maximum of $1,500 a month. Certainly, you aren't likely to leave a $1,500 check uncashed, but it is awfully hard to live the way you want on $18,000 a year. To help put that number in perspective, consider that the average retiree living on at least $50,000 a year depends on Social Security for just 21 percent of his retirement income.

Also, you may not be receiving that money as soon as you think. Congress has raised the "full retirement age." That's when you get your full Social Security benefits.

Age 65, right?

Probably not. Recognizing that people are living longer and that the resources of the Social Security Administration are finite, full retirement age has been pushed back. The following table tells the story.

If your full retirement age is older than 65 (if you were born in 1938 or later), you still will be able to take Social Security early, but the reduction in your benefits will be greater than it is for people retiring now.

Here's an example. If your full retirement age is 67, the reduction for starting your benefits at 62 will be about 30 percent; at age 63, about 25 percent; at age 64, about 20 percent; at age 65, about 13 percent; and at age 66, about 6 percent. As a general rule, early retirement will give you about the

Age to Receive Full Social Security Benefits

Year of Birth	Full Retirement Age
1937 or earlier	65
1938	65 and 2 months
1939	65 and 4 months
1940	65 and 6 months
1941	65 and 8 months
1942	65 and 10 months
1943–54	66
1955	66 and 2 months
1956	66 and 4 months
1957	66 and 6 months
1958	66 and 8 months
1959	66 and 10 months
1960 and later	67

Source: Social Security Administration

same total Social Security benefits over your lifetime—but in smaller amounts, because you will be receiving benefits longer. This is something to keep in mind if you are thinking of retiring early or are counting on Social Security to make up a large part of your retirement income.

Conversely, it can pay you to wait to apply for Social Security. Let's use another table to show how this works.

While this is a good deal, there is a limit. There is no benefit to waiting beyond age 70. The yearly increase stops at that point, so you might as well take the money.

Increases for Delayed Retirement

Year of Birth	Yearly Rate of Increase for Waiting
1917–24	3%
1925–26	3.5%
1927–28	4%
1929–30	4.5%
1931–32	5%
1933–34	5.5%
1935–36	6%
1937–38	6.5%
1939–40	7%
1941–42	7.5%
1943 or later	8%

But whether you take the money early or late, the government is going to be hard pressed to maintain the current level of benefits. As the National Commission on Retirement Policy explained in *The 21st Century Retirement Security Plan,* the prognosis is grim:

The imminent retirement of "the baby boom generation," combined with longer life expectancies, will place extraordinary pressures on the economic resources necessary to sustain the rising standard of living that Americans have come to expect—and potentially fray the vital threads of the safety net programs the government provides for senior citizens.

Federal entitlement programs [which include Social Security] . . . consume an ever-increasing share of our country's financial resources. Spending on entitlements (principally federal health and retirement programs) has more than doubled since 1963 and now accounts for almost half of federal outlays. By the government's own estimates, at the current rate of federal spending, entitlements could absorb all government revenues by 2030.

Without significant public policy and social responses to the impending challenges, the standard of living for retirees after the first quarter of the 21st Century could decline. Society simply will be unable to afford all the promises we have made absent change.

Presently, inflows to the Social Security system exceed benefits paid out. The program's Trust Fund will begin to pay out more in benefits than it collects in payroll taxes soon after the baby boomers begin retiring, however, and will run even larger annual operating deficits thereafter. According to the Social Security trustees, if no action is taken in the interim, the Trust Fund will be entirely depleted by 2032.

The following table brings that problem vividly to life. As you can see, there has been—and will continue to be—a continuing strain on the Social Security system.

The commission (which included PaineWebber's chairman and CEO, Donald B. Marron, as one of its cochairs) made a number of recommendations—including privatizing part of the Social Security system—that can

Help Wanted

The Number of Workers Contributing to the Social Security System for Each Recipient

1945	41.9
1960	5.1
1995	3.3
2020	2.4

Source: OASDI Trustees Report

serve as a road map for reform. Those recommendations will be debated in coming years.

In the interim, the safest thing investors can do is acknowledge that Social Security benefits may not account for a significant portion of their retirement income, and plan accordingly.

Summary

Traditional views of retirement have meant that most Americans planned to accumulate only those resources they needed to live comfortably once they stopped working completely. As we enter the new millennium, however, the vast majority of investors want to remain active in retirement. They want to work, but at something they enjoy.

But as we have seen, there is a major disconnect between the way most investors view retirement and their recognition of the amount of savings and planning they will need to achieve their goals.

While retirement has different meanings to different people, everyone needs to develop his own unique plan to prepare for a retirement that will allow him to live as he likes.

The following seven guidelines have worked for investors who have been able to retire successfully, on their own terms.

Start early

The longer you put off preparing for retirement, the more you will have to save in order to maintain the standard of living you had while working. An early start is particularly important. Many investors underestimate the amount of money they will need during retirement, both because they don't know how much they will actually require—and they estimate too low—and because they misjudge how long their retirement is going to last. (It will probably be longer than they think.) And equally important, an early start gives you more time to enjoy the benefits of compounding.

Think long-term

Incorporate retirement planning into your current lifestyle, and plan on being retired for at least twenty years, and probably thirty years, if you are thinking of retiring early. Reap the benefits of your long-term time frame by taking advantage of stocks' greater returns over time.

Define needs and goals

Your age, time until retirement (or the point at which you expect to need the money), and your risk tolerance are key factors to consider in drawing up your retirement plan.

Rebalance when necessary

The values of your investments change over time. Stocks can soar, making the equity portion of your portfolio greater than you initially established. Periodically evaluate your portfolio's performance and rebalance the way your investments are allocated to make sure that they reflect your preferences and market conditions.

Remember that there are two kinds of risk: volatility risk and inflation risk

While you always want to keep in mind that the value of equities will fluctuate more than either bonds or cash, don't forget about the risk that inflation is going to erode the value of your money, when you are thinking about how your retirement money should be invested. Odds are you are going to be retired for longer than you think. That argues for having equities as a significant part of your investment portfolio.

Avoid overreacting to volatility

The markets will go up and down. Try not to be concerned by every move. Remember, you are in it for the long term. What happens today will probably have little effect on the value of your portfolio twenty years from now.

Be consistent

Stick with your savings goal and investment plan and avoid withdrawals from your retirement account if at all possible during the time you are building up your assets. As you learned a long time ago, the power of a retirement plan is derived from consistent regular savings; the effects of tax-deferred compounding; and the long-term trend of markets to move consistently higher. You want to take advantage of all three factors for as long as you can.

17

Wealth Preservation: Strategies That Work

One daughter an estate and tax lawyer, one a social worker, the third working on Wall Street—surely we would have worked with our parents on an adequate estate plan well in advance of it being necessary. But we sisters, "experts" in our fields, were all so uncomfortable with the subject, and equally reluctant to appear greedy for our parents' hard-earned assets, that when our several halfhearted attempts to broach the topic met with disinterest, we dropped the subject, knowing that we would pay dearly for our reticence.

Fortunately, after our mother passed away, our father did deal with estate planning in time to avoid paying unnecessary taxes. But as you can see, I know personally how hard it is to face the unpleasant task of planning for life's two certainties: death and taxes.

You may have the same problem.

Let's see if this describes you: You've always worked hard to provide for your family's well-being. You've put money away for your children's—or grandchildren's—education. You've reduced your current tax burden by investing in tax-free and tax-deferred vehicles. You've given more than your fair share to charity and your local community. You've set aside money for your own retirement.

So far, so good. But like many investors today you may have left out one important element in your overall financial plan—detailed wealth-preservation planning. While you probably have a will—and life insurance as well—that may not be sufficient to ensure your assets are distributed the way you want upon your death. And they certainly aren't the best way to reduce whatever estate taxes might be owed.

If you don't know very much about estate-protection strategies, you are not alone. Most people don't, and that is not surprising. Wealth preservation was once considered necessary only for the very well-to-do. Today, however, almost everyone can benefit from a properly planned estate—even though, as my sisters and I clearly demonstrated, there can be a natural reluctance to address the issue.

No matter how sophisticated or experienced you are as an investor, wealth-preservation strategies may be the most difficult—from both a legal and emotional point of view—part of all the financial planning you do. That's why estate planning is the area where getting professional help is virtually essential. Not only can it help you avoid having your estate pay more taxes than are necessary; having a professional involved in the planning part—everything from the creation of a will to the establishment of trusts—can make the process emotionally less wrenching. And the complicated legal issues require legal expertise.

In fact, it is becoming common for the person who is creating an estate plan to have his or her estate lawyer meet with the beneficiaries, once all the paperwork is complete, to help explain what provisions have been made and why. That helps reduce some of the emotional turmoil surrounding the process and can help eliminate hard feelings (or worse) later on.

Reducing the stress involved in creating an estate plan is one key reason you want to have a professional involved. Minimizing your potential tax burden is another. As you can see from the following table, estate taxes start at 37 percent and go even higher—much higher. For example, you'll notice that once your estate has reached $3 million, each additional dollar is taxed at 55 percent. Between $11 million and $21 million the incremental tax rate is 60 percent, although it "falls" back to 55% for estates over $21 million.

Not only is the tax rate high, it is due virtually immediately. Estate taxes must be paid within nine months of death. Any delay results in penalties equal to 5 percent of the money owed *per month,* and interest is charged on top of that.

You can ask for an extension, but they are extremely difficult to obtain.

Estate Taxes

Your Taxable Estate	Tax (Before Subtracting the Unified Tax Credit)*
$500,000–$750,000	$155,800 plus 37% of amount over $500,000
$750,000–$1 million	$248,300 plus 39% of amount over $750,000
$1–1.25 million	$345,800 plus 41% of amount over $1 million
$1.25–1.5 million	$448,300 plus 43% of amount over $1.25 million
$1.5–2 million	$555,800 plus 45% of amount over $1.5 million
$2–2.5 million	$780,000 plus 49% of amount over $2 million
$2.5–3 million	$1,025,800 plus 53% of amount over $2.5 million
$3–10 million	$1,290,800 plus 55% of amount over $3 million
$10 million–$17,184,000	$5,140,800 plus 60% of amount over $10 million
$17,184,000 and over	$9,451,200 plus 55% of amount over $17,184,000

Source: Internal Revenue Service
* The unified tax credit was $200,555 in 2000, eliminating taxes for estates valued at $675,000 or less. The Taxpayer Relief Act of 1997 provides for that credit increasing to $229,800 in 2002 and 2003; $287,300 in 2004; $326,300 in 2005; and $345,800 in 2006 and thereafter. At that point, the unified tax credit would have the effect of eliminating taxes on the first $1 million of an estate.

Even if the executor of your estate is able to persuade the IRS that an extension should be granted, interest still accrues until the estate tax is actually paid. (The late penalty, however, is waived.)

As dramatic as the financial consequences are, the human issues are even more compelling. Most people are concerned about what will happen after they are gone. Will their spouse be adequately cared for? Can they make sure their children don't receive their full inheritance until they are ready—in terms of both their investment knowledge and their maturity—to handle it? Can the family business stay in the family?

Dealing with all these issues requires extensive planning.

That planning begins, of course, with a will. But while it's a good first step, a will may not be enough to ensure an orderly, sensible, and timely disposition of your assets. What's more, a will can do very little to shield your assets from what could be substantial taxation.

Tax planning for your estate is mandatory unless you want to make Uncle Sam your primary beneficiary.

So, begin with a will. Use professional help here as well. While the do-it-yourself, software, download-a-will-from-the-Internet wills may, as their proponents argue, actually be valid in all fifty states, given the complicated laws and vehicles available, this is not a do-it-yourself proposition for most of us.

But even after creating your will, odds are you are going to have to do more. For tax reasons alone, if you have an estate over the amount exempted from federal estate taxes—$675,000 in the year 2000, gradually increasing to $1 million by 2006—you will need to establish a comprehensive estate plan. There really is no other choice.

Why a Will May Not Be Enough

Let's look at each piece of the estate-planning puzzle in detail. One of the biggest misconceptions about planning your estate is that a will is the best way to leave assets behind and provide for your heirs. That is simply not the case, unless your estate is below the threshold where taxation begins, that is, $675,000 in 2000.

It is true that a will can help develop the foundation of your estate plan. And a will can help direct the disposition of personal belongings (you can make sure your daughter gets your engagement ring after you die, for example) and lets you designate a guardian for your young children.

Clearly, all those things are beneficial. However, while a will outlines your wishes, there are several major problems with relying on just a will to leave assets behind and to provide for your heirs.

If you rely solely on a will, your estate may be subject to probate, and because of the way probate works, the result could be that the disposition of your assets is not exactly what you wish. Probate—the word is derived from the Latin for "to prove"—deals exclusively (if I may oversimplify) with two issues: Did the person making a will have the capacity to do so? Did he have a good idea of what he owned when the will was created? Until both those questions are answered to a judge's satisfaction—which could involve calling witnesses and introducing various kinds of evidence—none of your wishes can be carried out.

While procedures vary somewhat among states and various jurisdictions, the following facts are generally true if you rely solely on a will, and therefore are subject to probate:

- Your assets are frozen until the will has been probated, a procedure that can be done quickly (in states like Texas) or take more than a year (in other parts of the country, like New York, California, and Florida). During that time it will literally take an emergency court order to change the status of your assets, even if what needs to be done is as basic—but important—as replacing a roof on your house.
- Over many months, your assets and bequests are dragged through a public probate process, subject to the claims of heirs and creditors. Estates passed through wills are publicized and examined, particularly by relatives, and sometimes by neighbors, friends, and individuals seeking to take advantage of possible business opportunities.

  Although many people don't know this, wills are a matter of public record once they are filed with the court. (Indeed, periodically someone publishes a book reprinting verbatim the wills of the rich and famous. Those books are always entertaining—unless it is your family they are writing about.) And while the exact value of your assets is not disclosed, it is fairly easy to determine from both the will itself and the probate filings how much money you left behind. For example, many jurisdictions use a sliding scale for probate fees, based on the size of the estate. Those fees are a matter of public record. All someone has to do is look at what your estate paid in fees, and they can get a rough idea of what it is worth.
- Estate settlement costs increase with the size of the probated estate. (Indeed, some attorneys charge based on the size of your estate.) The

probate process, as we have seen, can take months or even years, depending on the jurisdiction. In the meantime, your assets may be tied up and could lose market value (if we suffer through a bear market, for example, or there is a sudden downturn in real estate prices.) This is a truly hidden cost of estate settlement.

- And finally, there is the issue of estate taxes, which a will can only partially address. You may pass any amount of property to your surviving spouse without paying federal estate taxes, through what is known as the unlimited marital deduction. In addition, you can pass to your heirs up to $675,000 (in 2000—and this amount gradually will be raised to $1 million by 2006) free of federal estate taxes. (This is on top of the $10,000 a year you can gift to anyone with no tax consequences.) However, any amount passed to a surviving spouse is subject to federal estate taxes upon the spouse's death. Federal estate taxes, as the table earlier in the chapter shows, are as high as 55 percent for taxable estates of $3 million or more, and the assets of large estates are taxed at the rate of 60 percent between $11 million and $21 million. In addition, state inheritance or death taxes also may apply.

If you have a relatively simple estate, and one valued at less than $1.35 million in 2000 (if you are married; $675,000 if you are not), a will may be all you need. (That's assuming that if you are married you establish a credit shelter trust. Details on page 266.)

But for more complicated and/or larger estates, given the extensive, cumbersome, and time-consuming process of probate, a will alone is an inefficient way to pass many assets to your heirs, and it does nothing to minimize estate taxes. What's more, if you become incapacitated, your will does nothing for *you*. In fact, a court may appoint an administrator to oversee your well-being.

I don't want to leave the impression that having a will lacks value. Far from it. Everyone with assets or dependents needs a will. For estates of any substance, a will serves to codify a variety of instructions, distribute miscellaneous property and personal belongings, and govern how you would like your funeral to be handled. However, the job of passing serious financial assets is best left to a trust or a series of trusts (you can have an unlimited number).

Trusts: A Review

Available for hundreds of years—since the rise of common law in England, in fact—trusts today combine investment and possible tax-saving opportunities with the ability to provide for the well-being of loved ones even after your death. Trusts can ensure that your assets will be used exactly as you intended. And if you have a trust you can make certain your heirs are not forced to liquidate valuable assets—the home that has been in your family for generations, your privately held business—to pay estate taxes that could have been avoided with judicious planning.

A trust may be the most essential component of an effectively constructed estate plan, because it allows you to

- **Manage estate taxes.** A trust can be an important part of strategies to minimize estate taxes. Through proper planning, a married couple can protect $2 million—$1 million each—from estate taxes in 2006 and beyond. The limit in 2000 is $1.35 million: $675,000 each. (We will talk about how to do this through a credit shelter, also known as an A-B trust, in a moment.)
- **Protect family assets.** When you leave assets to your spouse, and there is no trust, and your spouse remarries, the new spouse could eventually dictate the distribution of what were your assets. A trust can keep that from happening.
- **Minimize expenses.** Assets passed by trust avoid probate—and probate-related expenses. Since a trustee can move quickly to distribute assets to beneficiaries, assets passed by trust avoid the hidden expense of being tied up in probate court while they potentially lose value due to a change in market conditions.
- **Avoid publicity.** A trust is a private document and is not subject to public scrutiny. That is why people traditionally have used trusts to shield their financial affairs from public access. Trusts not only keep the details of your affairs out of the press; they also make it harder for people to present your heirs with "can't miss" business opportunities after you are gone.
- **Plan for incapacity.** A will has no effect until your death, but a trust allows for your assets and financial affairs to be managed temporarily

should you become incapacitated. Without a trust, a family member or an attorney must petition the court to declare you legally incapacitated or incompetent. If that petition is successful, the court will appoint someone to manage your affairs. Planning for this unfortunate circumstance is no small thing. If you are a baby boomer, the odds of your becoming incapacitated for some period within the coming year are ten times greater than the chance you will die.

Selecting the Right Trusts

The trusts you select will, of course, depend upon your personal financial situation and future objectives. But among the ones you probably want to consider—or reconsider—using are the following.

Revocable Living Trust

This is the simplest of all trust types. In a revocable living trust you, as the grantor of powers to the trust, may change or revoke all terms of the trust at any time. (Since the grantor retains this power, any assets placed into the trust continue to be taxed to the grantor. In fact, the trust uses your Social Security number for tax purposes.) You, the grantor, retain the power to

- cancel the trust
- change the trustee or any beneficiary
- add or remove assets
- add or revise any term of the trust

The revocable living trust can hold assets, as well as provide a number of other important advantages. You don't have to worry if trust assets will be available should you become ill or incapacitated. Anytime you require the use of trust assets, you can simply withdraw the money—or have the person you designated do it—just as if it were a personal account. Meanwhile, the trust will continue to hold the remaining assets and continue to administer them as you instructed. The trust can also instruct how the assets in the trust are distributed after death. The assets pass directly, avoiding probate and its costs and delays.

As you can see, the revocable living trust offers numerous benefits, including the saving of time and money. (The revocable living trust is tax neutral. There are no income, gift, or estate tax advantages or disadvantages to setting one up.)

Anyone can establish a revocable living trust. The only requirement is that you be legally sane and over age 18.

Credit Shelter Trust

These are also called bypass trusts. No matter what you call them, the idea behind them is simple: they are designed to preserve the maximum amount of money a couple can pass along *tax-free*.

As we have said, there is no tax due on the first $675,000 (in 2000) of the assets a person leaves in his estate (and that figure increases steadily to $1 million in 2006). At the same time, there is an unlimited amount of money that one spouse can leave to another *tax-deferred*.

I chose that term carefully. While assets pass to the surviving spouse tax-free, taxes are ultimately due when that spouse dies. You see the problem with that. The first spouse could have passed along a certain amount of assets—$675,000 in 2000—tax-free. By leaving everything to his wife, however, he forfeited the $675,000 credit to which he was entitled.

Let's use some numbers to show exactly how that happened. Let's say a husband had $675,000 in assets and his wife did as well. And let's further suppose that the husband died in 1999 leaving everything to his wife. She now has an estate worth $1.35 million and she doesn't have to pay any taxes on what she received from her husband's estate.

However, if the wife died later in 1999, leaving that estate valued at $1.35 million, only $675,000—the deduction *she* is entitled to—is free of estate taxes when it is passed on to her heirs. The estate has to pay taxes on the rest. The $675,000 credit the husband was entitled to is lost.

To get around this problem, credit shelter trusts, or bypass trusts, were created. At the time of death of the first spouse, property equal to the estate tax credit—$675,000 in 2000—is placed into a trust. The trust is usually set up to provide lifetime income to the surviving spouse, and when the second spouse dies, the principal passes to another heir or heirs, often the children. This way, the full estate tax credit of each spouse is preserved. Also, this assures that, should the surviving spouse remarry, the principal will go to the designated heirs of the first spouse.

Gifting

There are other ways of using trusts to reduce estate taxes, but first let's consider a wealth-preservation strategy that most investors know about but don't use to full advantage. I am talking about gifting. After all, if you don't own it, it can't be taxed.

You already know that anyone can give to anyone $10,000 a year with no tax consequences. And you also know that means a husband and wife can give $20,000 a year to the same person ($10,000 from the wife, $10,000 from the husband) with no taxes owed at either end. And that is true whether they own the asset jointly or not.

You may also know that money used directly for tuition or medical expenses is not subject to gift taxes. So, if you pay the $30,000 a year it costs to send your granddaughter to college, neither you nor she have to pay any gift taxes. (And your decision to make a gift of tuition or medical expenses has no impact on either your estate tax credit or the $10,000 you can gift to other people.)

But most people don't understand how quickly that $10,000 exception allows them to reduce the size of their taxable estate. And they certainly don't fully understand how there can be substantial benefits from giving away more than $10,000 a year per person—a strategy that, in essence, uses up your federal estate tax credit while you are alive.

Let's take the points one at a time. Assume, for example, that you are single and have two grown children, Dick and Jane; your children are married, and they each have two children of their own. You can gift $80,000 a year to them with no consequences forever. You give Dick $10,000, his wife $10,000, and their two children $10,000 each; and you do the same for Jane, her husband, and their two children every year.

Obviously, if you were married, the amount you and your spouse could gift away would double, to $160,000 annually. Your spouse could make the same gifts to Dick and Jane and their children as you.

Fact #1: Gifting can be an excellent strategy for reducing the size of your estate, while still keeping the federal estate credit ($675,000 in 2000) in place.

Fact #2: Sometimes using up that federal estate credit while you are alive is even a better idea.

What happens if you gift more than $10,000 to someone during a year? You have to pay gift taxes, but that is not necessarily a bad thing. But first, let's explain how the tax would work.

For every dollar you exceed the $10,000 gift exemption per person, your federal estate tax credit is reduced by a like amount. Give your daughter $25,000 in the year 2000, $15,000 over the limit, and your federal estate tax credit decreases by $15,000, from $675,000 to $660,000. Give your daughter $25,000 and your son $10,000, and there is no further deduction. Even if you give someone more than $10,000, you can keep giving other people $10,000 with no gift consequences.

Once you use up the federal estate tax credit, you have to write a check to cover the cost of the gift taxes. (For how large that check has to be, see the estate-tax table.)

As you noticed before, taxes and gifts are taxed at the same level. That isn't by accident. In establishing the tax rates, Congress quickly realized that if an individual could give away all of his assets and not pay a tax, but would be forced to pay a tax on the same assets at death, most people would give their assets away before they died.

It may sound counterintuitive, but using up your estate tax credit while you are alive can be a sound financial decision. Think about that "excess" gift of $15,000 you gave your daughter (the first $10,000 of the $25,000 was tax-free). Suppose she invests that money in stocks, which have returned on average 11 percent a year. If the historical rates of return continue, at the end of ten years that $25,000 would have become more than $71,000, even if she didn't invest another dime. If your daughter then sold the stock, she would have to pay 20 percent of that $46,000 increase in value—about $9,200—in capital gains taxes, leaving her with $61,800. (That's assuming you had paid the gift tax on the excess $15,000 in the first place.)

Now, consider what would have happened to that $25,000 if you had not given it away. Invested in stocks, it still would have grown to $71,000 in ten years, but this time it would be part of your estate. If your estate is sizeable, that entire $71,000 could be taxed at a rate as high as 60 percent. At 60 percent, you pay $42,600 in estate taxes on $71,000 in assets. So, after taxes there would be only $28,400 left.

As you can see, gifting money out of your estate can make a lot of sense. An annual gifting plan can reduce the size of even a big estate, especially if you have a covey of children and grandchildren.

Family Limited Partnership

The family limited partnership is another example of how you can reduce your estate taxes. You, in conjunction with your heirs, establish a partnership, and then you donate property—real estate, stocks, bonds, a painting, or some combination of assets—to the partnership, in essence for the benefit of your heirs.

Say you are married and have three children. And let's say you have a piece of property worth $2 million. You, your spouse, and the three children establish a family limited partnership, and you and your spouse place the $2 million property into the partnership. What you have basically done is make a gift of $666,666—the $2 million value of your property, divided by three— to each of your three children.

If this had been done without creating a partnership, taxes would be due.

But because you have set up the partnership, things work somewhat differently.

Partnerships have two classes of ownership. There are general partners (the people who make all the decisions) and limited partners (the people who reap most of the benefits of the partnership but have no say in how things are run). In our example, you and your spouse are the general partners. While you retain just a 1 percent limited partnership interest, you own 99 percent of the general partnership class of stock. Your children's interests are the mirror image of that. They each have a 33 percent limited partnership interest, but own just 0.333 percent of the general partnership.

As a result of the way the partnership is set up, you and your spouse have control over how the partnership is run. You decide what to do with the property—should it be sold, improved, left alone—and you alone decide how any income from the partnership should be distributed.

Certainly your children have received a gift—the one-third limited partnership interest—but what is that gift worth? If they each had full control of one-third of the $2 million property, we could say each of the three gifts was worth $666,666. But they have been given less than that, since they don't have any control over how the partnership is run and how the property should be handled.

So, each of the three gifts is worth less than $666,666. The question is: how much less?

That is a matter of interpretation. The IRS test is, in essence, this: what would a disinterested third party pay for the limited partnership interest? Experts—who, of course, can differ in the opinions they offer—are brought in, and you ultimately put a value on the gift.

You can see where problems with the government can arise. For tax purposes, the creators of the limited partnership will want the limited partnership shares valued as low as possible. The government, not surprisingly, has exactly the opposite interest. That's why what value you put on the interest is so important.

Let's say, in our example, you ultimately decide that because your children don't have any voting rights when it comes to what should be done with the property, the value of the gift to the limited partners should be discounted by a third. That would not be uncommon in this kind of situation.

As a result, the value of the gift you and your spouse made is not $2 million—the market value of the property—but two-thirds of that, or $1.33 million, the cumulative amount your children presumably could get if they sold their limited partnership interests. Since you and spouse are allowed to pass up to $1.35 million tax-free, as of 2000, you could set up the partnership this way with no gift taxes being due.

How? It is relatively simple. You and your spouse don't even have to own the property jointly. The IRS recognizes a concept that it calls "gift splitting"; they will combine your lifetime exemption with your spouse's for purposes of making a gift. In this case, they will add your year 2000 exemption of $675,000 to your spouse's exemption of $675,000, and the entire gift of $1.3 million will be tax-free. In fact, you could have actually given away a bit more, because the first $10,000 you and spouse gave to each of three children—$60,000 in total—was free of taxes. You don't lose that $10,000 per person exemption, even if you make gifts that exceed that amount in a given year.

And of course, once you have given the limited partnership interest away, virtually all of the appreciation in the value of the trust is outside of your estate, since your children now own 99 percent.

Limited partnerships are a leveraged form of gift giving. But they are also very complicated and require legal advice.

Other Options

There are numerous other trusts that you can establish, and obviously you want to go over all of your choices with your advisers. But let's at least highlight two more options here.

Charitable Remainder Trust

Many people today use the charitable remainder trust for two important reasons: It gives them a way to sell highly appreciated assets without paying immediate capital gains. It can also be a way to create a stream of income for the rest of their lives, and even for the lives of their heirs.

Let's say you own stock worth $2 million that you paid a total of $400,000 for during the course of your lifetime. You place the stock in a trust for a charitable beneficiary, and you get a deduction based on the stock's $2 million market value, discounted by an IRS formula that takes into account how long the trust will be paying income to you (and your heirs, if you set it up that way).

To generate the income, the trust sells the stock. That sale has no tax consequences to you, and the trust uses the proceeds to provide you with the agreed-upon income stream for a predetermined amount of time.

(How that income is taxed is incredibly complicated. The principal involved is called "tiered" taxation, and it is possible that parts of that income could be subject to four different tax rates. Part could be taxed as ordinary income, and part at the capital gains rate. Part of it could be considered tax-free, and part could be considered to be a return of principal. While you will need a professional to help sort it all out, the general rule of thumb to remember is that wherever possible, the IRS will use the determination that subjects you to the highest possible tax rate.)

The principal passes to the charity at the death of the last income beneficiary.

While this is an irrevocable trust—once you create it, the principal belongs to the charitable beneficiary—you can retain certain powers, such as the ability to change at any time both the charitable beneficiary and the investment selection that the trust uses to generate income.

Life Insurance Trust

With a life insurance trust you can reduce the size of your taxable estate by keeping the proceeds from life insurance policies outside of it. You simply place, or purchase, a life insurance policy inside a trust and, in essence, pay the premiums in the form of annual gifts to your beneficiaries. At your death, the trust receives the insurance proceeds, circumventing both estate taxes and probate proceedings. The life insurance proceeds may be distributed to your beneficiaries free of federal income and estate taxes. (*Note:* If you transfer an existing life insurance policy, there is one complication. You must live three years from the date of transfer. If you die before that, the policy is considered part of your estate.)

There are countless other trusts, such as grantor retained annuity trust, where you gift away an asset but receive a revenue stream during your lifetime, but the point here is simple. There are numerous steps you can take to reduce the potential estate taxes that you owe, and experts who specialize in this area are readily available. Take advantage of them. Estate planning is a complicated area, confusing to the layman. It requires the expertise of someone familiar with the laws.

And those include state laws as well. Several states have attracted high retiree populations with hospitable tax environments, often with no estate tax. Some of the high estate tax states, having watched their retirees flee to avoid these taxes, are reducing or gradually eliminating them. Be aware of this additional tax bite if it affects you.

Death, unfortunately, is inevitable. Dying without planning is a tragedy.

18

Where Do We Go from Here?

As we begin the twenty-first century, the prospects for the next one hundred years are bright. Are we without problems? Of course not. We see regional ethnic conflicts with devastating consequences. Around the world there are high levels of poverty and disease in many countries; women are still repressed in many areas, and economic chaos hinders development in the Third World. In our own country, many do not participate in the American dream.

And yet the prospects for global prosperity have never been greater. The fall of communism has freed economies throughout the world. Telecommunications and technology are making the global village possible. And with even more countries moving into the economic mainstream, the promise of global prosperity may become a reality.

If the Dow Jones Industrial Average appreciates in this century at the rate it did in the last, we can expect a DJIA of 142,000 by the year 2050, and close to 2 million by the year 2100. More realistically, at the DJIA's 5.3 percent appreciation of the last seventy-five years, the index would be at 17,600 in 2010 and 29,500 in 2020. (The S&P 500 index appreciated 11 percent over this time frame.) Will we achieve those levels? The future is ours to determine, since we live in a country blessed with abundant natural resources and, more important, a culture in which entrepreneurial effort and hard work traditionally translate into opportunity. Education levels have never been higher.

If we shepherd those resources, nurture entrepreneurs, and continue to grow and create new jobs, the market should reflect that growth. Why shouldn't stocks be more highly valued today than in the prior half of the century? And why can't they be even more highly valued in the future? There is reason to be optimistic.

Companies are better managed than ever before

During the late 1970s and into the 1980s, much of American corporate management grew lazy. In our capitalistic society, the negative results of a management that is indifferent and inwardly focused, one that ignores competitors down the street as well as overseas, are inevitable. These firms lost market share—think what happened to the U.S. car companies, agricultural giants, and consumer electronics firms—and in some cases lost a lot of money. That led to major changes in the way these companies are run. We saw the rise of activist shareholders vocally expressing their dissatisfaction and prompting boards of directors to act, often by replacing management, a move that served notice that companies would be run for the benefit of shareholders, not management.

Not only did these boards recruit new people, but they also implemented new pay policies. Today's managers receive a significant portion of their compensation in the form of stock and stock options. Their interests and those of the shareholders are now in alignment. That is a key reason we expect managers of these companies to continue to perform well. It is in their personal interest to make their companies successful.

Technology is making us more efficient

Slow growth and low inflation, the current economic environment, make it difficult for companies to show strong growth. Revenues are constrained by the slow economy, and with low inflation, few companies have any pricing power. Fortunately, the massive investments in technology are paying off in productivity increases that are driving earnings higher. With information power increasing, and the Internet accelerating productivity, we expect technology to spur growth for decades to come. This means that wages will rise, keeping the economy strong. As long as a worker is producing more, he can be paid more without an inflationary impact. That is the best of both worlds.

Gone Global

Clearly, the easiest way to keep a company and its earnings growing is to increase revenues. Today our corporations are selling to global markets growing more rapidly than our own, dramatically expanding their prospects. As a result, large-growth companies are steadily increasing the percentage of sales and earnings they receive from outside the United States. The five hundred companies that make up the Standard & Poor's 500 Index now get about 42 percent of their earnings beyond our borders.

Not only are they now firmly entrenched in foreign markets, but the global economic trends are in their favor as well. Communism is becoming less and less of a factor, and partially as a result, the standard of living around the world continues to rise. Both those trends favor American corporations, no matter what they are selling. So, we expect earnings—especially those of large-cap growth companies—to continue to climb.

Even the federal government, through the Federal Reserve, is performing well. The Fed knows more than ever before about maintaining price stability while accommodating growth. It seems inconceivable that we would return to the mistakes of the sixties and seventies that fueled inflation and devastated our economy.

Does this mean nothing can go wrong? Of course not. As long as human beings (particularly political ones) run the government, uncertainty remains. While unlikely, it is possible that federal policies could lead us back to the days of high inflation and slow growth. It was just seven years ago that we almost had a national health care plan. Whatever the arguments on the merits, it is clear that the increased spending would have us producing even larger deficits, not surpluses, and the accompanying inflation would have hit the market's valuation hard. Vigilance is ever required, but the current fundamentals favor a continuation of the bull market.

But Are There Going to Be Any Buyers?

It is clear that if you look at the fundamentals of the economy, and demographic trends, the market seems ideally positioned to benefit in the years ahead. First, the fastest-growing segment of the population through 2005 will be the 45-to-60-year-old group. In the United States, ages 45 to 54 are the peak earning—and investing—years. The baby boomers are flooding that decade right now, and true to form, they are sharply increasing their equity investments.

Historically, when Americans have chosen to invest, they have done so through common stocks, and that's what we've seen happen throughout the 1990s. This inflow of new funds should continue for quite a while. The youngest baby boomer won't turn 54 until the year 2018.

Today the total value of equities is about $15 trillion, and if people between the ages of 45 and 54 continue to invest as they have in the past, there will be another $25 trillion of money flowing into stocks, putting even more upward pressure on share prices. That pressure doesn't really start to abate until baby boomers start to retire, somewhere around the year 2012.

Does the Universe End in 2012?

Looking at the following chart, you may wonder what happens after the year 2012. Does the market fall off a cliff as the chart might indicate? It's not all that clear, although there is reason to believe that stock prices will hold up fairly well.

For one thing, there still will be baby boomers retiring until 2029, and even then they may not all retire. The age to receive full Social Security benefits has been increased for people born after 1937. The youngest baby boomers will have to wait until they are 67 to receive full Social Security benefits. That might keep them in the workforce a bit longer.

Simultaneously, something unprecedented will be happening. We will see the largest wealth transfer in U.S. history. Thanks to increased savings rates, Social Security, and Medicare, today's generation of retirees is the first that,

Stocks as a Percentage of Household Financial Assets
and
Percentage of U.S. Population Aged 45–54

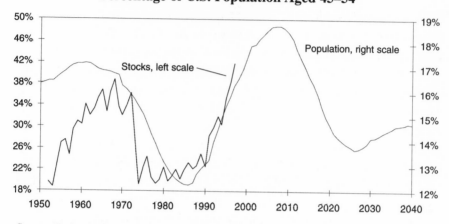

Source: *Federal Reserve; Bureau of the Census*

for the most part, isn't liquidating all its assets in retirement. In fact they will leave an estimated $8–10 trillion to their heirs over the next several decades. So, the baby boomers may enter retirement in better financial shape than their parents, and may not have to liquidate their equity holdings, or might do so at a gradual pace.

There are three other significant factors that would suggest there won't be substantial selling pressure, once the baby boomers retire.

First, today's baby boomers are only now beginning to save and invest in numbers equal to what their parents did. Once they get in the habit, we can hope that they will continue to invest in stocks right up until retirement and beyond.

Second, those same baby boomers know they are going to be retired—or semiretired—for a very long time. Someone who reaches age 65 can expect to live for at least another twenty years. If you have that kind of investing time frame, you are a long-term investor. (As we saw earlier, it is not your age that determines whether or not you are a long-term investor, it is your time horizon.) Long-term investors want to be in stocks, given the higher returns equities traditionally produce over time.

Third, today's boomers are not likely to retire in mass and live off their savings and investments once they turn 65. Indeed (see chapter 16), only 15 percent of them said they plan on a "traditional retirement." If they are continuing to work, there is less reason for them to sell their stocks—to live on the proceeds—or to shift much of their portfolio over to fixed-income investments. (People do that in retirement to generate a steady stream of income that serves as a replacement for their former paycheck. If they are working, there is no reason to generate that replacement income.) And even if they were to withdraw the bulk of their money, that wouldn't occur all at once, since the boomers will be retiring over a period of almost twenty years.

A Final Thought

Studying the history of the market can be illuminating and fascinating, but it is not necessarily predictive of the future.

Two examples come to mind. Up until the late 1950s, stocks, on average, provided a dividend yield that was 3 to 4 percent higher than bonds. After all, stocks were riskier than bonds, so investors should be compensated with higher dividend yields—so the thinking went at the time. A reasonable investment strategy was to sell stocks when the dividend yield got too low, under the theory that they must be overvalued and poised to correct. Conversely, a high dividend yield indicated that stocks were undervalued.

But in the late 1950s this yield relationship changed forever, and through the ensuing decades, dividend yields went down, and bond yields up, until 1982. Similarly, some investors watched during the bull market of the 1990s as stock prices went up, pushing dividend yields down. Assuming that the lowest yields on record must surely indicate an overvalued market, they sold much too soon. Other investors looked at another indicator. They focused on the highest price/earnings ratios since the 1950s, and also sold prematurely. In fact, one of the biggest mistakes of this market has been to sell too soon because prices exceeded historical averages.

Use history as your guide, but be prepared to alter your portfolio when market conditions warrant. Stocks have traditionally outperformed bonds and cash equivalents over time; and given current conditions, they are likely to outperform in the years ahead. Nothing on the immediate horizon suggests that the low inflation is going to change significantly. Similarly, corporate earnings, although subject to the business cycle, are likely to remain strong. In that environment, stocks are the place to be.

I wish you success.

Acknowledgments

With a full-time job and two teenagers, I knew from the outset that I would welcome any help I could get in developing this book. I have been very fortunate in the tremendous support I've received from many people, whom I wish to acknowledge here.

Edward Kerschner, Chairman of the Investment Policy Committee at PaineWebber, has been both mentor and friend. His record of success with long-term thematic research has been unmatched, and he has been inspirational in his drive for excellence. Much of his work, and that of our other strategists, Tom Doerflinger and Michael Geraghty, is reflected in the chapter on thematics as well as elsewhere in the book. Mike Ryan, our bond strategist, was generous with his insights on the bond market, for which I am grateful.

Belinda Couniotakis, my valued associate and friend, has been tireless in making everything happen and moving the book forward at each step of the way. Without her organizational and personal skills I would have been lost, and the last year would have been far less fun. Liz Greenfield, a brilliant quant, never failed to find the numbers and create the charts to make our investment case, and was thoughtful with her input on the book. I also owe a heartfelt thanks to others at PaineWebber, too numerous to mention, who generously gave of their time and expertise.

I have a special thanks for Donna Peterman. Although I had dreamed of writing a book for many years, it was Donna's vision and support that made it a reality, and her comments and guidance along the way were invaluable. Paul Brown amazed me with his broad base of knowledge and sources, and I am grateful for his significant contributions.

At Simon & Schuster, Fred Hills was an extraordinary source of expertise, valuable comments and guidance. His ongoing encouragement, shepherding of the project, and skillful editing contributed greatly, and he proved to be a wonderful resource bringing the worlds of finance and publishing together. I am also appreciative of Amanda Urban, Creative Artists agent extraordinaire, who took on an unpublished author.

Last, but certainly not least, thank you to my husband, whose unwavering support in this effort, as well as in all of life's endeavors, has been a gift.

Index

Page numbers in *italics* refer to charts and tables.